The God Who Lives

The God Who Lives

Investigating the Emergence of Life
and the Doctrine of God

Adam Pryor

◆PICKWICK *Publications* • Eugene, Oregon

THE GOD WHO LIVES
Investigating the Emergence of Life and the Doctrine of God

Copyright © 2014 Adam Pryor. All rights reserved. Except for brief quotations in critical publications or reviews, no part of this book may be reproduced in any manner without prior written permission from the publisher. Write: Permissions. Wipf and Stock Publishers, 199 W. 8th Ave., Suite 3, Eugene, OR 97401.

Pickwick Publications
An Imprint of Wipf and Stock Publishers
199 W. 8th Ave., Suite 3
Eugene, OR 97401

www.wipfandstock.com

ISBN 13: 978-1-62032-934-4

Cataloguing-in-Publication Data

Pryor, Adam

    The God who lives : investigating the emergence of life and the doctrine of God

    xviii + 202 p. ; 23 cm. Includes bibliographical references.

    ISBN 13: 978-1-62032-934-4

    1. Religion and science. 2. Evolution—Religious aspects—Christianity. 3. God (Christianity). I. Title.

BL240.3 P797 2014

Manufactured in the U.S.A.

For Rachael

Contents

List of Tables viii
Acknowledgments ix
Introduction: Inter-action xi

1 **What is "Life" Anyway?** 1
2 **Teleodynamics of Emergent Life** 36
3 **A Phenomenology of Life** 72
4 **Abstential Desire** 105
5 **Who Is This Living God?** 130
6 **Where Is This Living God?** 163

Bibliography 203

Tables

Table 1: Historical Account of Emergence Theory   45

Table 2: Clayton's Meanings and Approaches   62

Table 3: Comparing Deacon and Kant   68

Table 4: Correlation of Dynamics to Need and Desire   110

Table 5: Correlation Extended to Emergence Language   113

Table 6: Depicting Dynamics and Ontology   122

Table 7: Similarity & Difference between Divine & Creaturely Living   191

Acknowledgments

There are countless people who have helped to make this work possible. I am particularly thankful to the Lab Group at the Center for Theology and Natural Science who prodded me into thinking more deeply about living; to Inese Radzins, Terrence Deacon, and Wentzel van Huyssteen who read and offered invaluable suggestions to early drafts of the work; to David Drebes, Kayko Driedger Hesslein and Rajesh Sampath who challenged me to be clearer about what I really mean; and most especially to Robert Russell. Bob has offered ceaseless encouragement, support, and friendship in addition to invaluable insights. The fault is only my own wherever an argument lacks clarity or remains unpersuasive.

Last but not least, my family has lovingly supported me through all the ups and downs of writing and research. My parents have cheerfully listened to every spandrel of an idea floating through my mind. My wife has unwaveringly had more confidence in me than I do in myself. And our children continually remind me how to be in awe of what we can discover about life all around us.

Introduction

Inter-action

THE OFTEN USED APPROACH in creating dialogue between theology and science (especially as written by theologians) is to map with a cartographer's care the methodological landscape first and only then begin interdisciplinary research proper. However, each author that embarks on this interdisciplinary journey seems to feel the need to make their own set of pathways. It is as though each author ventures anew into what is believed to be an uncharted continent. At best, seeing ruts in the trails blazed by previous interdisciplinary explorers, new pilgrims on this journey may acknowledge the established roads, but ultimately abandon them. The result is an unwieldy plethora of pathways that all veritably have the same goal in mind.

I hope to *not* contribute here another method to the rapidly proliferating choices already available; however, I admittedly do not follow one established method with sustained rigor. Instead, my work is guided by three methodological values that appear often in the dialogue between theology and science: narrative, interaction, and transversality. I find these values expressed in a number of different ways through the plurality of methods proffered by other scholars with interdisciplinary aims, but my explication of these values is most explicitly influenced by Wentzel van Huyssteen and Robert Russell.

What is critical about the three methodological values used here is how they begin to press beyond strict interdisciplinarity: where traditional fields are scrupulously separated into specialized areas of discrete research, only subsequently to be in dialogue with one another. Instead, my use of these values is always aimed towards the constructive potential of inter-action: where strict interdisciplinarity gives way to problem-solving that holistically integrates various epistemic approaches.

Let me explain what I mean by beginning with narrative. If our aim is to draw together the insights of many different fields in order to deepen our understanding of the world in some way, we must delve deeply into the thought-world of the disciplines we seek to bring together. I think of this as telling the history of a discipline or offering the biography of a field. This is not an aimless story being told, wandering in many different directions. The story should lead the reader to the way various thinkers address a critical problem. The problem orients the way the story is told. In light of my specific interest in science and theology, the stories I narrate tend to lead to the primary thinker or concept within various disciplinary contexts that best addresses the orienting problem. I find this most akin to Husserl's sense of the "teleology of historical becoming." In his text *The Crisis of European Sciences and Transcendental Phenomenology*, he insists that to account for the depth of self-understanding that drives philosophical inquiry, one must attempt to discover the unity that runs through the history of philosophical projects. It is an effort to get behind the historical facts and discover a meaningful harmony that can only be established through a critical and over-arching view of the field. This is sometimes referred to as his "teleological consideration of history."[1]

Methodologically, there ought to be no doubt this is where I begin. With each of the fields of study treated here, the goal is to tell a story about the field that explicates the underlying unity in its development. The story then points to an indispensable thinker, theory, or concept epitomizing this unifying feature. In telling the story of the principles of life and emergence theory, the reader is led towards Terrence Deacon's model for self-organizing complexity. In terms of ontology, the story leads towards the insights of a "phenomenology of life" as described by Renaud Barbaras. Finally, in terms of the doctrine of God, the story leads to themes drawn from Paul Tillich, Jan-Olav Henriksen, and Simone Weil.

Telling these stories is only the beginning of this project. Ultimately, these various narratives are weaved together in order to generate a better account of the events in question than any single narrative can provide of its own accord. This represents the goal of an "interactionist" account of theology and science as articulated by Robert Russell. His method of "Creative Mutual Interaction" (CMI) builds upon the work of Ian Barbour. Slightly modifying Barbour's diagrams of religious and scientific reasoning laid out in his Gifford lectures, Russell develops eight paths that connect these analogous modes of reasoning.[2] The details of these paths in CMI are not

---

1. Husserl, *Die Krisis Der Europäischen Wissenschaften Und Die Transzendentale Phänomenologie*, in *Husserliana*, vol. 6, § 15.
2. See Barbour, *Religion and Science*, chap. 4.

of concern here. It is the to-and-fro movement between theological and scientific research that these paths signify that most influences my approach.[3]

It is crucial to understand that CMI depicts three distinct approaches to addressing research problems. There is the independent scientific research program, the independent theological research program, and the interaction there between conceived of as a third research program.[4] There is an epistemic gamble between these three research programs CMI identifies. First, it wagers that interactionist research will address interdisciplinary research questions better than either theology or science alone. Second, it bets that research done by the independent theological and scientific research programs (when answering questions not of interdisciplinary relevance) become more fertile when they consider the insights of the opposite discipline.

What is immensely important about Russell's approach is the epistemic bet it places on mutual interaction. This to-and-fro motion of his approach inculcates a crucial emendation to the teleological histories I tell. In addition to laying out the narratives of the emergence of life, a phenomenology of life, and an understanding of God as living, I will emphasize points of consonance in the way these distinctive narratives develop the theme of "life." By emphasizing these points of consonance in crafting the three narratives, I can weave them together into a whole with an interactive potential. The points of consonance become nodes by which to move back and forth between the various narratives. They are the points at which one narrative can shape the suppositions of another narrative.

In order to integrate moments where the narratives demonstrate interactive potential, I rely on Wentzel van Huyssteen's use of "transversality." For van Huyssteen, transversality is the mode of human rationality by which we integrate diverse and sometimes conflicting narratives into a reasonable whole. It describes a process that gathers and binds; he calls it an "extending over, lying across, and intersecting."[5] van Huyssteen's account of transversality relies heavily on the work of Calvin Schrag and the rich philosophical tradition that informs his discussion of this concept.[6] Schrag

3. R. Russell, *Cosmology—from Alpha to Omega*, chap. 10.
4. Ibid., 21.
5. van Huyssteen, *The Shaping of Rationality*, 135; see also Schrag, "Transversal Rationality," 64–66; and *The Resources of Rationality*, 149.
6. The philosophical background behind Schrag's use of the transversal (and the way it is taken up by van Huyssteen) is beyond the scope of this introduction. I will give only the briefest summary of the relevant points here as an extended aside and direct the reader to key sources for better understanding the philosophical implications of this topic if it is unfamiliar.
Jean-Paul Sartre uses the idea of the transversal to describe the intentionalities that provide for the longitudinal unity of temporal consciousness. His work on this point is

locates transversal rationality within communication. This is important because it means that transversal rationality never enjoys the security of being a foundationalist, self-constituting, or originating principle. Instead, the sense of transversality, as it is used here, is deeply contextualized both socially and historically.[7]

Thus, making an appeal to transversality as the mode of human rationality by which narratives of various disciplines are woven together is explicitly *not* to give recourse to a foundationalist supposition. Transversal rationality occurs between people in events of communication. With van Huyssteen, I am emphasizing the *praxial* quality of transversality. Transversal rationality describes something we *do*. It entails engaging, enacting, expressing, or otherwise wrestling with the various narratives I am bringing together in a dynamic way. I image this process of transversal reasoning to be like dogs herding sheep. The sheep, our various narratives, are constantly developing and changing; they may wander without abandon and be scattered across a meadow if isolated from one another. The shepherding dogs, akin to transversal rationality, herd the sheep together directing them away from eating planted crops and moving them away from roads or other dangers. Once brought together the herd instinct of the sheep is likely to keep them together and the shepherding dog gathers back the occasional stray.

---

a direct response to Edmund Husserl, who argues that the unity of consciousness across time can only be established, according to phenomenological analysis, by positing the transcendental ego as the personal facet of transcendental consciousness that accounts for the uniqueness of our experience phenomenologically reduced. Contra Husserl, Sartre affirms that the unifying play of transversal intentionalities is itself sufficient to account for the flow of temporal consciousness and recourse to a transcendental ego unnecessarily fractures our subjective experience. Thus, the unifying play of transversal intentionalities describes the binding together of past and present moments in the flow of transcendental consciousness.

Two problems arise (according to Schrag) with this account, though only one is particularly significant for my purposes. (1) Schrag asserts that the Sartrian philosophy of subjectivity is founded upon the primacy of consciousness and the resultant privileging of the present means Sartre lacks any protentional intentionality towards the future. (2) Schrag finds the subject-centered work of Sartre untenable. Instead, he resists the Sartrian emphasis on the primacy of consciousness in order to try to acknowledge both the plurality of interpretations that form interpersonal dialogue of great fecundity *and* to acknowledge the effects of this form of dialogue on participants in the dialogue. In so doing, he follows Félix Guattari, Gilles Deleuze, and Michel Foucault in locating transversal rationality within events of communicative praxis.

Key sources to consult on this topic might include Schrag, *The Resources of Rationality*, 148–56; Husserl, *Zur Phänomenologie Des Inneren Zeitbewusstesens (1893–1917)*, in *Husserliana*, vol. 10, pt. 1; Sartre, *La Transcendance De L'Ego*, pt. 1; Sartre, *L'Être Et Le Néant*, pt. 2, chap. 2; and Morrison, "Kant, Husserl, and Heidegger on Time and the Unity of 'Consciousness,'" 182–98.

7. Schrag, *The Resources of Rationality*, 152.

Once the various narratives are gathered together (transversally bound), a natural and productive relation can arise (like the natural herd instinct) that generates better research.

In an effort to bring together these various methodological features of interdisciplinary research under a single heading, I would use the term inter-action. The term is indebted to the recent writings of Mark C. Taylor. In an op-ed for *The New York Times*, Taylor argues against what he calls the "mass-production model" of the university, claiming it has led to untenable specialization and fragmentation.[8]

Against this failing model for university and graduate education, Taylor calls for a restructuring that emphasizes cross-disciplinary study and research. His call for restructuring the university reflects a fundamental change he perceives in the structure of knowledge production itself. As we move beyond a modern industrial model of production (both in goods and education) to what he calls an "information society," interdisciplinarity is no longer a luxury but a fundamental feature of knowledge production. Instead of generating intra-disciplinary narratives relevant only to members of a given disciplinary subfield, he advocates for a problem oriented approach that allows us to produce knowledge at the interstices of traditionally conceived fields. Taylor advocates for an understanding of areas of inquiry as nodes in a web that are willing to equally draw from various disciplinary resources.[9] He is issuing a call for scholars to realize how easily disciplinary boundaries can become a hindrance to meaningful inquiry instead of an aid.

This shift in thinking away from fields and towards problem driven inquiry is key to my use of inter-action and how I understand it to be related to the three methodological influences I have outlined above. The *inter-*action always occurs in the interstitial space between traditionally conceived disciplines. It plays betwixt and between the teleological narratives it constructs, looking for any point of relation even as those narratives are being recounted. The inter-*action* is a praxis of inquiry. It requires a careful articulation of *problems* to guide research that transversally binds together the variety of ways and means at our disposal for wrestling with those problems. That praxis of transversal binding is a thoroughly social process: we

8. Taylor, "End the University as We Know It." Taylor provides us with an excellent example of what he means. "Unfortunately this mass-production university model has led to separation where there ought to be collaboration and to ever-increasing specialization. In my own religion department, for example, we have ten faculty members, working in eight subfields, with little overlap. And as departments fragment, research and publication become more and more about less and less. Each academic becomes the trustee not of a branch of the sciences, but of limited knowledge that all too often is irrelevant for genuinely important problems."

9. Taylor and Raschke, "About *About Religion*: A Conversation with Mark C. Taylor."

are reliant on one another in this praxis. Finally, the inter-action harkens us back to Russell's interactional method in two ways. First, I find the greatest strength of Russell's method to be its emphasis on a clear and analytically precise approach for relating science and theology. Even as the boundaries between disciplines are becoming more porous, inter-action must not cease to strive for the precision that CMI challenges us to pursue. Second, inter-action must continue to pursue the spirit of the to-and-fro movement previously discussed; a movement constitutive of their mutual interaction. The nodes or areas of inquiry must remain open to being changed and developed in the course of being transversally gathered together.

As an example of inter-action my research uses various areas of inquiry to transversally address a research problem: to begin plumbing the depths of what it means to live. The areas of inquiry are recounted as three narratives. The first narrative will focus on life as an emergent phenomenon. After briefly identifying key developments to a philosophical history of life and identifying the continued impact of this history on contemporary scientific approaches to the principles of life in chapter 1, chapter 2 will examine emergence theory as providing an especially promising contemporary approach to articulating principles of life. Specifically, this chapter will focus on the recent work of Terrence Deacon. He develops a three-fold schema of emergence theory with orders of increasing dynamical complexity: homeodynamics, morphodynamics, and teleodynamics.[10]

What is most crucial to my work is Deacon's model of the autogen[11] as an example of a basic teleodynamic process. For now, let me simply note that what is most fascinating about his work is that teleodynamics (as in the autogen) provides a rudimentary "self" that emerges in contrast to its surrounding world. Given Deacon's model of the autogen, this "self" is distinct from the rest of its environment and can reproduce. Yet, the autogen may only be called proto-biotic: it does not meet all of the sufficient conditions entailed by contemporary scientific definitions of life—such as engaging in a self-propagating work cycle.[12]

The second narrative considers contemporary work in the philosophy called "phenomenology of life." This area of research is beginning to

10. See Deacon, "Emergence: The Hole at the Wheel's Hub," 111–50; and *Incomplete Nature*, chaps. 7–9.

11. In work previous to *Incomplete Nature*, Deacon has called this model an "autocell." In his latest work he has made this name change in order to avoid any confusion regarding the fact that the model is not necessarily cellular. Despite the name change, there is not a significant change in the model itself. See Deacon, *Incomplete Nature*, 307.

12. For instance, see Kauffman and Clayton, "On Emergence, Agency, and Organization," 501–21.

generate new ontological resources and conceptual schemas that call into question some of the sufficient conditions of the strictly biological understanding of life. Asserting that "[b]iology speaks not of life but of the mode of functioning of organisms recognized as living,"[13] philosophers such as Renaud Barbaras, free themselves from a commitment to definitions of life as articulated in biology (definitions of life that implicitly rely primarily on identifying specific substances and processes that resist death). Instead, they seek to identify how we recognize something as a living entity in order to better understand what it means to be alive.

Following this line of thinking, chapter 3 will explicate some of the dense philosophical language and history that pervades Barbaras's writing and subsequently consider Barbaras's position itself. He finds that living entities are those wholes that are *nothing* more than the perpetual operation of their parts. This seems so similar to the oft quoted aphorism, "the whole is *more* than the sum of its parts," that its implications can be easily overlooked. With Barbaras, I will emphasize that the whole is *nothing* more than its parts, granting a certain reality to the idea of nothingness; nothingness not conceived as the pure negation of being (*ouk on*) but an essential absence organizing its constitutive parts (akin to the idea of *me on*).[14] In chapter 4, I will explore how this understanding of a living entity could easily be concomitant with Deacon's account of emergence, particularly his notion of "constitutive absence."[15]

The third narrative will focus on theological discourse about the living God. Theology addressing this topic often, though not exclusively, takes its cue from narratives of salvation. Whether God is classically conceived as *eternally* alive (being without change, completely self-sufficient, and the source of all created things) or as the living empowerment of praxes of justice,[16] this religious symbol is squarely soteriological in its theological explication. Given the insights developed in the narratives about emergence and the phenomenology of life, I intend to shift the course of the theological narrative in a constructive way. Taking seriously the potential value of the inter-action of these diverse modes of inquiry for theological reflection, I will examine what it means to affirm that God is living in terms of the doctrine of God instead of

---

13. Barbaras, "Life, Movement, and Desire," 5; see also "A Phenomenology of Life," 206–30.

14. This distinction is well described in Tillich, *Systematic Theology*, 1:253–54.

15. "Constitutive absence" is the name that Deacon gives to the emergent quality that organizes (not as an additional effective cause but as a teleological end) its constitutive parts.

16. For instance, compare Oden, *The Living God*, 64ff.; and Johnson, *Quest for the Living God*, chap. 4.

soteriology. To that end, chapter 5 will consider five twentieth-century theologians (Karl Barth, Jürgen Moltmann, John Zizioulas, Sallie McFague, and Paul Tillich) who treat life and God's living in three distinct ways. What I find is that Tillich is particularly amenable to the highly dynamic account of life I have developed in the other two narratives.

However, the treatment of these theologians also reveals that the relationship between life and absence, so critical to the two previous narratives, remains theologically underdeveloped. As a result, in the final chapter I attempt to imagine what it means to understand the affirmation that God is living in terms of absence and desire—the critical themes developed from Deacon and Barbaras. In this process, the work of Jan-Olav Henriksen and Simone Weil proves to be invaluable. In the end, I find that to affirm that God is living theologically provides a way to imagine God's absence from the world, but an absence that is far from inert or inactive.

I

What is "Life" Anyway?

Research into the origins of life has a long and divergent history. A part of this divergence stems from the distinctive challenge of giving an account of the principles of life. These principles are notoriously difficult to define. What separates the living from the non-living? Is it behaviors? Is it the possession of a vitiating substance? Is it the organization of matter? Is life really distinctive and worthy of study or is it just a complex set of mechanical relations?

The answers to these kinds of questions have varied greatly in philosophical and early scientific history. However, in the contemporary scientific study of the origins of life the problems these conceptual challenges might pose is somewhat muted. On the contemporary scene, the question, "What is life?" seems to have given way to a different question: "How does life work?" The assumption is that if we know how life works then defining what it is will become obvious. This shift from "what" to "how" is really not so surprising. After all, life as we know it involves some very complicated processes even in the simplest of creatures. How do these processes that are essential for life arise? How can we determine what order they develop in? How does the very different environment of the early earth affect this formation and how have living things subsequently transformed that environment?

Detailing the array of answers to these questions from the contemporary scientific scene is not my primary focus. Instead, here the concern is for those muted conceptual questions: identifying core principles of what constitutes a living thing and its identification. Being clear about what is at stake in these philosophical distinctions can reveal where these concerns, though muted, are not entirely silenced in the contemporary scientific scene. In fact, there remains a surprising diversity in recent research programs with regard to these conceptual distinctions, with important ramifications for the way research questions are framed today.

I will begin by outlining the relevant points of three key philosophical thinkers who make essential contributions to identifying what constitutes a living thing: Aristotle, Descartes, and Kant. Let me be clear that my treatment of these three thinkers is not strictly historical. I am weaving together points from each to generate a teleological history of major philosophical efforts to establish principles of life. This history follows a pendulum-like motion regarding the role given to teleology. There is a shift from the critical role played by final and formal causes in the Aristotelian perspective on ensoulment to the abolishment of teleology in the mechanical explanations of the Cartesian account of bodies. Kant's work represents a distinctive shift back towards the relevance of teleological explication through his account of purposiveness. The lessons garnered from this teleological history will be used in a typological fashion to identify trends within the conceptual foundations of contemporary scientific research programs. My goal is to make clear why emergence theory and its use in principles of life research will be my focus for the rest of this work.

Aristotle and the Soul

Though Aristotle's work will not feature directly into my typological distinction, his *On the Soul* remains an essential early work to be consulted in any description of life and its origin. It provides a number of basic insights into what it means "to live" that shape biology, philosophy, and theology for millennia. Particularly, his work is fundamental to any understanding of the Scholastic development of this concept, the impetus behind the Cartesian approach, and contemporary neo-Thomist theologies. What I will focus on are the basic features of hylomorphism and the various faculties of the soul—especially the nutritive—because these are the features of Aristotle's work that Descartes most stringently contests.

Understanding where the study of living things falls within the wider corpus of Aristotle's philosophy gives greater depth of meaning to his account of hylomorphism and the faculties of the soul. With that in mind, it is important to realize that the modern way of understanding biology, as a study of living things in their own right, is quite different from what Aristotle envisions. *Instead, Aristotle accounts for the study of biology as a subset of physics; it is not a distinctive study of the domain of living as opposed to non-living things.* Why make biology a subset of physics? For Aristotle physics is the study of natural things. Living things are a species of natural things, and the study of biology is most properly understood as a means to understanding how exactly a living thing is a subset within the wider class of natural things.[1]

Thus, it is critical to know what Aristotle tells us about natural things: they are a union of matter and form where the nature, or substance, is that which persists through all incidental change.[2] Living things are understood in this context of natural things. They are those natural things (a union of matter and form) that consist of a more specific union of soul and body.[3] In sum, living things are natural things where the soul is that which persists through all incidental forms of change.

However, the soul always shares a special relationship to the body, the form and matter of living things, in Aristotle's work. The soul is not capable of a separate existence from the body (just as form relates inseparably to matter in natural things). Aristotle reasons that to demonstrate such a separate existence for the soul we would need to find some way by which only the soul acts or is acted upon. However, any such affection of the soul seems to always involve the body.[4] This is important because we cannot simply dismiss Aristotle's account of the soul as a kind of vitalistic, other-worldly energy: the soul is not a special ingredient that vitiates otherwise inert matter. Instead, we have a much more nuanced relation between body and soul

---

1. Of course Aristotle is much more specific about how living things are a subset of natural things. This is clear in terms of three distinctions. First, natural things are a type of substance. Substances are distinguished by whether or not they move. Natural things are those substances that move (in contrast to Aristotle's well known "unmoved mover"). Second, moving substances can be divided into those that move eternally and those that come to be and pass away. Traditionally those that come to be and pass away are said to be subject to "substantial change." Finally, things that are subject to substantial change can be divided into those that have an *internal* principle of motion and rest and those without such an internal principle. In sum, while all natural things move, living things are the subset of natural things that have an internal principle of motion and are subject to substantial change; living things are perishing self-movers. See Aristotle, "Physics," 192b 9–23 and 258b 26–259a 19; and "Metaphysics," 1026a 10–20 and 1069a 30ff.

2. Aristotle, "Physics," 192b 9–193b 6.

3. Aristotle, "On the Soul," 412b 27.

4. Ibid., 403a 3–19. Angels do not have a place in the Aristotelian picture. However, integrating angels into the wider natural philosophy of Aristotle provides a significant point of challenge for later Christian Aristotelians. This is a discussion that takes us well beyond the bounds of our primary focus, however. For a helpful secondary source related to this issue, see Kreeft, "Aquinas and the Angels."

being developed here in terms of Aristotle's four causes: material, formal, efficient, and final.[5]

According to Aristotle, proper knowledge of a thing only comes when we have grasped all its causes, of which Aristotle identifies four.[6] Imagine this in terms of a house. The material cause of the house would be the timbers, bricks, mortar, etc. It is that out of which the thing is made. The formal cause for the house might be the blueprint, since it is the cause of the form of the house or an account of what it is to be. The efficient cause is what we are most familiar with as a cause after the explosion of modern science and the Enlightenment. The efficient cause describes primary sources of change; for the house, this would be the workers who erect it. Lastly, the final cause is that for the sake of which a thing should be. The final cause of the house could be to provide shelter. Just as we might apply these four causes to the complete explanation of any object in Aristotle's conception of nature, even an inanimate object like the house, the four causes may also be applied to living creatures. "A monkey, for example, has matter, its body; form, its soul; an efficient cause, its parent; and a final cause, its function."[7] Note how body and soul appear in this account of the four causes as applied to a monkey: the body and soul stand for the material and formal cause respectively.

This particular, and repeating, relationship between the material and the formal in Aristotle is called "hylomorphism." It is characteristic of all generated compounds both natural and artificial. Think back to the house, since in its existence it too is hylomorphic. Its matter is the various brick and mortar while its form is the shape of the house (indicated by the blueprint in the schema above). The brick and mortar is never a house without being arranged into the proper shape; vice versa, the shape of a house must always be "en-mattered." The form and matter are inseparable in their realization, but we must also remember that they are *contingently* related. A house could be made of wood or stone instead of brick, and the bricks in our example could be used to make a retaining wall, driveway, or outdoor grill.[8] The relation of the body and the soul as a union in living things falls into this wider set of hylomorphic relations that characterizes all generated things for Aristotle; they are inseparable in their realization but only contingently related.

To be clear about the contingency of the hylomorphic relationship between form and matter, matter could be called potential. The potentiality

---

5. For a great secondary source on this philosophical concept, see Falcon, "Aristotle on Causality." The most important general accounts of the four causes can be found in Aristotle's "Physics," 2.3; and "Metaphysics," 5.2.

6. Aristotle, "Posterior Analytics," 71b 9–24.

7. Shields, "Aristotle's Psychology."

8. Cohen, "Hylomorphism and Functionalism," 58–59.

of matter is relatively clear; lumps of bricks and mortar are not necessarily a house even if they may become a house: the material *potentially* has the form but does *not necessarily* have the form. This indicates that not any type of matter can simply take on any form. The matter needs to have a certain set of qualities in order that it is amicable to being en-formed in a particular way. By contrast, the form is the primary substance or actuality of the generated thing.[9] This is particularly important because it means that it is the presence of this form, soul, and not the particular matter the soul en-forms that separates living things from other generated things.[10] Still, form must be en-mattered and matter must have qualities that make it amenable for the form to which it is related. While the relation between matter and form in hylomorphism is characterized by contingency, the relation is not completely arbitrary or accidental.[11]

However, there is a rub in the contingency of hylomorphic relations when applied to living things. In Aristotle's work, for the thing to truly be what it is, it must be capable of performing its function (where "living" is the function that definitively separates living and non-living things). The classic example of this point is *an eye that cannot see is not actually an eye*, it is an eye in name only. This is the *homonymy principle*. Aristotle not only applies this principle to particular organs (like the eye), but also to the whole body of a living thing. "So just as a dead or detached eye is only homonymously an eye, a 'body' having lost its soul is only homonymously a body."[12]

The homonymous body sets up a problem that John Ackrill clearly formulates. First, remember for hylomorphism generally the material element only needs to be potentially en-formed; in a hylomorphic compound form and matter are contingent to one another. In a living thing, this would mean the body as the matter of this hylomorphic compound should be potentially, but not necessarily yet, en-souled. Now the homonymy problem rears its

---

9. See Aristotle, "On the Soul," 412a 6–413a 10; and "Metaphysics," 1032a 28–1033a 22, esp. 1032b 1.

10. Aristotle makes this point explicitly: "We resume our inquiry from a fresh starting-point by calling attention to the fact that what has soul in it differs from what has not in that the former displays life" ("On the Soul," 413a 21).

11. Of course, this relationship of contingency but not arbitrariness between matter and form should not be surprising for those familiar with Aristotle's *Physics*. The accidental quality of the changes characterized by chance and spontaneity eliminates them from being fundamentally applicable to substances. Only quantitative, qualitative, and locomotive changes are applicable as incidental changes maintaining natural substances. Living things, as a specific class of natural things, cannot violate this broader principle of nature in their substantial formation. See Aristotle, "Physics," 198a 1–13.

12. Whiting, "Living Bodies," 77. See also Aristotle, "On the Soul," 412b 21–23; and "Generation of Animals," 734b 24–27.

head. To identify a body as the matter in the hylomorphic compound of a living thing, the body must already be a *living body*. A body (i.e., matter) without its soul (i.e., form) is only homonymously a body—a body in name only. Thus, the problem is that it is not quite right for us to affirm that the matter of the hylomorphic compound of a living thing is the body. Instead, to be a body, which means an actually functioning body and not just homonymously a body (as with a corpse), is already to be a living, en-souled body. The upshot of Ackrill's argument is that the body and soul are not truly analogous to the class of hylomorphic compounds indicated by Aristotle because the relation of body and soul can never truly be contingent.[13]

Many have offered solutions to Ackrill's problem and the corresponding trouble it makes for interpreting Aristotle on this point. These solutions are largely variations on a theme: they try to more clearly delineate the contingent and functionally necessary features of the body in relation to the soul in order to clarify how the living thing is a type of hylomorphic compound.[14] This involves making a distinction in what it means to say that the body is the matter of the hylomorphic compound that is a living thing.

Jennifer Whiting introduces terms to clarify how the body as the matter in a living thing has two senses: functional flesh and compositional flesh. The functional flesh represents the body as matter necessarily related to the soul as its form; the compositional flesh represents the body as it is contingently related to the *functional flesh*. The functional flesh becomes an intermediary: functional flesh is necessarily en-formed or en-souled, while the compositional flesh is contingently related to the functionally defined whole of en-souled functional flesh. Whiting calls this en-souled functional

---

13. Ackrill, "Aristotle's Definition of *Psuchē*," 65–75. One could argue back to the basic elements as the compositional structure of the material part of the hylomorphic compound to establish potentiality, but this is put out of bounds by Aristotle. See "Metaphysics," Θ, 7.

14. There is a tremendous volume of writing that has been done on this topic. However, I have excluded much of it because it takes us far afield from our present interest in Aristotle into the relationship of hylomorphism and contemporary functionalism in the philosophy of mind and functionalism's relation to teleology. I follow the language and approach of Jennifer Whiting, which I find to be particularly clear and well put for my primary interest in issues of life and not mind. Other critical sources to consult for a more in depth analysis of this point would include at least the following: Burnyeat, "Is an Aristotelian Philosophy of Mind Still Credible? A Draft," 57–73; Charlton, "Aristotle's Definition of Soul," 170–86; Code, "The Persistence of Aristotelian Matter," 356–67; Cohen, "Aristotle's Doctrine of the Material Substrate," 171–94; Cohen, "Hylomorphism and Functionalism"; Hartman, *Substance, Body, and Soul*; Irwin, "Homonymy in Aristotle," 523–44; Jones, "Aristotle's Introduction of Matter," 474–500; Modrak, "An Aristotelian Theory of Consciousness?," 160–70; Putnam, *Representation and Reality*; and Sorabji, "Body and Soul in Aristotle," 63–89.

flesh the organic body. In sum, the organic body is the functional flesh and the soul, which stand in necessary relation to one another, while the compositional flesh is contingently related to the functional flesh of the organic body.[15]

Two points about hylomorphism need to be emphasized: (1) the soul is not a separate force that vitiates the body apart from matter and (2) matter is understood in a highly nuanced way. Matter is much more here than the minimalist idea of extension that we inherit in a post-Cartesian period. Aristotelian matter is pluriform—appearing in various guises according to its conjunction with specific forms to which it is well suited. Whiting's interpretation is helpful because it helps bridge the Aristotelian hylomorphism (through functional flesh) to our inherited post-Cartesian sensibilities about matter (through compositional flesh).

Now if the soul is the essential form or substance of a living thing, as we have already noted above, then an analysis of the soul can deepen our understanding of the Aristotelian conception of the principles of life. His work *On the Soul* is critical to such an analysis, but it can be a bit tricky to interpret. Nonetheless, Aristotle makes two points very clear in that work. First, different living things possess various faculties of the soul. The soul of a plant exhibits different abilities from the soul of an animal that are different than the soul of a human being. The faculties that he describes as particular to each of these expressions of the soul (nutrition to plants, sensation to animals, and mind to human beings) appear to be nested one within the other.[16] Second, the presence of any one of the faculties Aristotle enumerates indicates a thing is living.[17]

How are these two points to be interpreted in relation to each other? What does it mean that these faculties are "nested"? What is the relationship between different faculties? These questions can be helpfully framed in a more technical way: if there is to be one essential form, "soul," across these various faculties such that en-mattering this form constitutes being alive, what would be the unifying principle that cuts across the faculties? What can indicate why the soul is the form of living things, while also not doing violence to the real differences that the faculties' variations indicate?

It would seem Aristotle could be interpreted in one of two ways regarding these questions. First, to be a living thing is to possess the nutritive faculty as a foundational power. This faculty would be the foundation upon which all the higher faculties accumulate. The "nesting" being described

---

15. Whiting, "Living Bodies," 77–85.
16. Aristotle, "On the Soul," 414a 29–414b 1 and 434a 24–434b 8.
17. Ibid., 413a 21–25.

would then be something like an inverted pyramid, where the more and more complex faculties rest on this most basic feature of the soul.[18]

This interpretation is not satisfactory on two accounts, but to understand why we need to examine the nutritive faculty in more detail. As the name would imply, the nutritive faculty is concerned with consuming food; however, it is also related to reproduction. Why group these two seemingly different behaviors together? It has to do with the four causes. The soul is the form of those hylomorphic beings that are alive, but a full account of a particular thing needs to address all four causes. Aristotle identifies that the goal (or final cause) towards which living things strive is to participate in what is eternal and divine. Since living things are perishable and subject to substantial change, they cannot live into this final cause themselves; thus, reproduction is the only means by which a living thing can attempt to achieve this end.[19]

If reproduction (as a substitute for participating directly in the eternal) stands as the final cause of the living thing, consuming food is an efficient cause that maintains the living thing and eventually allows reproduction to take place. Here, nutrition involves three factors, "what is fed, that wherewith it is fed, and what does the feeding; of these what feeds is the first soul, what is fed is the body which has that soul in it, and that with which it is fed is the food."[20] This structure is typical of Aristotle's analysis of faculties of the soul. The general power or faculty (the nutritive faculty of the soul—the "what does the feeding") is described in terms of an action (the consuming of the en-souled body—the "what is fed") that must be understood in terms of its correlative object (food—the "that wherewith it is fed").[21]

What about this account makes our first interpretation (the nutritive faculty as a primordial power) untenable? First, it seems unlikely that Aristotle intends his work to be read this way, if one has a suspicion that there are non-mortal beings (a suspicion which Aristotle appears to hold). He describes non-mortal beings that are alive since they *have* the power of one faculty of the soul (rationality) but do not need the nutritive faculty since they do not need to reproduce or grow in order to achieve the end of participating in the eternal.[22] If these non-mortal beings are "alive" according to Aristotle, it would seem highly unlikely that this first reading—the nutritive

18. Ibid., 415a 23.
19. Ibid., 415a 31–415b 8.
20. Ibid., 416b 20.
21. Ibid., 415a 14–22.
22. Ibid., 415b 7–12; see also Matthews, "De Anima 2. 2-4 and the Meaning of Life," 190.

faculty as a primordial power for en-souled, living things—is what Aristotle intends.

Second, even if the nutritive faculty is understood as the primordial power at work in all living things against Aristotle's intention, there is an irreducible quality to Aristotle's description of the nutritive power. Food is defined in terms of the en-souled body; food is something consumed by a living thing.[23] Thus, food, by definition, is conceived in terms of what is living. To subsequently give an account of what is living in terms of nutrition (i.e., a living thing is what consumes food) would be circular. What this indicates is that Aristotle's account of life, even in its description of this most basic of faculties, appeals to some presupposed concept of life that is irreducible to any one of the faculties.[24]

What then of the second interpretation. This reading posits an alternative unifying principle that does not make what it means to be a living thing foundationally reliant upon a most primitive faculty. The "nesting" of the various faculties could be thought of more like matroyshka dolls rather than an inverted pyramid. The faculties relate to each other in such a way that the more complex faculties can include simpler faculties, but are not necessarily constituted by the simpler faculties. The critical power of being a living, en-souled thing will be different across the various types of living things we can identify, but what it means to live will entail a common aim or goal that the varying powers help fulfill.

The part reproduction plays in the analysis of the nutritive faculty, on this interpretation, is important. In the account of the nutritive faculty Aristotle reveals that the final cause, the end towards which living things have their being, is participation in the eternal or the divine. This drive for participation in the eternal can be the unifying principle for the second interpretation. Thus, the nutritive, sensitive, and rational faculties of the soul all serve as powers that contribute to the various classes of living things best enacting this final cause—a drive to participate in the eternal.[25]

23. Aristotle, "On the Soul," 416b 9–13.

24. Shields expresses this point well: "[A] living system is the sort of thing which can take on nutrition, while nutrition is whatever stuff is such as to sustain a living system. So, if living systems cannot be reductively defined in some other way, it will follow that no reductive account of life will be forthcoming. Consequently, Aristotle's discussion of nutrition provides some reason for thinking that he will resist any attempt to define life in terms which do not themselves implicitly appeal to life itself" ("Aristotle's Psychology," § 5).

25. See especially Matthews, "De Anima 2. 2–4 and the Meaning of Life," 191–92. Put in terms of species survival (instead of participation in the eternal) and psychic powers (instead of my use of faculties of the soul), Matthews is able to offer us a more formal definition that helps identify just how this second reading actually envelops the

This second reading can elegantly identify all four causes constituting a proper knowledge of living things. The body is the material cause of the living thing joined in hylomorphic fashion to the soul as its formal cause. The contingency of this hylomorphic relation is preserved in the relation of the constituting flesh to the functional flesh of the organic body. The faculties of the soul are the efficient causes that promote how a living thing achieves its final cause of participating in that which is divine and eternal. It is noteworthy that this reading places a strong correlation between final causes and the principles of life. The final cause of the living thing is the unifying principle across the various manifestations of the faculties of the soul in actual living things. Final and formal causes share an intimate relationship in this interpretation that makes the inner teleology of Aristotle essential to giving an account of the principles of life. The soul, as the formal cause of self-movement in living things, constantly strives to perpetuate itself, fulfilling the final cause of participating in the eternity of the divine.

Descartes and Mechanical Life

A typical account of Cartesian philosophy would begin with his methodological approach: radical doubt. It is known by that oft turned phrase, "I think, therefore I am" or his *cogito* argument. It intends to set out an indefeasible foundation upon which to build his philosophy. Descartes is not actually applying doubt to everything for the sake of doubting it; instead, he is treating as doubtful anything that might make a claim to being the indefeasible foundation for knowledge. This even includes doubting our own perceptions and sensations, in order to generate the certainty that Descartes seeks.

---

first reading. This formal definition has been highly influential on my reading of the two potential ways to interpret Aristotle on this point.

"Now we can say (going beyond any claim explicitly stated in Aristotle, though I think something like this is suggested by what he says) that what it means to say that an organism is alive is that it can exercise at least one psychic power; that is, at least one of the powers that organisms of its species must, in general, be able to exercise for the species to survive.

"x is alive =df there is a species s, and a psychic power p, such that x belongs to s, p is a psychic power for species s, and x can exercise p.

"Because of nesting it will turn out that any mortal organism that is alive will have the power of self-nutrition. Still, 'is alive' does not *mean* (on this reconstruction of Aristotle) 'is capable of self-nutrition.' What it does mean is 'can exercise a power such that members of the organism's species need to be able, in general, to exercise that power in order that the species may survive'" (191–92).

However, here the concern is for what it means to be alive, and the *cogito* argument—critical to a general account of Cartesian philosophy—is only significant in terms of its implications for understanding what "living" means. What suppositions must be doubted in order to indefeasibly ground the principles of life? In the Aristotelian framework Descartes inherits during his lifetime the power of the soul is associated with the powers of life as the essential form of a hylomorphic compound. It is this power of the soul *regarding life* that Descartes comes to doubt. Instead, he supposes a radical disjunction between the mental and the physical, associating the mental with the soul. In the Cartesian framework the power of the soul is associated only with the rational. There is then no place for the Aristotelian vegetative or sensitive faculties in the Cartesian account of the soul (these faculties are not mental powers). Instead, the Cartesian account—in order to succeed when compared to the Aristotelian account—needs to demonstrate how the vegetative and sensitive powers are best ascribed to the body and the physical realm.[26] Moreover, remember that by Descartes's reckoning such a physical account consists only of those attributes that empirically and quantifiably characterize matter's extension: motion, size, shape, and their interaction.[27] Even the human body is not distinctive in this sense; its operations are to be explained in light of completely physical mechanisms. In Aristotelian terms, the explication of living things is being moved out of the realm of final causality and into efficient causality.[28]

Since the veracity of the Cartesian descriptions of bodies is simply laughable in light of contemporary scientific accounts, it is important to keep this contrast with the Aristotelian mode of explanation in mind. The Cartesian account of the body in mechanical terms provides a "proof of concept" argument.[29] The mechanical explanations are intended to demonstrate

26. Code and Moravcsik, "Explaining Various Forms of Living," 139–40.

27. As relevant details from Descartes's physics appear in the text, these key sources will have been indispensable for my interpretation. Garber, "Descartes' Physics," 286–334; Garber, *Descartes' Metaphysical Physics*; Gaukroger, *Descartes' System of Natural Philosophy*; and Shea, *The Magic of Numbers and Motion: The Scientific Career of René Descartes*.

28. "When dealing with natural things we will, then, never derive any explanations from the purposes which God or nature may have had in view when creating them <and we shall entirely banish from our philosophy the search for final causes>. For we should not be so arrogant as to suppose that we can share in God's plans. We should, instead, consider him as the efficient cause of all things" (Descartes, *Principles*, pt. 1, §28).

As is standard, page references will be made to the Adam and Tannery edition of the complete works of Descartes as AT followed by volume and page number. The only exception will be the *Principles*, as cited here, which are customarily cited by part and section number.

29. Des Chene, *Spirits and Clocks: Machine and Organism in Descartes*, 17.

that the Aristotelian reliance on formal powers and final causes is otiose in explaining nutrition, growth, reproduction, and sensation. Keeping in mind this proof of concept approach clarifies the intent of the Cartesian accounts of digestion, circulation, and respiration as means of replenishing blood: these mechanisms of the body account for the self-movement of nutrition and growth in the Aristotelian nutritive soul. It is worthwhile to review these unfamiliar Cartesian accounts of the body.

Beginning with digestion, Descartes describes a process of fermentation and sifting. In the stomach, food particles are broken down by "certain liquids" brought from the heart that separate, shake, and heat the food particles. Descartes compares the food particles to new hay that when shut in a barn before being dry begins to break down under heat; one can presume that the heated liquids coming from the heart and the stomach provide the food particles an analogous environment to the barn for the new hay. The agitation of this heating creates a sifting action, whereby the relative size of different food particles are sorted out by the tiniest particles descending into the smallest holes of a fibrous tube that carries these particles to the liver.[30] Once in the liver, this mingled liquid of food particles is further "subtilized" and part of the liquid is blended with the blood that passes through the liver.[31] Here the food particle liquid takes on the form of blood; this process (which converts the whitish liquid of the food particles to the red color of blood) is likened to the fermentation of white juice into light red wine.[32]

Descartes proceeds with a description of circulation. From the liver, the blood recently comingled and subtilized with the food particle liquid passes via the veins to the right cavity of the heart. The heat of the heart, a common concept of the time, inflates and dilates the blood into a kind of vapor. From the right cavity, the heated blood travels to the lungs. The lungs are so soft, cool, and rare from respiration that they re-condense the blood and it passes back into the left cavity of the heart. This re-thickened blood serves to stoke the fire within the heart that is the source of its heating. The blood now in the left cavity of the heart is again inflated and dilated (in

---

30. As an example of this sifting, Descartes often makes an analogy to an agricultural trick: "[J]ust as when one shakes meal in a sack all the purest part runs out, and only the smallness of the holes through which it passes prevents the bran from following after" (*Treatise of Man*, AT 11:122).

31. Ibid., AT 11:121–23. My account combines the formation of *chyle* and *chyme* that are usually separate in a Cartesian account of digestion. This eliding is not detrimental for my purposes. More on the historical development of this distinction can be found consulting Des Chene, *Spirits and Clocks*, 19n13; and Hall's notes in his edition of *Treatise of Man*, n18.

32. Descartes, *Treatise of Man*, AT 11:123.

addition to stoking the fire of the heart) and is pushed out of the heart and to the rest of the body via the arterial system.[33]

What Descartes is developing in these passages is the rudiments of a circulatory system and an account of the pulsing of blood. He suggests that this pulsing is a product of the dilating and rarefying of the blood, which causes a series of membranes to open and close "like little doors" at the four veins and arteries that open into the chambers of the heart. Rather than envision this as the product of muscular contraction, like today (or like William Harvey in his own time), he imagines it to be a product of the dilation of the blood. The heated and dilated blood vapors expand rapidly and suddenly, thereby closing the venous membranes and opening the arterial membranes, subsequently inflating all of the blood in the arterial system. Once released from the chamber there is a deflation of the heart that closes the arterial membranes but allows the venous membranes to open and have rarefied blood enter that can then be subsequently heated.[34]

Understanding the pulse is important because of its critical role in the Cartesian account of growth. The inflated blood of the arteries is constantly pushed away from the heart as the chambers of the heart dilate the blood. As the heart deflates, the particles of blood in the arterial system stop wherever they may be. Descartes envisions that the tissues of the body are fibrous; further, little threads of these fibrous body tissues extend into the furthest reaches of the arterial branches. Growth and maintenance of the tissues of the body occurs by blood particles assimilating to these threads. The force of the pulsation of dilated blood from the heart pushes blood particles past these threads of fibrous tissue, but as the heart deflates and fills with new cool blood the blood particles in the arterial system remain still and some of these particles become entangled with the threads of the fibrous tissues, while others will continue circulating with the next dilation of blood in the heart. Thus, with his account of circulation, Descartes has manufactured an explanation of growth.[35]

Finally, by offering a mechanistic account of hunger that drives living things to find food, Descartes is even able to make the self-regulation of his digestive and circulatory cycles mechanical. At root, hunger occurs when

---

33. Ibid., AT 11:125. Descartes also has an explanation for how the rarefied blood of the lungs that sustains the fire in the heart is made accessible for fetuses that do not breathe. For this description see the same reference above.

34. Ibid. A much more thorough account of the pulse and the anatomical details that Descartes understood in its regard can be found in his "La Description Du Corps Humain," AT 11:228–32.

35. Descartes, *Treatise of Man*, AT 11:127; and "La Description Du Corps Humain," AT 11:239.

the digestive fluids cannot find food to dissolve, and they begin to work on the stomach. This stimulates and pulls on the nerve filaments that set in motion the rush of animal spirits in the brain that coordinate a series of movements to find food.[36] The general idea that this sensation be *called*

---

36. I have chosen not to enter into a full discussion of how Descartes offers a mechanical account of sensations stimulated from within and outside the body. To do so would take the reader too far from the primary focus. For those particularly interested, it is noteworthy that Descartes connects the work of the circulatory system to his mechanical account of sensation generally (which includes hunger).

The connection is made through his account of growth. As outlined above, Descartes envisions the arteries of the circulatory system to be like sieves. The fineness or coarseness of these various arterial sieves allow for Descartes to make a distinction amidst the subtlety and quality of the blood particles that are given access to the various tissues. For instance, when newly heated blood from the lungs leaves the heart, it moves first toward the brain. However, the arterial sieve towards the brain is so fine that only the subtlest of blood particles can pass towards the arterial ends where the tissue fibers reside. Blood particles unable to move toward the arterial ends in the brain cavity circulate to the next most subtle arterial sieve. This process continues repeatedly as the blood particles circulate to more and more coarse arterial sieves.

Descartes uses this sieving to separate particles to a nearly infinite degree. Even within the brain itself, there is an arterial separation of those blood particles that are coarser and "bathe" the surface of the brain and those that are the most fine and form the very important "animal spirits" that reside in the pineal gland (the Cartesian locus of the union of the body and the rational soul). These animal spirits are formed from the subtlest particles of the blood that best preserve the rapid movement given to them by being heated in the heart. They move through the pores in the substance of the brain and are thereby able to pass through the nerves. It is by the flow of these animal spirits that muscular movement occurs and sense organs are able to function. Nerves that proceed to muscles branch off into several loose membranes upon entering those muscles. These membranes are able to expand and contract according to the volume of animal spirits in them at a given moment. As these membranes fill with animal spirits they inflate and the muscle contracts; as the animal spirits withdraw these membranes deflate and the muscle elongates. Imagining muscles in antagonistic pairs, Descartes also imagines a simple valve system to prevent contraction of both muscles from occurring at the same time. This valve system is akin to that of the heart; only in the muscles instead of the inflation that causes the shutting of a valve to be produced by heating, the inflation is governed by the volume of animal spirits. The valve system in the antagonistic muscles and the connections between the antagonistic muscles are arranged in such a way that as the primary muscle fills with animal spirits, the animal spirits from its opposing muscle are also shunted into the primary muscle. The arrangement of these valves on the shunt and nerve tubules are also intended to prevent backflow; thus, as the primary muscle fills another valve closes the tube that would shunt its animal spirits into the opposing muscle. Muscle movement in the body is a highly coordinated system of pressure valves and backflow restrictors that operate based on the volume of animal spirits in the membranes within muscles at the ends of nerves.

For Descartes just as the nervous system controls muscle movement, it also controls sensation. In addition to the nerves being tubules for the transmission of animal spirits to muscles, they also contain fine fibrils that run from the central portion of the brain to all the various parts of the body with sensation. When nerve fibrils are moved by

"hunger" is a product of the soul when united with the machine that is the body. Naming the particular sensation "hunger" is the only place where the soul has entered into this account of the body.[37]

Put together, these descriptions form an interrelated series of mechanisms that present an alternative account of the fundamental powers of Aristotle's nutritive soul. The critical concept Descartes employs over and over in these descriptions are cycles that begin where they end. By essentially resetting themselves, these cycles create their initial casual conditions allowing for repetition. Further, the interrelation of these cyclic systems creates a means to self-maintenance and self-regulation. Digestion aids replenishment of the blood by sending food particles to the liver that are there mixed with the blood, which are heated by the heart, cooled and thickened by the lungs, and circulated through the body for growth and repair thereby being used up. This generates the need for more food to be transmuted into blood particles and the description of a synergistic cycle for the acquisition of food. To that end, the sensation of hunger, which is simply the digestive fluids—as heated by the heart—working against the stomach itself since no food is present, opens the pores of the brain for the animal spirits to generate muscle movements to search for satiating food.

There is perhaps one specter that remains in Descartes's body-machine to be vanquished: the heat of the heart. This is a concept that comes from the biological tradition preceding Descartes, and in that tradition it would hardly be considered as mechanical as Descartes's work would indicate it is. After all, the heat of the heart seems quite similar to that inner principle of self-movement so critical for the Aristotelian soul. So is the heat of the heart a remnant of the soul in the Cartesian account? Is it just a new name for the principle of self-movement? Is it a little homunculus that remains in his mechanistic body, leading to the failure of his account? To be an honest interpreter of Descartes's work is to answer these questions with a resounding, "No!"

Descartes calls this heat of the heart a "fire without light." The concept is immensely important because it relates intimately to his understanding of life and the beast-machine. In an oft noted letter to Henry More, Descartes

---

sensory stimulation they pull on the parts of the brain from which they come, opening the tubules for animal spirits generating muscle movement. Sensation becomes the tugging of nerve filaments that open the pores in the brain instituting the movement of animal spirits, something like strings attached to sliding doors.

On this relation of the circulatory, nervous, and muscular systems see Descartes, *Treatise of Man*, AT 11:128–30, 133–35, 141; see also Des Chene, *Spirits and Clocks*, 22–23.

37. Descartes, *Treatise of Man*, AT 11:164.

writes, "I do not deny life to animals, since I regard it as consisting simply in the heat of the heart; and I do not even deny sensation, in so far as it depends on a bodily organ. Thus my opinion is not so much cruel to animals as indulgent to human beings...."[38]

Even as Descartes endeavors to develop a mechanical explanation of animals (and bodies more generally), he does not deny that these things are alive. Instead, he is making it clear that the mechanical and the living are not mutually exclusive categories. The heat of the heart is the vital principle for Descartes; whatever mechanism can sustain the fire without light within itself is most certainly alive.[39] *Thus, mechanical bodies are living things, only for Descartes living is not a quality worth being excited about.* By contrast, the juncture of the rational soul and the mechanical body is significant for Descartes. It is here that freedom comes to be—with the rational soul and the peculiar union of body and soul that is the human being. The mechanical-living body lacks this freedom entirely, but it does not lack life. While it is much easier as interpreters to simply assert that Descartes does away with plants and animals as living things—relegating them to mere machines—this does not do justice to the tension of his perspective. It is important to acknowledge that Cartesian life is as inert as Cartesian matter.

In the spirit of this overlap of the mechanical and that which is alive, the heat of the heart—the vital principle—has a mechanical explanation. This explanation requires understanding a few points of Cartesian physics though. Dennis Des Chene makes clear why it is important to examine these features of Cartesian physics to completely understand his account of the heat of the heart. "Descartes agrees with many of his predecessors in holding that the principle of life is heat, the heat of the heart; he takes over many claims from older physiologies—that the heart is the hottest organ, for example.... But Descartes admits those claims only if they can be interpreted mechanistically: ideally, in terms of the laws of motion, but practically, by way of comparisons with nonliving systems whose mechanical nature he takes to be obvious."[40] Descartes is trying to explain the principle at work in the fire without light that heats the heart in terms of what can generally be said about fire in his account of physics.

Descartes asserts that all extended substance is a plenum: there is no vacuum or space, only extended substance divided into bodies based on

---

38. Descartes, "To More, 5 February 1649," AT 5:278–79; see also "Discourse on the Method of Rightly Conducting One's Reason and Seeking the Truth in the Sciences," AT 6:46, 48, 52–55, 59–60.

39. See Bitbol-Hespériès, "Le Principe De Vie Dans Les 'Passions De L'âme,'" 415–31; and *Les Principe De Vie Chez Descartes*.

40. Des Chene, *Spirits and Clocks*, 29.

the coordination of local motion.[41] As a corpusculist, not an atomist,[42] he identifies three elements of matter (paralleling the classic conception of air, fire, and earth) from which all bodies in the plenum are composed. The first element is violently agitated particles of indefinite smallness; the second element is spherical particles subject to division; and the third element is bulkier particles with non-spherical shapes that make them less suited for motion.[43] He suggests that fire is a fluid (as constituted by the rapidity of its particle motion) that can occur with or without light. Usually, fire consists of the first and second element particles.

I have already indicated that the fire in the heart is one without light. However, it has another special feature as well. The presence of fire's heat in solid substances (like the heart) indicates that the pores of that substance are so fine that only a fluid of first element particles (not first and second element particles as would be standard) fill the space of the plenum in these pores. The point to emphasize is that the fire in the heart can be described in terms of the same properties as any other fire; specifically, it consists of a fluid of first element particles continually fed by the recondensed blood that has passed through the lungs.[44]

Certainly, one could object that these processes and the heat of the heart are not nearly as mechanical as Descartes would have us believe. However, objecting to the Cartesian explanation is not the point of this description. Here the concern is to exemplify how a relatively few properties of mechanical and chemical processes can be arranged in a self-perpetuating series in order to make the functions of the Aristotelian nutritive sole otiose. If nothing else, there is something to marvel at in the Cartesian account in that it is largely based only on the arrangement of a remarkably few mechanical tools: fermentation, sieves for sorting, a series of valves, and the properties of fluid pressure under volume and temperature. The result of these simple, mechanical processes is to make the qualities basic to the nutritive powers of the Aristotelian soul (notably growth and nutrition) otiose: they are thus conceived as a function of the arrangement of systems and parts in this body-machine.[45]

41. On the challenges of this approach, see Slowik, "Descartes' Physics."

42. The difference between a corpusculist and an atomist has to do with the divisibility of matter. For the atomist there is a smallest unit of matter, but for the corpusculist matter is (at least in principle) infinitely divisible. Descartes is explicitly a corpusculist (see *Principles*, pt. 2.).

43. Descartes, *Principles*, pt. 3, §§48–52; and "Treatise on Light," AT 11:23–25.

44. On the relevant passages dealing with the Cartesian understanding of fire see Descartes, "Treatise on Light," AT 11:7–16; and *Principles*, pt. 4, §§80–100.

45. "I desire you to consider, further, that all the functions I have attributed to this

There is, though, a critical issue that remains open in the account of the Cartesian understanding of living bodies offered here. While the account above, taken largely from his *Treatise of Man*, addresses the formal powers of digestion, growth, and the senses that are a part of the Aristotelian vegetative and sensitive souls, the generation of the body is not addressed. If Descartes's work is to be a proof of concept against the necessity of final cause and formal powers in explicating what it is to be alive, it is reasonable to expect some response to all aspects of the vegetative soul, which must include reproduction.[46]

As to the formation (in both its development and generation) of the body, the best clue about Descartes's thinking appears in his *Description of the Human Body*. Here he gives a description of those parts of the body that are originally formed from the seminal material.[47] The seminal materials from the parents are fluids that in their interaction produce heat in a process Descartes again likens to fermentation. The heat causes certain fluid particles to gather together and begin forming the heart. The heart takes in surrounding smaller particles, causing them to expand and thereby function as blood. Once expanded, this newly rarified blood is expelled from the heart and follows a path of least resistance that takes it away from the space where the heart is taking in new small particles to expand. The direction this rarified blood flows is towards what will become the brain. This displaces

machine, such as [a] the digestion of food; [b] the beating of the heart and arteries; [c] the nourishment and growth of the members; [d] respiration; [e] waking and sleeping; [f] the reception by the external sense organs of light, sounds, smells, tastes, heat, and all other such qualities; [g] the imprinting of the ideas of these qualities in the organ of common sense and imagination; [h] the retention or imprint of these ideas in the memory; [i] the internal movements of the appetites and passions; and finally [j], the external movements of all the members that so properly follow both the actions of objects presented to the senses and the passions and impressions which are entailed in the memory—I desire you to consider, I say, that these functions imitate those of a real man as perfectly as possible and *that they follow naturally in this machine entirely from the disposition of the organs—no more nor less than do the movements of a clock or other automaton, from the arrangement of its counterweights and wheels. Wherefore it is not necessary, on their account, to conceive of any vegetative or sensitive soul or any other principle of movement and life,* than its blood and its spirits, agitated by the heat of the fire which burns continually in its heart and which is of no other nature than all those fires that occur in inanimate bodies" (Descartes, *Treatise of Man*, AT 11:202; emphasis my own).

46. See also Des Chene, *Spirits and Clocks*, chap. 2.

47. It is worth noting that Descartes's account on this point makes a distinction between seminal fluids of animals and the hard seed of plants. See "La Description Du Corps Humain," AT 11:253. If the goal was to systematically generate a Cartesian account of life, it would be important to search out a separate account of the generation of plants if they too are to fall into his mechanistic account of living things.

more small particles that are then pushed towards the entrance to the heart which rarefies blood from these seminal liquids. This circular motion comes as no surprise since it enacts one of Descartes's general rules for the motion of bodies.[48] A basic circulatory system is formed, and we already know from the description of how branches of the blood break off in order to facilitate growth, that the establishment of this circulatory system will allow for the development of the other organ systems and exactly enacts the circulatory path of blood particles maintained by the heart's pulsing in the fully developed body.[49]

Thus, while in *Treatise of Man*, Descartes's accounts of digestion and growth are simply givens since the mechanics of organ functions are described only in their developed entirety, when read in conjunction with the *Description of the Human Body* a principle of generation begins to emerge. The formation of organs, as mechanisms where the cycle performed begins where it ends, finds its generation in these seminal fluid dynamics.[50] Even the power of generation can then fall into the Cartesian mechanisms. As such, by employing the principles of displacement in the plenum and the circularity of motion that are established in Cartesian physics,[51] all of the powers of the Aristotelian nutritive soul can be explained without recourse to final causes. The reproductive fluids interact in such a way as to form the systems that allow for growth and digestion allowing for subsequent reproduction. To the contemporary mind, the problem of an initial generation may still loom in this account, but for Descartes, this can be dismissed since all created things are initially formed by God.

48. See Des Chene, *Spirits and Clocks*, 36; and Descartes, *Principles of Philosophy*, pt. 2, §33.

49. Descartes, "La Description Du Corps Humain," AT 11:254–57.

50. Making the connection even more explicit, Des Chene highlights a passage that comes just before the account of the formation of the heart out of seminal fluids I have rehearsed here. In this earlier passage, Descartes notes that in the living body there is no difference between parts that are fluid and those that are solid; the whole body is continually subject to change, and the quality of being solid or liquid consists only in the speed with which the constitutive particles move. This makes a more direct connection between the generation of such self-resetting systems and their developed mechanical operation as organs. As Des Chene aptly describes: "To think only of clocks and wind-up toys in imagining a Cartesian automaton is to be quite misled: the "machine of the body" is much more like a petroleum distillery or the system of pneumatic tubes for delivering messages that one still sees in some old buildings—but one which is constantly sloughing off and snapping up slivers of glass and metal" (Des Chene, *Spirits and Clocks*, 39–40). See also Descartes, "La Description Du Corps Humain," 248 and 254–57; and Pichot, *Historie De La Notion De Vie*, 381.

51. Descartes, *Principles*, pt. 2, §§37–44; and pt. 3, §57; and "Treatise on Light," AT 11:31–46.

Descartes's use of this mechanical conception of the body is a ubiquitous feature of his work. Moreover, it lays the foundation of a mechanistic and physicalist approach to defining life and its features, which continues to be widely adapted by many scientific models of life today. It is critical, though, not to divorce the mechanical arguments of Descartes from their historical trajectory. This trajectory is important in two senses—one moving forward and one looking back.

Moving forward from Descartes, the mechanical account of the body actually clears the way for the subsequent development of more robust forms of panvitalism. By strongly separating the material body and the rational soul, Descartes's mechanisms press the property of life into the realm of matter. However, this does not entail that one needs to follow Descartes in his view of inanimate matter in order to take the mechanization of life from his philosophy. In thinkers such as Leibniz, La Mettrie, Diderot, and Herder this is exactly what happens. These thinkers espouse an understanding of matter that lives. Thus, following Descartes life is not dependent in this perspective on the union of body and soul: life is a fully material property that ultimately ought to be describable in terms of mechanics. However, instead of accounting for that property in terms of the organization of things recognized as alive, in panvitalist materialism all material things have life and the organizational disposition of matter is only more or less complex. In looking at the work of Immanuel Kant, he will be responding to both of these Cartesian inspired approaches: mechanical and panvitalist materialisms.

Looking back from Descartes, we must remember that his mechanisms serve as a proof of concept against the Aristotelian vegetative soul. Remembering this conceptual problem is at stake in the Cartesian writing on living bodies prevents one from treating this work as merely antiquated anatomical musings. Instead, Descartes puts forward key criteria that subsequent mechanical explanations need to overcome if they are to rid "life" of its more than physical characteristics—its mysterious en-souled vitalism. In this regard, perhaps one of Descartes's greatest achievements is his realization that *the systemic mechanisms of living things need to be self-perpetuating*. Cyclic systems of automated causes—systems that reset themselves by ending where they begin—are able to do this particularly well. By arranging various smaller cyclic systems into a larger cyclic system one can generate breathtaking complexity: a living machine.

Kant and Natural Ends

If my reading of Descartes is a proof of concept against the Aristotelian vegetative soul, my reading of Immanuel Kant is a proof of concept against the fervently mechanistic approach of Descartes. However, at first glance Kant's approach appears to be very similar to the Cartesian organization of systems in the body. Pursuing two questions can clarify how there are elements of both continuity and discontinuity with the Cartesian vision of life in Kant's approach. First, Kant rejects the idea that living things are merely simple mechanisms; how does Kant reject this point? The rejection entails a retrieval of teleology for understanding the principles of life; but what is the quality of the teleology Kant invokes in this rejection and how is it related to the idea of teleology from Aristotle that Descartes rejects? Second, how does the Kantian account of living things preserve the use of simple mechanisms and cycles so fruitfully constructed by Descartes? I could borrow Aristotelian language to ask these questions: how does Kant give due credit to Descartes's account of living things in terms of efficient causality while preserving some conception of final causality?

Kant's concept of "end" or "purpose" is crucial to his argument that living things are not simply machines. Living things represent a special form of teleology he calls "natural ends." These natural ends are a self-causing form of organization wherein (1) the parts that yield the natural end are only recognizable in terms of the whole to which they belong and (2) the various parts are arranged so as to reciprocally be means and ends for one another.[52]

When Kant uses this term, "end," it has a technical meaning that represents a distinction he draws between an "end" or "purpose" proper on the one hand and "purposiveness" on the other (a difference between *Zweck* and *Zweckmässigkeit*).[53] In a dense sentence he lays out this distinction. "[A]n end is the object of a concept insofar as the concept is regarded as the cause of the object (the real ground of its possibility); and the causality of a *concept* with regard to its *object* is its purposiveness (*forma finalis*)."[54] This can be a bit confusing, so it is worth taking the time to work slowly through these important definitions.

---

52. Kant, *Kants Gesammelte Schriften*, 5:373. As much as possible, references to Kant's work are taken from this edition of the collected works and subsequently abbreviated *KgS*. The edition will be cited by volume and page number.

53. On the challenges of translating these two terms see the editor's introduction to Kant, *Critique of the Power of Judgment*, xlviii. I will frequently use both "end" and "purpose" for *Zweck*.

54. *KgS*, 5:220.

Kant's idea of an "end" needs to be contrasted to the four causes in Aristotle: material, formal, efficient, and final. Hopefully, the description above has already made the Aristotelian picture quite clear. I imagined the Aristotelian causes in terms of the example of a house: the material cause is the stuff used to make it, the formal cause is the blueprint, the efficient cause is the labor of construction, and the final cause is the purpose for which it is built. Kant tells us an end or purpose [*Zweck*] occurs where something comes to be as a result of having an idea of it. In terms of our house example, we could say the house exhibits an end because the idea of the house precedes the actual construction of the house.[55] Moreover though, for Kant it is not the "idea of the house" that is the end or purpose, but the constructed house itself ("an end is the *object* of a concept"). Kant's end or purpose cannot be separated from its actual instantiation as an object, and for that object to be an end the concept of the object needs to be the cause of its being.

A Kantian end appears to be very similar to an artifact (i.e., something made by design); what about his concept of purposiveness [*Zweckmässigkeit*]? For purposiveness the concept *need not* cause the existence of its object. Something is purposive so long as the very possibility of its being cannot be understood except that it was produced according to some concept of it. The example of the house might be helpful in distinguishing an end and purposiveness. The difference between the house, as an end, and the purposive object is that the house is produced by design: the concept of the house is causative of the existence of the house. However, the purposive object is not necessarily designed: the concept of the purposive object is not causative of it.[56] An end or purpose is an object caused by its concept; a purposive object can only reasonably be understood *as if* it were an end.

This account of purposiveness is important because of the way Kant imagines living things to be one instance of this purposiveness without end or purpose: what he calls a "natural end."[57] How are we to understand

---

55. We might think of this as a kind of amalgamation of the formal and final Aristotelian causes: the idea of the house includes both its purpose for being built and the plan for building imagined to realize this purpose.

56. Kant lays this point out explicitly: "But an object or a state of mind or even an action is called purposive, even if its possibility does not necessarily presuppose the representation of an end, merely because its possibility can be explained and conceived by us only insofar as we assume for its ground a causality according to ends (i.e., a will), which has regulated it according to the representation of a certain rule. Purposiveness, thus, can be without an end, insofar as we do not place the causes of this form in a will but can only make the explanation of its possibility conceivable to ourselves as we educe it from a will" (*KgS*, 5: 220). See also Ginsborg, "Kant on Understanding Organisms as Natural Purposes," 251.

57. Additionally, purposiveness provides a means for conceiving of final causality

living things to be natural ends? Moreover, what does it mean that natural ends exhibit purposiveness without purpose?[58] Kant identifies two critical

---

even within the strictures of Kant's previous writing on the single direction of causal sequences (always moving from cause to effect) that operates as a law of nature. Without a concept of purposiveness, living things would seem to violate the single direction of causality Kant so firmly establishes. *KgS*, 20:237–39; and Kant, *Critique of Pure Reason*, A198–99/B243–44.

58. It is helpful to keep in mind that the arguments Kant makes with regard to organisms as natural ends I am reviewing represent a very small piece of his larger argument made in the *Critique of the Power of Judgment*. There he makes a distinction between two types of judgment: determining and reflecting. Determining judgment subsumes a particular to a universal principle or law; reflecting judgment begins with a particular and seeks out a universal principle or law under which to subsume it. Determining judgment is the form of judgment Kant describes in the *Critique of Pure Reason*, where the *a priori* categories of the understanding are schematized making possible the judgment of any experience. Never does the determining judgment have to generate its own law or universal principle; these laws are transcendental. However, there are a tremendous number of forms in nature that are underdetermined by the transcendental categories of pure understanding. There is a need then for a principle by which to establish universals or laws that, although empirical and contingent to our understanding, can accommodate the diversity of nature. Reflecting judgment fits the bill in this regard: moving from particulars to universal laws it can flesh out those universal laws that remain underdetermined by the categories of pure understanding.

The reflecting judgment requires a transcendental principle by which to move from particulars to universal laws (akin to the categories of understanding). The rub is that this transcendental principle cannot come from experience, since the principle is to ground the systematic interrelation of empirical principles at work in experience. Nor can this transcendental principle be derived from anywhere else outside the reflecting judgment because then it would be a principle of the determining, not reflecting, judgment. To develop this transcendental principle of reflecting judgment, Kant makes an analogy to the universal laws of nature that arise from the categories of our understanding. These broad laws are grounded in our understanding and prescribed to nature; the empirical laws underdetermined by these broader laws should also be thought of as though they were given over from an understanding. This allows for a unity to be assumed amidst these empirical laws that would make our experiences that accord to laws of nature possible. This operating as if empirical laws are given over by an understanding is *purposiveness*, as was already outlined above. The transcendental principle of reflecting judgment is the general purposiveness of nature conceived as a logical necessity for the use of reflecting judgment.

Since the transcendental principle of the reflecting judgment is a necessary presupposition and not a category of the understanding as in determining judgment, the quality of the judgments made is different. There are three typological polarities for characterizing the purposiveness demonstrated by those things considered by reflecting judgments: subjective-objective, formal-material, and direct-indirect (or inner-outer). Not every combination of these typologies is explored by Kant, but they are useful in separating out his main arguments. The distinction between subjective and objective determines the two major parts of the *Critique of the Power of Judgment*: aesthetic judgment deals with subjective purposiveness and teleological judgment with objective purposiveness. My focus is on purposiveness as applied to living things. This

points. First, natural ends relate to themselves reciprocally as both cause and effect.[59] This is intended to demonstrate that a teleological sensibility is required for the possibility of a natural end;[60] the parts of the natural end are significant in terms of their participation in the whole—a significance that is in no way figured in the part alone. However, this criterion by itself is insufficient to characterize a *natural* end. It could equally well apply to any work of art or other designed object (i.e., anything exhibiting purpose not just purposiveness). Thus, Kant lays out a second criterion of those things that are *natural* ends which separates them from being mere artifacts:

> But if a thing, as a natural product, is said to contain in itself and its internal possibility a relation to ends,—i.e., is only to be possible as a natural end and without the causality of the concepts of a rational being outside of it—then it is required, *secondly*, that its parts be combined into the unity of a whole by being reciprocally the cause and effect of their form. For only in this way is it possible, that conversely (reciprocally) the idea of the whole, in turn, determine the form and combination of all the parts: not as a cause—for then it would be a product of art—but, for someone who judges it, as a cognitive ground of the systematic unity of the form and the combination of all of the manifold contained in the given material.[61]

By explicitly indicating that the parts of a natural end are the cause and effect of their own form, the specter of a designer can be removed. The natural end is an organized and self-organizing being that reciprocally produces

---

falls within the objective purposiveness of teleological judgment discussed in the second part of *The Critique of the Power of Judgment*. Here there is a distinction between the formal and the material. Objective formal purposiveness relates to the judgment of things such as geometrical figures, and objective material purposiveness relates to living things. Judgments concerning objective material purposiveness can further be divided between those that are indirect, where an organism remains in a means-end relationship to another thing, and direct, where the purposiveness describes a self-referential cycle of means-ends relations. My concern is only with Kant's work on an analysis of judgments related to objective-material-direct purposiveness; this is only a sliver of his far larger analysis of reflective judgment, which itself is only one of two forms of judgment Kant characterizes. See *KgS*, 5:179–81 and 362–69; 20:212–16, 224, and 249–50; and *Critique of Pure Reason*, §§19–20. An immensely helpful secondary source in this regard is Ginsborg's "Kant's Aesthetics and Teleology," §3.1.

59. *KgS*, 5:370.
60. On Kant's description of efficient and final causes see ibid., 5:372.
61. Ibid., 5:373.

its own parts. Kant calls this formative power of self-organizing being an analogue of life.[62]

It is important to understand that Kant is in no way devaluing or asserting that mechanical explanations should not be pursued with regard to living things. Living things are, after all, natural. As much as possible scientific knowledge should press on the bounds of mechanical explanation for this is a prime means for generating knowledge of the natural world. However, the concept of purposiveness relies on a fundamental disjunctive point beyond which mechanical explanation can never insert itself.

In order to be as specific as possible about this threshold the mechanical cannot cross, it is important to consider Kant's antinomy of teleological judgment. Roughly stated, the antinomy indicates that there is an *apparent* contradiction between two approaches to judging material things and their forms. First, one could affirm that all material things and their forms arise only in accordance to mechanical laws. Second, one could affirm that some material things and their forms cannot be judged in accordance only with mechanical laws, but also require an account of final causes.[63]

For Kant this tension does not represent an authentic contradiction. Instead, we must pursue the judgment of material things by mechanical laws in order to generate the best cognition of the world around us, but this does not exclude the possibility that other modes of causality can contribute to this process. Moreover, Kant is quite specific about what an understanding in terms of other modes of causality provides: the mechanical laws can only produce an *aggregate of parts* for analysis, while an account by final causes can yield *a self-formative whole*. He assures us that the teleological and mechanical explications may be unified in terms of a single principle; however, such a principle would be supersensible and beyond the cognitive limitations of our reason.[64]

In interpreting the meaning of this intersection of the mechanical and teleological in organisms as natural ends, there is much agreement in the secondary literature on two points. First, when Kant affirms that to understand the very possibility of an organism requires an account by purposiveness, he means that this concept is essential to the very nature of a living thing.[65] Second, there is wide held agreement that the antinomy between the mechanical and the teleological cannot be resolved by simply emphasizing

62. Ibid., 5:374.
63. Ibid., 5:387.
64. Ibid., 5:388 and 412.
65. See for example McLaughlin, *Kant's Critique of Teleology in Biological Explanation*, 133–37; Allison, "Kant's Antinomy of Teleological Judgment," 31–32 and 37–39; and Ginsborg, "Kant on Understanding Organisms as Natural Purposes," 236.

that this tension is a product of reflective, not constitutive, judgment.[66] Beyond these general points of agreement, there is variation amidst different interpreters on how best to treat this portion of Kant's work.

I follow Hannah Ginsborg, who identifies the importance of the purposiveness of organisms in terms of its contrast to what Kant means by mechanical explanation. Of course, identifying what Kant means by mechanical explanation is not straightforward.[67] However, the exegetical details of such an argument are not of concern here. Instead, what is critical is to understand that when Kant affirms purposiveness in the face of mechanical explanation, he contends that mechanical laws by themselves are insufficient for giving an explanation of a living thing. Mechanical explanation is not being rejected as a means of explaining the formation of a living thing from its organized parts; it is being used to reject the sufficiency of mechanical laws alone to explicate the occurrence of a living thing from unorganized matter (i.e., without consideration of the organized parts on which they are acting). Ginsborg gives an exceptionally helpful example to illustrate this difference.

> Thus the claim that organisms are inexplicable on mechanical laws—at least in the context we are considering—does not itself entail that we could never explain the origin of an individual bird as a lawlike consequence of the precise arrangement of matter to be found in an intact egg (as we might explain the ringing of an alarm clock as a lawlike consequence of its state just after having been wound up). It entails only that we cannot explain the origin of a bird by appeal to the powers of unorganized matter, say the powers of the same egg after it has been beaten.[68]

At stake is an issue of contingency and normativity. The mechanical inexplicability of living things points to a fundamental problem for biological investigation in general; the purposiveness of living things, their biological regularity, is *contingent* with regard to mechanical explanation. For example, I have tomato plants in my garden. In August, I share a portion of my harvest with the local bunnies; eat some of it with my family; pick at the wrong time and put this rotten fruit in my compost bin; and occasionally

---

66. See for example McLaughlin, *Kant's Critique of Teleology in Biological Explanation*, 137–40; and Friedman, "Regulative and Constitutive," 73–102. On the difference between reflective and constitutive (or determining) judgment see note 58 above.

67. Ginsborg clearly identifies five distinct ways we might understand what Kant means by "mechanical" and two distinct ways we might understand the meaning of "explanation" with regard to this problem. See "Kant on Understanding Organisms as Natural Purposes," 239–40.

68. Ibid., 242–43.

find that some fruit makes its way into the ground to produce new plant shoots for the next year. Despite the various ends my tomatoes might see (be it bunny food, a new plant, or bruschetta), they would always be described biologically as being for the reproduction of the plant. Biology privileges a teleological end for the tomato (producing a new plant) that according to the mechanical laws of matter alone is not necessarily any more likely to occur.[69]

The point is that living things exhibit patterns of regularity; they appear subject to rules even if these rules are contingent with regard to mechanical laws alone. This fact—living things appear subject to rules even though they are mechanically contingent—makes purposiveness an ineliminable feature of living things. Purposiveness indicates that living things are subject to a set of normative standards and constraints. Living things, or natural ends, are purposive because they are subject to normative rules that govern how they *ought* to behave, and these rules can never be reduced to mechanical explication alone.[70]

The *ineliminable* place of the purposive in Kant's account of living things is well exemplified by contrasting his work with one of his contemporaries: the Göttingen biologist Johann Blumenbach.[71] The idea of a self-formative power is crucial to both thinkers' constitution of the object of biological study: biology is a study of natural ends. Purposiveness, and its relationship to self-organization, was also critical for both thinkers. For Blumenbach though this purposiveness and the reflecting judgment from which it is generated only provided a *heuristic* that guides the course of future mechanical explication. In his account, purposiveness should give way to efficient causal explication; the purposive serves as a placeholder for underdeveloped mechanical explanations. However, Kant was adamant that purposiveness can never be reduced to a series of mechanical laws, and disagreed with Blumenbach on this point. For Kant, purposiveness is *fundamental* in providing the normative regularity that guides biological investigation and is contingent to mechanical explication.

69. Ibid., 245–48.

70. "Like the laws of physics and chemistry, they [normative generalizations] enable us to understand nature and its working by grasping the regularities characteristic of observable natural processes. But understanding nature, in the context of biological investigation, is a matter of grasping not how things *must* be, but how they *should* be" (ibid., 253).

71. See especially Richards, "Kant and Blumenbach on Bildungstrieb," 11–32; and for relevant primary sources by Blumenbach, see *Über Den Bildungstrieb*; and *Handbuch Der Naturgeschichte*, §2.

It is important to note the critical differences that have developed in this account of Kant as compared to Descartes. First, natural ends (organized and self-organizing organisms) possess a level of interrelation amidst the parts constituting a whole that goes beyond the mechanical account. *The parts of an organism are not decomposable as in a machine.* That is to say that one piece of an organism as a natural end cannot simply be removed and replaced like cogs in a machine. The parts of a natural end are constitutive of one another and importantly the whole is constitutive of the parts and their action: to remove a part is to have the whole cease to be.[72] In Kant, a final cause is conceived through the integral connection of efficient causes—purposiveness is a self-formative force. Still, this purposive teleology is *not* a constitutive principle as in the determining judgment. That is to say that purposive teleology is not like an efficient cause operating from the future in the Kantian perspective outlined here. The curious place of purposiveness as a regulative principle in the reflecting judgment is a function of how our human understanding relates to the faculty of judgment more generally. However, as a regulative principle this teleology is certainly not otiose—in significant distinction to Descartes.

To put a sharper point on it, think back for a moment to the very organized (and potentially self-organizing) systems of the Cartesian living machine. The systems in the body are arranged in such a way that they are reciprocally cause and effect, much like the Kantian criteria. What a Kantian would claim to be absent from the Cartesian account is the implicit role that purposive teleology plays as the *ground of the systematic unity* of the form of the organism as a whole: the second Kantian criteria. While Descartes treats the animal-machine as a unity, how is he justified in this treatment? Why not treat each mechanical system separately? Why not treat each mechanical system only in terms of its constituent parts? How can Descartes justify treating a system of many mechanisms as a unified object? The Kantian response would be that there is an unacknowledged debt to purposive teleology in making these judgments. Purposiveness is required as a norm for judging what constitutes the unified system.[73]

---

72. *KgS*, 5: 406–8.

73. Ibid., 5:398; see also Des Chene, *Spirits and Clocks*, chap. 6. While Des Chene does not follow the specifically Kantian track I mention here, he does offer an immensely helpful typology for better understanding the implicit reliance on teleology and ends in the Cartesian account of bodies—particularly, the relation between norms, ends, dispositions, and unity.

Continuity and Holarchy

The tension identified in Kant's antimony between the mechanical and the teleological helps give shape to the philosophical and conceptual history I have offered here. From Aristotle to Descartes to Kant there is an oscillation in the emphasis on mechanical and teleological explication with regard to the principles of life. I would suggest this is an oscillation that does not stop with Kant; rather, it is a tension that pervades even approaches to investigating life's origins and principles in scientific discourse today. What principles are sufficient to characterize a living thing? Do those principles include an inherent point of teleological explication or are they mechanically reducible? These questions have not been resolved (nor does it seem as though they will be any time soon). Examining a few key concepts from origins of life research can demonstrate that this tension concerning the place of teleological thinking with regard to the principles of life persists. Evidencing the persistence of this tension helps make clear how the conceptual history laid out above is not merely adiaphorous; the tensions of the conceptual history continue to be relevant to the explication of principles of life today.

What Iris Fry has called the "continuity thesis" is an immensely helpful tool in illustrating the juxtaposition of the mechanical and teleological. She claims this thesis is a philosophical presupposition of scientific research into the origins of life. The thesis assumes "there is no unbridgeable gap between inorganic matter and living systems, and that *under suitable physical conditions the emergence of life is highly probable.*"[74] As an epistemologically necessary philosophical assumption the thesis does not have any scientifically methodological power: the thesis does not spawn particular rules for origins of life research, but must be assumed for these rules to be formed. The continuity thesis (epistemic) does not describe a specific principle of continuity (methodological and scientific).[75]

Fry uses her thesis to typologically separate various approaches to the origins of life: those adhering to the continuity thesis (the "law camp") and those who do not (the "almost miracle camp"). The scientific group that most often disagrees with the continuity thesis takes issue with the "highly probable" character of the emergence of life given appropriate conditions. These scientists propose instead that the occurrence of life is a chance event that is highly unlikely to be repeated even in suitable conditions. The prototypical representative of this camp is Jacques Monod and his firm assessment that the chance association of a specific sequence of nucleotides in amino acids

---

74. Fry, "Are the Different Hypotheses on the Emergence of Life as Different as They Seem?," 389.

75. Ibid., 391–92.

that would be needed to give rise to life is nearly inconceivable: the fact that life does arise is a unique and happy accident.[76] The crux of the typology that Fry establishes is that the "almost miracle camp" adherents deny the high probability of the formation of life given proper conditions *by refusing to acknowledge the possibility of ascribing any features to inorganic matter besides chance association*. Without an organizational principle besides pure chance, the origin of life is deemed highly improbable and becomes a singular event that is therefore off-limits from scientific analysis.[77]

By contrast, the "law camp" affirms the high-probability of the formation of living things given the proper conditions. In large part, this camp is identified in its response to the chance and improbability affirmed by thinkers like Monod. The line of reasoning is as follows: given that (1) life is an extremely improbable singularity given only the occurrence of chance molecular association and that (2) life nonetheless exists, then (3) it follows that we should seek out other explanations than just chance occurrences.[78]

The key is this idea of seeking out explanations besides chance occurrences. In the wide variety of, sometimes disagreeing, positions and key concepts that Fry places in the "law camp" (including random replicators, hypercycles, clay organisms, error-tolerance, protenoid microspheres, phospholipid vesicles, and various forms of non-equilibrium thermodynamics),[79] all hold to a relaxed view of chance occurrence. While chance for Monod and the "almost miracle camp" is a form of pure statistical randomness, the randomness of the "law camp" is directed by some means. How this direction of randomness is explained constitutes the various principles of continuity on which these approaches may disagree widely, but there is broad coherence amidst their commitment to reformulating our understanding of

---

76. Monod, *Chance and Necessity*, 96 and 135–36.

77. Fry, "Are the Different Hypotheses on the Emergence of Life as Different as They Seem?," 395–401. Fry associates this position with Kant's approach to organisms. Noting the similarity in their positions with regard to the inertness of matter, Fry asserts that the "almost miracle camp" and Kant create a strong distinction between biology and physics insofar as both indicate the scientific study of the origins of organization in biology goes beyond the bounds of the proper subject of biology. See especially 398–99.

78. Ibid., 401; see also Bernal, "Discussion," 65–88.

79. Descriptions of these models can be found in the following: Cairns-Smith, *Seven Clues to the Origin of Life: A Scientific Detective Story*, chap. 11; Dyson, *Origins of Life*; Eigen, "Self-Organization of Matter and the Evolution of Biological Macromolecules," 465–523; Eigen, *Steps Towards Life*; Fox, "Protenoid Experiments and Evolutionary Theory," 15–60; Kauffman, *The Origins of Order*; Kauffman, *Investigations*; Morowitz, *Beginnings of Cellular Life*; and Wickens, *Evolution, Thermodynamics and Information*.

statistical randomness to directed randomness, leading to self-organization by physical mechanisms.[80]

Fry's continuity thesis is helpful in two ways. First, it is an immensely powerful typological schema. It identifies an underlying philosophical concept for a wide segment of contemporary projects in origins of life research that can be vastly different in their details. Second, it provides a clear indication of the shift regarding chance encounters in scientific approaches to the origins of life.

Fry primarily deals with the role of probability in the continuity thesis; however, for my purpose there is another implication worth considering. The "law camp" invokes various material properties to explain the formation of an organized whole. If something like Kantian purposiveness is invoked in these continuity thesis approaches, it would only be as a heuristic tool. The purposiveness of the "law camp," where it is invoked, is much akin to the approach of Blumenbach: purposiveness standing as a place holder for undiscovered mechanical explication. This point can be pressed even further though: given the way Fry constructs the continuity thesis, these approaches appear most akin to Cartesian mechanism.[81] In both cases there is a striking out of teleological features as otiose via systems of organization; this point is rather obvious. More importantly, *in both cases there is an assumption that matter is potentially self-organizing.* Think back to the formation of the fire without light residing in the heart. This principle of life arises only from the action of those smallest and fastest moving particles in the plenum as they are concentrated together by the seminal liquids; but once they are concentrated together they are loathe to dissimilate from one another. This collection of particles causes the matter of the plenum around them to behave in a way that perpetuates the fire. Though the Cartesian account in this regard is distinctly pre-Newtonian, what is important is that his plenum describes matter as ripe for organization. Though the view of the material world for continuity thesis adherents is certainly post-Newtonian, their account of this material is not inert. A driving assumption of these approaches is that life is explicable in terms of the organized arrangement of underlying physical and chemical processes; these processes, given appropriate conditions, are likely to spontaneously occur because matter is not strictly governed by chance alone. Proponents of this view affirm "directed

---

80. Fry, "Are the Different Hypotheses on the Emergence of Life as Different as They Seem?," 411–12.

81. In making this claim there is an important caveat. The continuity thesis approaches employ a model of the organism that is far less decomposable than Cartesian living machines. In that regard they can be said to be "organismic" instead of "artifactual." However, there remains much in common with the Cartesian approach.

randomness," which implies matter is more than just inert. I think it is fair to claim that Fry's continuity thesis, as a means of organizing contemporary scientific approaches to the origin of life, resembles Descartes's approach with a shift regarding decomposability.

Above, I suggested that the real difference between the Kantian approach to life as a natural end and the Cartesian approach to the mechanical body lies in the credence given to purposiveness. The role of purposiveness in identifying which system of interactions count as interactions remains silently unacknowledged in the Cartesian account. The Kantian approach, by contrast, affirms that systems need to be organized for self-maintenance and self-organizing in origin. The parts of the system need to be reciprocally cause and effect of one another as to form and generation in order that the purposive influence of the whole is acknowledged as the ground for natural ends.

This role of purposiveness also finds a parallel in our contemporary account. I believe this is well-exemplified in the work *What is Life?* by Lynn Margulis and Dorion Sagan. Borrowing a term from Arthur Koestler, Margulis and Sagan use the idea of "holarchy" to describe the myriad of systems that demonstrate the biotic potential of life. Holarchy designates the "coexistence of smaller being in larger wholes."[82] It is a nesting concept, wherein parts are not only the parts for the larger whole, but they also represent wholes in and of themselves (so they rename these parts "holons"). Utilizing this concept, Margulis and Sagan claim "[l]ife on Earth is not a created hierarchy but an emergent holarchy arisen from the self-induced synergy of combination, interfacing, and re-combination."[83]

The implication is that holarchic life takes on a much wider scope. Holarchic life is not limited to five kingdoms; the systems of organization that produce life-like functions happen across a wide spectrum of scale and complexity. For instance, on this view life even occurs at a global scale. As Margulis and Sagan poetically describe it:

> The act of viewing Earth from space echoes that of a baby glimpsing, and really seeing, itself in a mirror for the first time. *The astronaut gazes upon the body of life as a whole.* The French psychoanalyst Jacque Lacan posits a stage in human development called "the mirror stage." The infant, unable to control its limbs, looks into the mirror and perceives its whole body. Humanity's jubilant perception of the global environment

---

82. Margulis and Sagan, *What Is Life?*, 9. This concept is intended to do away with the hierarchical thinking wherein human beings stand as the pinnacle of creation.

83. Ibid.

represents the mirror stage of our entire species. For the first time we have caught a glimpse of our full, planetary form. We are coming to realize that we are part of a global holarchy that transcends our individual skins and even humanity as a whole.[84]

Do not let the poetic language allow you to imagine this to be some simple simile. There is a literal quality to their use of the phrase "life as a whole." This literal quality is also reflected by their encouraging the revival of the term "organic being," as is found in Darwin's *On the Origin of Species*. They advocate for this term because it does not prejudice our investigation into living things with the preconceived biases associated with "organism." "Organic being" is, conceptually, better able to help us imagine how everything from cellular organelles to ecosystems might be alive.[85] If, as with their view, concepts so wide as the biosphere (i.e., the earth as a whole) can count *as a living thing itself and not just a rock with life on it*, then what constitutes "life" in Margulis and Sagan is significantly different from what we have been examining so far.[86]

What I suggest is that the definition of life in Margulis and Sagan is one that is distinct, though quite similar to the schema of the continuity thesis. Life is still a material phenomenon, investigating the origins of its organized and self-organizing features is necessary for a thorough understanding of its principles, and it can be investigated as a predictable process given specific conditions. However, there remains a subtle, though immensely important, distinction regarding the principles of life. Whereas the continuity thesis finds sufficient explanation for the behavior of an organized system as a whole in terms of their constitutive substantial parts, the holarchy of Margulis and Sagan's approach is not amenable to this inherently leveled approach.

Margulis and Sagan play on the overlap between realms of scale at which features of life appear. Living things are parts of other living things in their approach. Still, this is not a naïve return to vitalism. Instead, it is an approach conceived fully in terms of "behaviors." The result is a muddying of the neat distinction between a living whole and its constitutive parts. Here there are *living parts within living wholes* so long as each exhibits the requisite behaviors.

> Life is distinguished not by its chemical constituents but by the behavior of its chemicals. The question "what is life?" is thus a linguistic trap. To answer according to the rules of grammar, we

---

84. Ibid., 11; emphasis mine.
85. Ibid., 14.
86. On the earth as alive, see ibid., 20–24.

must supply a noun, a thing. But life on Earth is more like a verb. It repairs, maintains, re-creates, and outdoes itself.[87]

This emphasis on life as "verb" and "behaviors" rekindle Kantian purposiveness as it is appealed to against Cartesian mechanics. Living systems cannot be accounted for without at least an implicit appeal to purposiveness as a principle that is irreducible to mechanical explication. What Margulis and Sagan provide, through their account of life by behaviors that are holarchically nested, are examples of the way organized systems of life-processes appear widely, once the purposive facets of articulating principles of life are acknowledged and thoroughly employed to define what constitutes a living thing. In their terms, life's behavior is specifically metabolic autopoietic behavior: self-maintenance through energy expenditure that works locally against the global entropic tendency. From cells to biospheres, they argue this type of behavior is exhibited and represents a variety of holarchic living systems.[88] By indicating how life nests within life, the principles of life are not reducible in every instance to their physico-chemical bases; something about the quality of life is not directly explicable in terms of the physical properties of the matter that constitutes it.

Now I have offered two examples of how the tension between Cartesian mechanism and Kantian purposiveness continues to have ramifications in current scientific work. The research into origins of life presupposing Fry's continuity thesis was associated with Cartesian mechanism. This was contrasted with the work of Margulis and Sagan who highlight the potentially continued relevance of purposiveness for understanding wholes as more than an aggregate of parts through concepts like "holarchy." The robust presence of Kantian purposiveness and its use in contemporary scientific study with regard to life is an indicator of a significant disjunction in the aims of contemporary research programs: a disjunction between those that use purposiveness only in terms of its heuristic value (as with Blumenbach and the Cartesian approach of the continuity thesis) and those who use it in a robust sense (as with Kant and modeled in Margulis and Sagan). This distinction regarding purposiveness indicates a useful distinction between research focused on investigating the *origins* of life versus the *principles* of life. Though the two concepts often intermingle, being clear about this distinction could help us in moving forward. Origins of life research must be principally concerned with our only known examples of living things—those that have arisen here on Earth. By contrast, an investigation into the principles of life, while not being able to violate the findings of origins of life

87. Ibid., 14.
88. Ibid., 17–20.

theorists, need not dogmatically hold itself to an analysis of living things as we traditionally think we know them. Here the concern is to focus on how we articulate the distinction between the living and the non-living. This is a point that is always already assumed in origins of life research, but must be subjected to critical scrutiny by principles of life research.

My subsequent focus will be on the *principles* of life. Eventually the aim will be to indicate how theology has a stake in the establishment of these principles. Since these principles are assumed in the way origins of life research is conducted, establishing principles of life provides theology and natural science a fertile ground for interaction that is largely underdeveloped. To develop this fecund potential, I want to look back at purposiveness as a potential principle of life. For Kant the teleological power of purposiveness is irreducible to mechanical explication; however, as the antinomy of teleological judgment indicated, this does not entail it is in conflict with mechanical explication (even though the unification of teleological and mechanical judgments is supersensible and always beyond human rational power). The next chapter will begin to examine what a unity of the teleological and mechanical might entail with regard to the principles of life and what challenges exist in this endeavor as Kantian ideas are brought out of their larger framework of transcendental idealism. This process will proceed in terms of one promising means of investigating principles of life today: emergence theory.

2

Teleodynamics of Emergent Life

Establishing the unity of a system as an object for investigation is not necessarily difficult. Commonsense criteria can delineate a system of study based on its intuitive appeal or useful structure regarding the problem being investigated. However, simple appeals to commonsense criteria seem a bit more dubious and frustratingly tautological when you are trying to identify the systems of organization that appear essential to giving a thorough description of principles of life. The commonsense reasoning might sound something like this: I study that organized system because it is used by all living things, but I know that thing is living because it enacts that organized system. Do I study the organized system because it is demonstrated in living things in this case or because living things are constituted by the organized system? Each half of the reasoning in our commonsense scenario reduces to the other without showing how the organized system, by its principles of organization, is related to the end it produces and for which it does the production. While the system of efficient causes is here conceived as radically independent from any final cause, the problem of the commonsense scenario is similar to the challenge we identified in giving a strictly mechanical account of life: I already had to possess an intuitive sensibility about what a living thing is or does to identify the organized system as living. Technically speaking, the epistemology of physics does not include the needed categories to adequately account for living things

Kant's idea of purposiveness is a promising concept for establishing the phenomenal unity of a self-organized and self-maintaining system because it intrinsically linked purposiveness to the study of particular systems of organization. In these systems, the form and existence of parts are only conceivable in terms of the whole and the parts are reciprocally cause and effect of their form exhibiting the novel occurrence of end-directed behavior. However, purposiveness is a broad criteria and its contemporary investigation has occurred in terms of technical concepts with greater specificity in scientific parlance. These have included concepts such as replication, reproduction, metabolism, embodiment, negentropy, and autopoiesis.

In this chapter, I move away from the strictly conceptual realm of the philosophical accounts of the principles of life. Instead, I will pursue one model for investigating the principles of life: emergence theory. This model has great potential as a partner in the inter-action of theology and science because of its serious engagement with the previously reviewed philosophical accounts and their implications. In using emergence theory, I will specifically be following the work of Terrence Deacon. He has developed a three-tiered dynamics of emergence and a particularly important model called the "autogen."

I will begin, though, with a brief explication of the historical origins of emergence theory and the importance of strong emergence theory. This will be followed by a thorough explication of Deacon's model of emergent dynamics in relation to other contemporary projects considering strong emergence theory.[1] Finally, I will conclude with a comparison of Deacon's work and Kantian purposiveness. This analysis will demonstrate how Deacon's work could be augmented by deeper philosophical conceptualizations of critical ontological criteria that will be the focus of the next chapter.

Strong and Weak Emergence

Characterizing emergence theory is difficult. The term has become an umbrella for a wide variety of projects and research programs spanning many different traditional scientific fields. As Philip Clayton has rightly identified, at first blush emergence theory is not itself a scientific theory, but a meta-level concept seeking to explain iterative causal patterns that appear across many different scientific disciplines.[2]

The complexity of emergence theory is amplified when we clearly articulate the philosophical distinction at stake between various emergence theorists through history. Typically this distinction has been labeled epistemological versus ontological, or weak versus strong emergence. In accounts of weak emergence, the iterative or emergent processes identified describe *properties* of a single ontological reality. No ontologically new things arise

---

1. Some pieces of the description of Deacon's work in this chapter appeared in Pryor, "Tillichian Teleodynamics," 835–56.
2. Clayton, *Adventures in the Spirit*, 64–66.

from weak emergentist accounts; only a single (usually physico-reductionist) ontological reality exists upon which *descriptive* properties indicate greater complexity. The entire causal work of weak emergence accounts occur at the most fundamental microphysical levels. In strong emergence accounts, an emergent process yields an ontologically new causal agent or causal process. It is not only a property that emerges; instead, the emergent whole possesses *irreducibly* new causal capacities.[3] It is quite easy to slip into a vacillating language about emergence that inadvertently tries to entail both of these incommensurable positions at the same time.[4] However, both positions rely on different ontological levels being recognizable by novel causal production.[5]

Before delving into any correlation there might be between our earlier account of the conceptual foundations for life and emergence theory, it is important to understand strong and weak emergence as they have developed on their own terms. There is no better way to understand the philosophical nuances of this distinction than to examine the historical development of emergence theory in five thinkers: two key thinkers prior to the British emergentists, J. S. Mill and G. H. Lewes, as well as the British emergentists proper, Samuel Alexander, C. L. Morgan, and C. D. Broad.[6]

---

3. See Clayton, "Conceptual Foundations of Emergence Theory," 8–9; and Silberstein and McGeever, "The Search for Ontological Emergence," 182–84. Silberstein and McGeever provide one of the clearest and most stringent definitions of ontological emergence: "By this [ontological emergence] we mean features of systems or wholes that possess causal capacities not reducible to any of the intrinsic causal capacities of the parts themselves" (182). This definition should be kept in mind to best realize the vast extent of what "irreducibly" means above. For a more logically formal set of definitions developed out of C. D. Broad's work on emergence theory, see Beckermann, "Supervenience, Emergence, and Reduction," 100–106.

4. For an example, see Silberstein and McGeever, "The Search for Ontological Emergence," 186–87.

5. I would suggest this tension between weak and strong emergence exhibits in a specific way the general tension already identified between the role of the mechanical and the teleological in living things. The disagreement over the efficacy of novel causal production as a criterion for the existence of ontologically new things is akin to determining if teleological powers are otiose in giving an account of living things. Further, the sheer incommensurability that Silberstein and McGeever identify between weak and strong emergence parallels the contradiction that Kant finds in the antinomy of teleological judgment when its theses are moved from the reflective to the constitutive register. On this point, compare the following: *KgS*, 5:395–96; and Silberstein and McGeever, "The Search for Ontological Emergence," 182–87.

6. Any number of sources can be consulted in constructing such an historical introduction. My approach is most shaped by Clayton, *Mind and Emergence*, chap. 1; Deacon, *Incomplete Nature*, chap. 5; O'Connor and Wong, "Emergent Properties"; and McLaughlin, "The Rise and Fall of British Emergentism," 49–93. What I will avoid is a synthesizing approach that makes British Emergentism into a monolithic body of

Each of these thinkers is wrestling with the scientific and philosophical conflict of their time between vitalism and reductionism. They sought to clarify the relationship between higher-level science (biology and chemistry) and lower-level sciences (physics). Each wanted to articulate an emergent vision of life that gave credence to reductionist opponents without giving away the vitality of living things as distinct from their constitutive physico-chemical properties and materials; in short, they worked at the intersection of the mechanical and the teleological.

Mill, earlier than Lewes but without using the term emergence, sets this story in motion with his examination of "homopathic" and "heteropathic" effects. Homopathic effects are characteristic of mechanical causes (pushes and pulls). Since, a mechanical cause produces a directly given effect a number of different mechanical causes will produce an effect that is the sum of individual mechanical causes. Specifically, he thought of mechanical causes in terms of the addition of forces in physics. Even multiple mechanical causes added together remain homopathic. Playing off the additive principle of vectors in physics, called the composition of forces, Mill calls the mechanical quality of homopathic effects the "composition of causes."

These are different from heteropathic effects, which are characteristic of chemical causes. *These effects violate the additive quality of mechanical causes.* One of Mill's examples was that the combination of sodium hydroxide and hydrochloric acid (two agents with mechanical causes detrimental to living things) produce table salt and water (two agents with mechanical causes needed for life). The combination of two detrimental mechanical causes does not just produce double detriment. Instead, we have an emergent effect: what Mill calls a heteropathic effect.[7]

The import of these effects is made clear in considering a brief statement Mill makes about the living body. "To whatever degree we might imagine our knowledge of the properties of the several ingredients of a living body to be extended and perfected, it is certain that no mere summing up of the separate actions of those elements will ever amount to the action of the living body itself."[8] The living body is produced as a series of heteropathic causal effects; no sum-total of homopathic effects will ever be sufficient to describe the working of living beings. The heteropathic is not

---

doctrines.

7. Mill, *A System of Logic*, 3.6.1–2. The language of a "chemical cause" is clearly not germane to natural science today. We have to remember, however, that electrons were not even discovered until 1897, over fifty years after the first edition of Mill's work and over a decade after he died.

8. Ibid., 3.6.1.

limited to the level of chemical action (as with our example of table salt and water); it describes an irreducible mode of causality.[9]

While it is Lewes who introduces the term "emergent," he is using it in the same sense as Mill's heteropathic effect. "Thus, although each effect is the resultant of its components, the product of its factors, we cannot always trace the steps of the process, so as to see in the product the mode of operation of each factor. In this latter case, I propose to call the effect an emergent. It arises out of the combined agencies, but in a form which does not display the agents in action."[10]

Unlike many other emergentists though, Lewes is not interested in clarifying biology's distinction from physics. Instead, his concern (and use of the term emergent) is for a rejoining of cause and effect that he believed had been separated by the radical skepticism of David Hume. By Lewes's account, the problem in Hume's interpretation of causality lies in misnaming events: the cause and effect are two parts of *one* causal event for Lewes not *two* events as in his reading of Hume. What can make Lewes's approach so confusing is that he stresses there are two classes of effects—resultants and emergents. Since products and effects are related as a single event, he uses different classes of effects to surmise that there are distinct modes of causal processes.[11]

In both Mill and Lewes there is a tendency toward strong emergence. Whether through the language of heteropathic effects or emergents, both thinkers propose that it is through a distinct causal topology that new and unpredictable things come into existence. The emergent has a new series of properties for causal interaction that are not the same as their preceding constitutive causes.

Alexander in *Space, Time, and Deity* gives a very different account of emergence than what is developed by Mill and Lewes. For Alexander, terms like "life" and "mind" represent emergent "qualities" that sum up the complex constellation of lower-level structures.[12] However, these qualities do not represent a different causal logic (as in Mill and Lewes). Instead, the

---

9. This is balanced by his continued affirmation that all phenomena are subject to the composition of causes (i.e., a living thing is still subject to at least some mechanical causes). For more, see ibid., 3.6.2.

10. Lewes, *Problems of Life and Mind*, 412.

11. "Hume and his adherents gratuitously puzzle themselves with the imaginary connection of two events which are not two events but two aspects of one. The causes exist only in abstraction until realized in the effect" (ibid., 2:411; see also p. 415 and 421). Certainly Lewes is making too simple a case out of Hume's skepticism, but that is not the focus here.

12. Alexander, *Space, Time, and Deity*, 45–47.

roots of the emergent quality remain firmly in lower-level structures. This is clear in his correlation of neural and mental phenomena.[13]

What also makes this work notably different from that of Mill and Lewes is the expanse of Alexander's investigation. Alexander develops a hierarchical ladder of emergent levels that represents an immensely complex, and holistic, metaphysical system, though it is undeniably a reductive-physicalist system.[14] In Alexander's work, the increasingly complex organization of parts indicates emergent levels of order, but there is no new causal power introduced. By contrast, for Mill and Lewes the logic of causal topologies never stratified into an emergent evolutionary system: it was concerned with singular transitions between complex systems.

I find Alexander's position easiest to imagine in terms of the Laplacian demon (named for Pierre-Simon Laplace who first imagined this scenario). The demon, which has complete knowledge of the laws of the universe and its initial state, is able to calculate from this knowledge alone all future distributions of matter and energy. In Alexander's vision of emergence, the Laplacian demon is given his due—no new causal powers evade the demon's detection; however, just because the demon would know distributions of matter and energy, it does not mean that the demon could predict emergent qualities. These are truly novel—the logic of their emergence is beyond computation even if their component ontological parts are determinable by the Laplacian demon.[15] Historically this is an important point. Even the Laplacian demon could *not* predict emergent qualities on Alexander's account. If the demon could predict the property then it would be difficult to make the case that the property actually emerges: to borrow Mill's language, the property would be a homopathic effect whereby our inability to discern the connection between causal parts and the new property would be a merely epistemic limitation. However, in the case of the Laplacian demon all of the epistemic limitations are cleared away and still the property is unpredictable.

In terms of the development of emergence theory, Alexander's work is triply important. First, subsequent to Alexander a leveled view of reality becomes a cornerstone of emergence theory as an evolutionary mechanism. Second, novelty or unpredictability is crucial to identifying emergent properties. Finally, this represents the first explicit account of weak emergence: emergent properties do not possess the causal agency characteristic of strong emergence per our definition above. The emergent properties on

---

13. Ibid., 5–26.

14. For a clear summary of this material, see Clayton, *Mind and Emergence*, 27–28; and Dasgupta, *A Study of Alexander's Space, Time and Deity*.

15. See Alexander, *Space, Time, and Deity*, 73.

Alexander's model of emergence are unpredictable and completely novel, but causal efficacy remains only at the lowest-level indicating the properties are epistemologically but not ontologically valuable.

Morgan is clearly indebted to the "emergents" and "resultants" schema of Mill and Lewes,[16] but develops this in terms of emergent levels of increasing complexity, much like Alexander. As Clayton rightly points out, however, Morgan's turn to levels is scientifically and empirically motivated—it does not represent a series of metaphysical distinctions initially.[17] What is notably different from Alexander's view is that these levels indicate a fundamental discontinuity for Morgan. The ascending levels of complexity are not subject to a complete causal description in terms of their component parts and represent substantially different instantiations of reality. As he puts it, "there is redirection of the course of events at each level."[18] These redirections are conceived of so strongly that emergent levels represent different sets of ontological substances for Morgan. What begins as a scientifically motivated turn to describing reality in terms of levels of increasing complexity *yields* a distinct metaphysical insight.

What is most crucial in Morgan's development of emergence is his early articulation of a notion that appears to be much like downward causation. The emergent property or feature that Morgan describes is a new kind of relation amidst the constitutive parts.[19] This emergent relatedness affects the parts at the lower level of complexity, biasing the lower-level laws. Thus, the emergent mode of relatedness involves the lower-level laws but is unanticipated by these lower-level laws themselves (it is thus an emergent or heteropathic causal law). Moreover, the course of events for the lower-level laws relies upon the higher-level modes of relatedness.[20] It is with Morgan that we gain a first glimmer of the modern concept of strong emergence: a leveled ontological schema wherein each level has distinctive causal powers that are best described in terms of higher-level biasing of lower-level laws in unpredictable ways.

Finally in *The Mind and its Place in Nature*, Broad gives another classic account of emergence that distinctly shapes the course of subsequent use of the term. He addresses the concept of emergence in a slippery way in

---

16. Morgan, *Emergent Evolution*, chap. 1.

17. Clayton, *Mind and Emergence*, 14–15. Clayton's text is immensely helpful on this point since Morgan's conception of levels could easily be misread as a metaphysical primer.

18. Morgan, *Emergent Evolution*, 207, and see especially 203–8.

19. Ibid., 7 and 64.

20. Ibid., 64–69. See also McLaughlin, "The Rise and Fall of British Emergentism," 68.

terms of our distinction between strong and weak emergence. He affirms a fundamental monism about the physical world that is leveled according to irreducible properties that emerge from lower-level predecessors. This is well described in his oft quoted phrase, "[w]e might, if we liked, keep the view that there is only one fundamental kind of stuff. But we should have to recognize aggregates of various orders."[21] For Broad, the emergence of these "aggregates of various orders" is the product of what he calls trans-ordinal laws. These laws are only articulated *after* the appearance of the higher-level aggregate: they can *never* be deduced from knowledge of the properties or intra-ordinal laws of the lower-level aggregates.[22] The result is that trans-ordinal laws are completely unpredictable from lower-level states (they are not metaphysically necessitated in any way).

While it is certain that emergent features and trans-ordinal laws are quite novel on Broad's account, the causal efficacy of these emergent features is more difficult to judge. The emergent substance has irreducible causal powers once the emergence account moves beyond the physical realm (i.e., it is a form of strong emergence). However, as emergent features relate to the physical world, they do not represent novel, irreducible causal powers. In sum, he seems to be a weak emergentist in relation to the physical world and categorizing the difference between life and non-life, but he appears to be a strong emergentist in characterizing the emergence of mind in living things.[23]

What is most important is that, different from his predecessors, Broad lays a great deal of emphasis on the post-appearance quality of emergence: its utter unpredictability. He seems to take on the logic of downward causation like we find in Morgan's account,[24] but identifies the occurrence of trans-ordinal laws by the emergence of "ultimate characteristics"[25] that are only identifiable after their occurrence. In sum, downward causation is fine as a principle for Broad, but identifying the important trans-ordinal laws that actually characterize the distinction between emergent levels is restricted to an *a posteriori* account. The unpredictability and newness of ultimate characteristics become the indicators of discontinuity between emergent levels. In this way Broad's work almost reads like a tenuous stand between Alexander and Morgan. Like Alexander, Broad emphasizes the role

---

21. Broad, *The Mind and Its Place in Nature*, 77.
22. Ibid., 79–81.
23. Ibid., 81. Key texts for comparison on this point include §§A and E.
24. See the discussion of "Emergent Vitalism," especially ibid., 68–69.
25. Ibid., 78.

of novelty to an exceptional degree; however like Morgan, Broad finds at least an *a posteriori* place for a form of downward causation.

In these early emergentists we see the basic philosophical structures of emergence theory, in its characterization as weak or strong, begin to appear. In the case of Mill, Lewes, Morgan and (tentatively) Broad, we see a strong emergentist argument, while in Alexander we have the prototypical weak emergentist argument. Amidst the strong group, emergent structures possess new causal capacities irreducible to their lower-level constitutive elements, while in Alexander the emergent qualities are descriptive of a causal logic that is ultimately singular and reductionist.

However, there are distinctions to be drawn between the strong emergentists as well. Broad's argument is ultimately based on a metaphysical assumption: we tend to overestimate the ontological unity of reality. The trans-ordinal laws, because of their non-deducible character, seem really only to function in a descriptive capacity. The causal distinctiveness of different emergent levels is ultimately rooted in a hunch that these trans-ordinal laws can never be explained by the inter-ordinal laws of the previous level from which they emerge.

For scientists interested in minimizing the role of metaphysics in their work on emergence theory (while not yielding to the causal reductionism of weak emergence) Morgan must be a kind of patron saint. It is probably safe to claim that most scientific accountings of emergent phenomena (that seek to describe ontologically emergent phenomena) are placing themselves within the tradition of Morgan's approach to this issue and emphasize the role of downward causation.

Finally, Mill and Lewes, though quite differently from one another, make their strong emergentist argument based on two distinctive causal architectures. For Mill especially, it is not retrospection from an emergent substance that generates his account, but a desire to articulate distinctions in the dynamics of causal logic itself. A strong emphasis on this distinction in causal architecture is not to be found in the work of Morgan or Broad.

This historical overview can help us better understand why there is such diversity amidst thinkers claiming to be emergentists. Over the course of 80 years (and in the case of Alexander, Morgan, and Broad a decade) there was a rapid accretion of related but distinct features that came to categorize what emergence theory meant. While there is certainly conceptual similarity across the use of these accretions, sometimes the same conceptual tool was employed in various and incommensurable ways. I would suggest that contemporary writings on emergence theory (as in its resurgence since the 1960s) have not until very recently begun to critically examine and articulate how they make a claim on the various and divergent facets of these historical accretions. Being aware of the historical diversity allows (1) for a clearer understanding of what current articulations of emergence theory hold to be most essential in this conglomeration of ideas and (2) for the avoidance of intellectual mires wherein mutually incommensurable articulations of these conceptual tools results in logical contradiction.

As a minimum, therefore, I suggest three rules for proceeding into contemporary accounts of emergence given an awareness of the historical diversity.

1. Emergence theory is fundamentally monistic in terms of substance (i.e., a substance dualist could not be an emergentist).
2. Whatever account of emergence is formulated today, it must struggle with articulating the character of the continuity and discontinuity between various emergent levels (so there cannot be a naïve historical return to the work of Mill and Lewes).
3. Any analysis of contemporary emergence theory must be vigilant in clearly explicating how to identify an emergent structure (novelty, causal architectures, the occurrence of downward causation, etc.).

Although the historical recounting I have offered is structured in terms of conceptual accretions, not all of those concepts will be necessary for contemporary accounts—as indicated in point three above. Thus, to falsify or argue strongly against one aspect (i.e., novelty as essential to any account of emergence theory) will not be enough to do away with the variety of accounts that characterize emergence theory as a field of research.

Table 1: Historical Account of Emergence Theory

Emergentist	Critical Feature
John Stuart Mill	Identifies homopathic and heteropathic causality: Emergence as Distinctive Causal Topologies
G. H. Lewes	Directly relates effects to causal topology: Emergence as Distinctive Causal Topologies
Samuel Alexander	The complex constellations of lower-level structures: Emergence as Epistemic Novel Qualities of Lower-level Phenomena
Conway Lloyd Morgan	The discontinuous levels between emergents: Emergence as Downward Causation
C. D. Broad	The non-deductive character of trans-ordinal laws: Emergence as Ontological Novelty

To illustrate this point I have included table 1 above, which summarizes the development of key features by each historical emergentist in terms of the three rules I have generated. As to the first rule, we can affirm that all of the historical accounts of emergence we have investigated are sufficiently monist. As to the second rule, we find a divide between the earliest emergentists and the British emergentists as indicated by the shading on the table. The shaded area indicates the earliest emergentists who do not offer a tiered account of emergent levels; the non-shaded area includes the British emergentists who very carefully consider the role of emergence across increasingly complex epistemic or ontological levels. As to the third rule, I have sketched the critical feature of each emergentist. This makes clear the disparate ways in which contemporary emergence theory might appeal to an "essential" feature of emergence.

Before moving directly into more contemporary accounts of emergence, it is important to understand why I have dwelled so long on historical accounts of emergence to make this distinction between weak and strong emergence theory clear. As a Christian theologian interested in preserving the possibility of God's interaction with the world, I find it is the account of strong emergence that provides the most interesting and a potentially robust partner for interdisciplinary dialogue. Niels Gregersen's five-fold typology of interaction between theological thinking and emergence theory, which moves from those least religiously committed to most, helps illustrate this point.[26]

Gregersen's first three types (Flat Religious Naturalism, Evolving Theistic Naturalism, and Atemporal Theism) are all amenable to either a weak or strong account of emergence theory. It is only with his fourth type, Temporal Theism, that strong emergence appears more apt for interdisciplinary dialogue.[27] Why is this? What about the distinction between Atemporal and Temporal Theism makes such a difference for using weak or strong emergence theory in interdisciplinary investigation?

---

26. Gregersen, "Emergence," 279–302.

27. These four types are very specifically described in Gregersen's work. To briefly summarize, "Flat Religious Naturalism" refers to the position where nature is constitutive of our ontological reality and the divine is understood as equivalent to nature. "Evolving Theistic Naturalism" affirms that nature is prior to God and that God is a subsequent complex development that emerges from nature. "Atemporal Theism" is his name for the classic position of philosophical theology that affirms God as prior to nature as its creator and unchanging. Finally, "Temporal Theism" affirms that God is prior to nature, but allows for change in God. See ibid., 288–96.

One may also note that I am only dealing with the first four parts of Gregersen's typology here, leaving off "Eschatological Theism"—a position whereby possibilities result from the interplay of the creaturely and the divine. I am not opposed to eschatological theism, but the necessity of a strong emergentist account for interaction with Eschatological Theism is beyond doubt. My focus is on the border at which strong instead of weak emergence becomes apropos for accounts of Christian theology.

Gregersen's distinction between Atemporal and Temporal Theism turns on the classic concern about the impassibility of God. Atemporal Theism preserves this impassibility, while Temporal Theism affirms (at the least) a dipolar notion of God that includes a part of God that is affected by the changing world.[28] In relation to emergence theory, there is not a strict demarcation between these positions (i.e., atemporal theists always use weak emergence while temporal theists must use strong emergence), but I see an increasing correlative tendency in Gregersen's typology: while Atemporal Theism might interact with either weak or strong emergence, the more robust a version of Temporal Theism one affirms, the more theological interaction with emergence theory becomes increasingly confined to strong emergence.

This correlation has to do with the intertwining of God and nature that is a part of Temporal Theism. In Atemporal Theism the aseity of God is given a theological primacy of place and the concepts of emergence (be it weak or strong) is not in any way *necessarily* correlated to our understanding of God. By contrast, in Temporal Theism as the distance between God and nature is diminished, or vice versa as it is increasingly affirmed that "[n]ature equals God-and-nature,"[29] affirming accounts of strong emergence is increasingly important as a model for preserving the continuing creative power of God. If God is increasingly conceived as God-and-nature, then restricting the ontological relevance of emergent phenomena limits God's continued creative acts.[30] If one wishes to generate interaction between theology and emergence theory that allows for God's continuing creation, then it is imperative to be able to articulate a version of strong emergence. Finding such a suitable strong emergentist account is my aim for the rest of this chapter.

How Strong is Emergent Teleodynamics?

Granted that strong emergence is, for the purposes of this interdisciplinary dialogue, my primary interest and that Deacon is serving as my scientific conversation partner, it should come as no surprise that I read his work as

---

28. Ibid., 287, 290, and 293.

29. Ibid., 297.

30. "Although some form of temporal theism—understood as a passive divine responsiveness—is indeed possible on the premise of an exclusively weak emergentism, the view that God interacts with a developing world is particularly congenial to the notion of a God whose experience grows along with the emergent realities in relation to which (or whom) God is seen to be actively involved" (ibid., 294). See also Clayton, "Emergence from Quantum Physics to Religion," 319.

an example of strong emergence. Still, there are a wide variety of contemporary theories that could claim the title "strong emergence" and make a claim to it in distinct ways (as the conclusions of the historical investigation indicated). Further, one could argue that I have misread Deacon's work and that it actually represents a variety of weak emergence. As such, my task in explicating Deacon's approach to emergence has a double challenge. First, I have to consider if his approach resists the most stringent contemporary critiques of strong emergence (sublimating it to weak emergence) such that Deacon's strong emergence is a viable partner for my interdisciplinary dialogue. This will be accomplished in consideration of the work of Jaegwon Kim. Second, I must defend this choice against critics who would argue that it is not a strong enough form of emergence for the kind of interdisciplinary dialogue I envision. This will be accomplished in conjunction with the work of Philip Clayton.

Is Strong Emergence Really Weak?

Without a doubt, the philosophical work of Kim represents the most stringent contemporary critique of strong emergence. While his approach—as I follow it here—has been well responded to in philosophical circles,[31] it remains a critical argument for us to consider because it relates so directly to oft held philosophical suppositions from literature in theology and natural science. The nuances of his critique are tied intimately to his corresponding critique of non-reductive physicalism, which he sees as *logically concomitant* to emergentism. Consequently, he focuses on the account of the emergence of mind from physical matter, but I will generalize the argument to an account of the laws of emergent phenomena. To understand the force of Kim's critique, one must examine the four-tiered development of his argument.

First, Kim argues strong emergence inherently requires an account of downward causation. He constructs this argument out of four premises he takes to be constitutive of emergence theory, all of which are consistent with the account of ontological emergence outlined above; they could quite reasonably be maintained as necessary in either Broad's or Morgan's account of emergence. His premises are:

1. Emergence theory represents a form of physicalist ontology; it is concerned with material entities and their physical properties.

2. Genuinely novel properties can emerge given sufficient lower-level structural complexity.

---

31. See O'Connor and Wong, "Emergent Properties," §3.3.1.

3. The novelty of these emergent properties is irreducible to their emergent conditions.[32]

4. Causal status accords ontological reality.[33]

From these premises, he concludes not only that an account of an ontologically emergent feature must have irreducibly novel causal power, but he adds a second-tier to his argument: emergentism entails downward causation. This part of the argument relies on the logic of the third premise above: irreducibility of the novel causal power. The implication of the third premise is that for any emergent property (EP) to be ontologically emergent, it must demonstrate how it has an irreducible causal effect on a lower-level phenomenon (LLP) or on another emergent property of the same level (EP*). If EP has a causal effect on LLP then we have perforce an example of downward causation. In the case of EP causally effecting some subsequent EP* we also always enact downward causation. *This occurs because any instance of an emergent property relies upon the instantiation of its lower-level structural complexity* (per premise two above). To say that EP brings about EP* is actually to say that EP brings about LLP*.[34]

In the third part of the argument, Kim wants to show that emergent properties are actually epiphenomenal, and irrelevant to a causal account. He does this by invoking the logical movements within his account of downward causation. If the causal efficacy of EP is always directed towards LLP* (and thereby also to EP*), and the causal relation is understood in terms of nomological sufficiency, then LLP (as the sufficient cause of EP) can be said to be the sufficient cause of LLP*. EP can be removed as a middle term in this causal chain since the emergent property is not construed in terms of causality, but irreducibility (per the third premise above).[35] Essentially, EP becomes a redundant feature, otiose to giving an account of the sufficient causality of LLP*.

Finally, the fourth-tier of the argument brings us to his *conclusion* about the difficulties that advocates of strong emergence theory must address if Kim's account holds. There is a deep problem for emergence theory related to the physicalist assessment of the causal closure of the world. In a nutshell, the "causal closure of the world" simply means that physical events have sufficient physical causes. The ultimately physicalist ontology of emergence theory (point one of Kim's premises) makes for a short logical

32. Kim, "'Downward Causation' and Emergence," 122–25.

33. Ibid., 134–38.

34. Ibid., 136.

35. Kim, "Making Sense of Emergence," 32–36; and "Being Realistic About Emergence," 200–201.

deduction to the causal closure of the physical world. The sting of Kim's critique is that based on the premises of strong emergence and an account of sufficient logical causality, emergence theory is shown to *entail* the causal closure of the physical world. This point cannot be overemphasized since it is so different from many other physicalist arguments: *Kim does not assume causal closure of the physical world against emergence theory, emergence theory provides the premises for constructing an argument that concludes in favor of the causal closure principle.* Given this causal closure conclusion and Kim's account of the inherent place of downward causation in emergence theory, then a gauntlet is laid down that sets the agenda for advocates of strong emergence: "you must either provide sufficient and compelling reasons for rejecting the closure principle or else show that downward causal efficacy of irreducible emergent properties is consistent with physical causal closure."[36]

Dynamical Strong Emergence

If it is Kim's critique that articulates the problematic of strong emergence for contemporary research, Deacon's approach is all the more exciting because it rebuffs the *structure* of the critique. Kim's account of strong emergence relies upon the efficacy of top-down mereological reasoning (whole-part or EP-LLP), which is to be expected if we look back to the emergence theory of the British Emergentists. Deacon, however, wants to rethink emergence theory in dynamical terms while respecting the causal closure principle.[37] In this way, he will use facets of complex systems theory to describe iterative, nonlinear processes that can self-organize. In terms of our historical account of emergence, Deacon harkens back to Mill and Lewes—conceiving of emergence in terms of distinct causal schemes, while trying additionally

---

36. Kim, "Being Realistic About Emergence," 199–200. Responses to Kim's challenge are typified by articles found in the same volume such as Silberstein, "In Defence of Ontological Emergence and Mental Causation," 203–26; and Murphy, "Emergence and Mental Causation," 227–43. Silberstein contests the assumption of the causal closure principle, while Murphy accepts the causal closure principle but seeks to show its consistency with downward causal efficacy.

37. Deacon is using the term "mereology" in a highly specific way. It does not only refer to part-whole reasoning generally conceived; instead, it refers to part-whole reasoning where wholes are decomposable to their parts. The implications of this will be expanded upon in what follows. Certainly though, mereology could be used with a much broader meaning than my use of the term here as I attempt to follow Deacon's work closely. On Deacon's understanding of the causal closure principle and mereology see *Incomplete Nature*, chap. 1, and pp. 164–69.

to build in the evolutionary logic of emergent levels as found in the later British emergentists, especially that of Morgan.[38]

To reimagine emergence theory in terms of dynamical, instead of mereological, reasoning has some significant consequences—notably two. First, if emergence theory shifts to dynamical reasoning instead of mereological reasoning, the typical understanding of lower-level parts accumulating into emergent, higher-level wholes has to yield to some other descriptive taxonomy for identifying when an emergence occurs. Second, if Deacon is to be interpreted as advocating a strong emergence account, then whatever new language he introduces for his dynamical approach still must demonstrate causal power.

Responding to the first consequence, Deacon, introduces "dynamic regimes" of process and organization. The simple higher-level/lower-level structure of supervenience remains, but any force given to its mereological logic is stripped away. This is because interrelated levels of dynamical organization are not decomposable: a higher-level of organizational process is in no way the sum of a series of lower-level organizational processes. Deacon offers specific explanations of the *change in organizational structure* that yields a higher-level organizational process from lower-level organizational processes.[39] In order to respond to the second consequence, Deacon explicates how these organizational processes themselves are a causal topology: how particular structures of the organizational process generate property regularities.[40]

What should already be clear is that Deacon's approach to emergence theory disallows any definition of emergence by the appearance of novel properties (as with Alexander or Broad). What is curious though is that a classic sense of emergent properties does not entirely fall out of the picture. Remembering that, for Deacon, emergence is dynamical—referring to various causal topologies of distinct dynamic regimes—the appearance of a novel structure is really a symbol indicating the potential presence of a constitutive emergent topology. The ordered features of novelty are the

---

38. The connection really lies in the close correlation that Mill and Lewes draw between causal processes and effects. As Deacon's approach is unfolded, how it (at the very least stylistically) echoes the approach to emergents as effects that Lewes summarizes will become clearer: "Finally, let me say that the search after causes is the search after the special conditions which enter into and compose the effects, and not the idle search for *something else*. A phenomenon is a *process*; its *causation* is its *procession*; and this may be viewed analytically in its component causes, conditions, and synthetically in the resultant effect" (*Problems of Life and Mind*, 2:421).

39. Deacon, *Incomplete Nature*, 175–81.

40. Deacon, "The Hierarchic Logic of Emergence," 280–84.

structural traces of *"regularities in the dynamics of a process,"*[41] wherein it is the *process* that is emergent. Thus, for each order of the dynamic regimes we can identify corollary structural traces or particular substantive effects.

Now, Deacon identifies three-orders of dynamic regimes in his account of emergence. First-order emergent processes have non-recurrent causal topologies and produce homeodynamic effects. Typical examples of this "simple" set of emergent properties are surface tension in a liquid or viscosity. Surface tension of water is a good example to examine. Here, it is the shape of water molecules themselves (think Mickey Mouse ears) that bias the way many water molecules near each other can interact (i.e., the Mickey Mouse ears of one molecule can only touch the head of another producing a lattice-work of water molecules). The bias limits the "freedom" of the water molecule such that a particular orientation of the molecule is iteratively favored creating a holistic property (surface tension). The bias reduces the potential distribution of difference in the system, constraining the unbiased tendency of a system to spontaneously even out. Thus, even in these homeodynamic effects there is an underlying set of regular dynamics that are emergent of which the effect is a trace.[42]

I also noted that these first-order processes are non-recurrent. This means that the amplification of biases is actually canceling out the perturbations of the system and moving it toward greater entropy and uniform distribution. Two terms Deacon introduces might help to clarify what this means: orthograde and contragrade change. Orthograde changes are those that appear natural. It is the tendency of a system "to change, irrespective of external interference."[43] By contrast, contragrade changes are those "that must be extrinsically forced, because they run counter to orthograde tendencies."[44] Homeodynamics represent a form of orthograde change. As in the example of surface tension, the shape bias of the molecules encourages the orthograde tendency toward asymmetric change as described by the second-law of thermodynamics: homeodynamics generate uniform distribution that accords to the orthograde tendency towards an increase in entropy.

Second-order emergent processes have simple recurrent causal topologies and produce morphodynamic effects. A typical example of this second-order emergence would be the appearance of hexagonally symmetrical Bénard cells in an evenly heated liquid of uniform depth. In this

---

41. Deacon, "Emergence: The Hole at the Wheel's Hub," 118.
42. Ibid., 127–30; and *Incomplete Nature*, 213–19.
43. Deacon, *Incomplete Nature*, 223, and fig. 7.1.
44. Ibid.

example, the liquid begins in a state of equilibrium. The even heat on the bottom of the system perturbs this state, so that liquid molecules on the bottom of the system have a decreased density through the continual influx of thermal energy. This lighter liquid on the bottom moves to the top in an effort to convey its heat and return to a state of equilibrium. This movement, given the finite space, presses the cooler top liquid down to the bottom which is then heated. Initially, the molecules may simply rise and fall, but with ever-increasing thermal energy input, a convection dynamic has to form in order for there not to be a local accumulation of heat. The result is the macroscopic effect known as Bénard cells—whose hexagonal shape is incidental to being geometrically most dense, but necessitated by the rapidity with which the heat must be conveyed.[45]

How are second-order emergent processes different from the first-order processes described above? In the first-order dynamic example given above, the constraining feature is the shape of the molecule itself. This bias alone enacts a homeodynamic process that persists in an orthograde fashion towards entropy (where entropy represents the most statistically even disbursement of molecules given the conditions). In the example given for the second-order emergent processes, it is a homeodynamic process itself that enables the morphodynamic formation of Bénard cells. Without the constant input of heat causing perturbation in the system that otherwise strives to regain a state of equilibrium, the morphodynamic feature could not form. In sum, the convection cycles that create these hexagonal cells are the product of two homeodynamic processes in a specific relationship to one another (the input of heat that causes iterative movement of the molecules and the shape constraint spontaneously formed by the agitated molecules continuously bumping into each other and then forming currents so as best to convey the heat).

This example can also be thought of in terms of orthograde and contragrade tendencies to illustrate the relationship between homeodynamics that yield a morphodynamic system. As a whole, the morphodynamic system represents an orthograde tendency towards change: it will spontaneously form given the persistence of lower-level homeodynamic processes. In terms of the Bénard cells, this means the cells will form again even if the system is perturbed in some way so long as there is a constant input of heat. This is why I initially stated that the morphodynamic, second-order emergent feature is called simple recurrent: it relies upon the recurrent input of heat (in this example) for the emergent effect to form. In the first-order

---

45. Deacon, "Emergence: The Hole at the Wheel's Hub," 130–31; and *Incomplete Nature*, 250–52.

emergent process, no recurrence is needed for the property to emerge since the shape of the molecule itself provides the constraint for the emergent property.

However, this orthograde tendency of the morphodynamics relies on synergistic reciprocity[46] producing contragrade local tendencies in the homeodynamics. In terms of our example, the continuous heat input and the formation of currents by agitated molecules represent local constraints that propagate across the system. The orderliness of the hexagonal Bénard cells is a drastic simplification of the possible states of unconstrained orthograde tendencies of each homeodynamic process by itself.[47] This is important to emphasize, because the synergistic reciprocity of contragrade change producing higher-level regions of orthograde dynamics is a motor to Deacon's dynamical model of emergence. This relationship of contragrade to orthograde tendency is again exhibited in the final dynamical order.

These final, third-order emergent processes have hyper-recurrent causal topologies and produce teleodynamic effects. It is at this stage that, at the very least, a proto-biotic entity[48] with a lineage subject to evolution by natural selection comes to be. Just as morphodynamic, second-order processes rely on homeodynamic, first-order processes, so also teleodynamic, third-order processes rely on morphodynamic processes. In parallel to what we discovered above, teleodynamic processes rely on the synergistic reciprocity of (at least two) morphodynamic processes. In sum, morphodynamics comes from the synergistic reciprocity of homeodynamics; teleodynamics comes from the synergistic reciprocity of morphodynamics. Deacon's example of an "autogen" is helpful in understanding this most complex emergent topology.

In its simplest guise, the autogen consists of two concepts related to ubiquitous features of life: autocatalysis and containment. Containment, being a bit more straightforward, is that feature of the autogen that separates it from the rest of its world. Without the separation caused by self-assembling containment, the complex molecular processes needed for life would fall prey to the thermodynamic tendency towards entropy. Autocatalysis is a

46. The term synergistic reciprocity is from Deacon. I use it to describe situations where the reciprocal effects of two lower order dynamics create a stable local relationship that perpetuates itself despite the general orthograde tendencies of the lower order dynamics.

47. Deacon, *Incomplete Nature*, 234–37, 245–46, and 261.

48. I call the entity proto-biotic in deference to origins of life research programs that would require a number of other processes to be in place before calling an entity alive. Notably, the autogen does not perform its own work cycle and possess a metabolism by which to repair parts that break down. I will deal with this gray space between the biotic and proto-biotic in subsequent chapters. See ibid., 315–19.

non-equilibrium chemical process where there is a circular arrangement of molecular interaction. Imagine six chemicals A-F, where A and B make C, while D and E make F. Now imagine further that F is a catalyst for the A and B reaction, and that C is a catalyst for the D and E reaction (as is diagramed in figure 1 below). In this simple hypothetical set we have the circular arrangement of autocatalysis: where the product of a first reaction is a catalyst for a second reaction and the product of the second reaction is a catalyst for the first reaction. Traditionally, all catalytic reactions are limited by the finite presence of a substrate material or a lack of energy in the system to continue the sets of reactions. When the morphodynamic processes of autocatalysis and containment reactions are reciprocally related to one another, there is the potential for an autogen.[49]

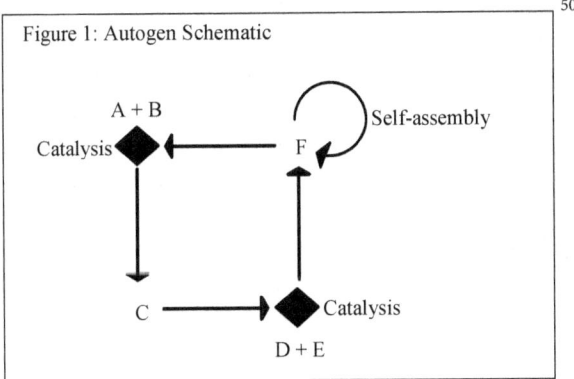[50]

Let me explain this in a bit more detail. Imagine one of the molecules produced in the process of autocatalysis has a tendency for self-assembly that leads to containment (assume product F from the example above). The great lack of self-assembly in the potential to form containers is sufficient amounts of substrate (meaning there is not enough substance F in a

---

49. It may be less than obvious why autocatalysis and containment reactions are morphodynamic processes. In both cases, a form of constraining self-organization is recirculated and amplified that biases the potential future states of the system *and* allows us to identify the morphodynamic features that distinguish the system itself. For instance, in the case of autocatalysis, the micro-configurational properties of the molecular components constrain the vast possibility of potential reactions and amplify this constraint by favoring particular allosteric reactions that will greatly influence the whole collection of components. With the continuous introduction of energy and raw materials to keep the cycle of autocatalytic reactions going (much like the need for the continuous input of heat for creation of Bénard cells), an autopoietic system is generated. For a more detailed description, see Deacon, "Emergence: The Hole at the Wheel's Hub," 135-36; and Kauffman, *Investigations*, chap. 2.

50. Figure is modeled off of Deacon, *Incomplete Nature*, fig. 10.2.

localized space), but in the setting of an autocatalytic cycle, more and more of the self-assembling substrate will be produced, greatly increasing the chance of containment. In forming a container, there is also a likelihood that some group of molecules will be trapped within the container separated from the rest of the environment (to extend our thought experiment imagine the new container encapsulates some of substrate A and D as well as product C). By forming containers, the cycle of autocatalytic reactions are prevented from being exhausted. If the container then breaks open in a new environment rich in substrate molecules for the autocatalytic cycle (in this case an environment with substrates B and E since the autocell already contains A and D), then more autogens can be formed.[51] "In other words, *the reciprocal complementarity of these two self-organizing processes creates the potential for self-repair, self-reconstitution, and even self-replication in a minimal form.*"[52]

By synergistically linking two morphodynamic processes, which each demonstrate a simple recurrent causal structure, the autogen exemplifies the hyper-recurrent causal structure of third-order emergence processes: a temporal causal structure that can recur despite temporal distance between instantiations. By linking autocatalysis and self-containment, the substrate and energetic limitations are removed (i.e., the autogen remains intact until a substrate rich environment is present so that neither morphodynamic process exhausts itself). This generates a "memory" for the autogen to a reference state—because of the interdependence of the morphodynamic processes. In a new substrate rich environment, the morphodynamic processes will persist in their interdependence and thereby allow for the teleodynamic entity to persist with a newly emergent identity. "Only a third-order emergent process has such an intrinsic identity."[53] Moving away from the description of a specific teleodynamic entity (i.e., the autogen and its process of autogenesis) and back to the dynamic logic itself, we can make a more general statement about the self-formative process at work in teleodynamics in terms of its orthograde and contragrade features. *The orthograde tendency of teleodynamics relies on the synergistic reciprocity producing contragrade local tendencies in its formative morphodynamics.*

---

51. For accounts of the autogen, earlier termed autocell, see Deacon, "The Hierarchic Logic of Emergence"; "Reciprocal Linkage Between Self-organizing Processes Is Sufficient for Self-reproduction and Evolvability," 136–49; "Emergence: The Hole at the Wheel's Hub"; Deacon and Sherman, "The Pattern Which Connects Pleroma to Creatura," 59–76; and Deacon, *Incomplete Nature*, chap. 10.

52. Deacon, *Incomplete Nature*, 305–6.

53. Deacon, "Emergence: The Hole at the Wheel's Hub," 138–39.

Hopefully, this description has begun to make clear how Deacon's approach is quite different from those emergent logics that rely on part-whole thinking. Most notably, by conceiving of emergence theory in terms of processes and organization, the teeth are taken out of reductionist critiques that often plague initial efforts at interdisciplinary dialogue between theology and science. If emergence is conceived in terms of processes and dynamics instead of substances (wherein we realize that substances are always representative of a process), the organization of these processes must be considered fundamental to the emergence of increasingly complex phenomena. Different emergent levels of complexity and scale, on Deacon's approach, represent the realization of different organizational possibilities.[54]

What remains is a difficult conceptual problem. How are these processes and organizational possibilities causally efficacious (if Deacon's account is to represent a form of strong emergence)? If organization is only thought of as a descriptive feature of processes, its causal implications can be rendered epiphenomenal.[55] Thus, what is critical to establishing the ontological efficacy of processes is *not* to think of organization descriptively. This is difficult; in our everyday interaction with the world, organization describes a form of redundancy or similarity amidst substrates. Organization gets conceived of as an idealized global property that describes the relationship amidst parts of a whole. In such an understanding the causal efficacy remains with the substrate being described in terms of the property of organization. By contrast, Deacon is calling for an account of causality by constraint.

He thinks of constraint in a technical sense as the diminution of possible freedom or variation. It is not an imposed limitation or merely descriptive feature; instead, Deacon is specifying the sense of the word so that constraint refers to the causal source of restriction in a measurable way. Constraint is the reduction of freedom as exhibited by unrealized states of a process; it is a state of the organizational system *as a negative property* and

---

54. Deacon, *Incomplete Nature*, 177.

55. "What must be explained then is how the organization of a process can be a locus of a distinctive mode of causality that is independent of the patterns of causal interaction among individual components of that process. Beneath this question lies another that is even more basic: Isn't organization merely a *description* of some relationships between components? Indeed, isn't it inevitably a simplification and an abstraction? We must still ask whether there is something about the organization of a process that is causally relevant over and above lower level processes and their causal influences. *If organization is not an intrinsic property, but rather merely a comparative assessment or idealization, it is rendered physically epiphenomenal*" (ibid., 179; emphasis mine).

not an extrinsically imposed boundary. "It is a way of referring to what is not exhibited, but could have been, at least under some circumstances."[56]

It is perhaps helpful to think back to the Bénard cell again in order to illustrate the importance of this shift in thinking. From the common-sense view of organization (i.e., organization as a global property describing the relationship amidst parts of a whole), we could say that the molecular parts within the Bénard cell as its whole are organized according to convection cycles. In this description, the term "convection cycle" provides organization as a kind of substrate neutral property with descriptive, but not causative, force. It describes a process applicable not only to the molecular movement but any other number of substances as well. Here, "convection cycle" represents a positive, extrinsic property that could equally well describe any number of different sets of component parts. From the constraint view of organization (i.e., organization as the reduced freedom exemplified by unrealized states of a process), the Bénard cell is organized because the molecular interaction is constrained. On this view the term "convection cycle" does not indicate an extrinsic, positive property beyond the components; rather, it is a negative property. It expresses what states of the component process could have been but are not because of the organizational principle. It indicates how the wide possibility spaces of the orthograde tendencies of the molecules have been narrowed. Here, "convection cycle" is a short hand for the causal force restricting the possibilities of the molecular free movement.[57]

This distinction, at first, may not seem very important; however, it is critical to understanding why Deacon's work is not simply subject to the criticism that Kim levies—reducing emergent properties to their lower-level parts without remainder. The question is why are Deacon's emergent dynamics not completely characterized in terms of the lower-level dynamics by an argument analogous to Kim's account of emergent properties as reducible to their lower-level parts and the arrangement of these parts? Would not emergent dynamics reduce to lower-level dynamics just as Kim's emergent whole reduces to its lower-level parts?

Constraint and its relation to characterizing the dynamical transitions that Deacon identifies in terms of an alternating logic of orthograde and contragrade change is the key to avoiding this criticism. The constraining synergistic reciprocity of lower-level dynamic regimes changes the

56. Ibid., 193.

57. A critical part of thinking about organization as a negative property is to consider the constitutive parts of a whole in terms of its future possibilities. This will be explored in more detail in chapter 4. For now, it is simply important to note that I find this to be a critical, if somewhat implicit, feature of Deacon's approach.

otherwise orthograde tendencies of the lower-level dynamics to being contragrade. From homeodynamics to morphodynamics and morphodynamics to teleodynamics this alteration from orthograde dynamic to reciprocal contragrade dynamic persists. This is why characterizing Deacon's work in terms of Kim's mereology, parts and wholes, is not quite adequate: the morphodynamic "parts" are transformed from orthograde to contragrade tendency by the causal power of constrained organization. *The part, in the context of the whole, is not the same as the part independently conceived.* This is why Deacon will affirm there is a basic supervenience relation between dynamical regimes but not a mereological relation.

Here again it is helpful to think of the Bénard cell. According to a constraint account of organization, we found that the organizational principle is causative in a preventive or constraining sense. The convection cycle prevents the free movement of molecules. That constraint is generated, as we have already covered in detail, through the reciprocity of two homeodynamic processes. However in the constrained morphodynamic relationship, the orthograde tendencies of the homeodynamics are made contragrade (i.e., in the cell the molecular interaction and input of heat that should normally continue to move the system towards even distribution suddenly constrain the system to a narrow possibility-space). Thus, while the morphodynamic supervenes on its homeodynamic components, it is not mereologically related to them because the tendency of the parts outside the context of the whole (orthograde) is not the same as for the parts in the context of the whole (contragrade).[58]

Finally, since Deacon's account makes dynamics the primary concern in an account of emergence, what place does this leave for the emergent property or substance more traditionally conceived? Deacon accounts for this in terms of constraint as it relates to order and habit: something is more orderly or more habitual as its degrees of freedom are increasingly constrained. I think of order and habit as Deacon describes them in terms of a symbolic relationship; the causal efficacy of constraint in the dynamic yields a symbol of itself—a structural trace indicating an emergent level of organization.

The notion of symbol I have in mind here is something akin to that described by Paul Tillich. He affirms what we could call a "translucency" model of symbol. The translucent symbol is like a stained glass that affects the light passing through it. The color of the glass makes visible the light that would otherwise be invisible; the translucent symbol manifests the infinite

---

58. Deacon, *Incomplete Nature*, 255.

through its existential distortion.⁵⁹ A translucent symbol requires its finite, existential embodiment to manifest the infinite through itself.⁶⁰

In a similar way, Deacon's emergent properties could be thought of as translucent symbols that reveal the ontological, causal topologies of constraint. Organized properties arise as symbolic windows to the habitual iteration of reciprocally related processes that in their mutuality constrain the possible free states of the component dynamics. It is important to note that this constraint is inherently a relational notion because of the reciprocal structure. Constraint is unrealized dynamical potentialities; potentialities that are suppressed by some bias in the probability of occurrence due to its synergistic reciprocity with another process. A dynamic does not constrain itself. This is important because the dynamic is what is ontologically significant, while the property itself is not constitutive or ontologically sufficient as a causal source.⁶¹

Is Teleodynamics Strong Enough?

Deacon's account rebuffs the critique of Kim by avoiding reliance on mereological reasoning in a traditional emergentist sense; instead, Deacon locates causal efficacy in the constrained organization of dynamical systems. However, does Deacon's logic of constraints represent a strong enough account of emergence for viable interdisciplinary work in science and theology? In making such an evaluation, the work of Philip Clayton provides an essential analytical tool.

Clayton helpfully identifies five different meanings of the term "emergence" across disciplines and four approaches to working with emergence theory today. There is an important correlation to be identified between these five meanings and four approaches, granting a greater degree of insight into how Clayton is using the concept of emergence in his theological investigation. It is worth briefly unpacking these nine concepts.

---

59. Tillich, "Rejoinder," 187.

60. Tillich, *Religiöse Verwirklichung*, 104–5. Of course, this understanding of the pane of stained glass is not consonant to the contemporary understanding as in physics. (I am indebted to Robert Russell for explaining this to me). White light, which has all frequencies of light, encounters a pane of glass that we perceive as stained because it absorbs all colors of the light *except* for the one frequency which it allows to pass through. It is an open question if this understanding changes the way we might constructively interpret Tillich's concept of symbol for theology more generally. Here, this minutia is not critical.

61. Deacon, *Incomplete Nature*, 197–205.

Beginning with the five meanings, the first meaning—E_1—represents a feature of a specified scientific system; however, the specificity of the claim prevents its extension to differing scientific theories. E_2 designates connections that may become part of a broader unified scientific theory. It is an explication of the basic correlative law or theory that is absent from E_1. These first two meanings are the only ones that are explicitly scientific. E_3 is a meta-scientific term that describes common patterns across a range of scientific theories. Here the connections identified in E_2 are extrapolated into poly-theory patterns that yield a heuristic function in postulating new emergentist hypotheses. E_4 is an attempt to explain why identified meta-scientific patterns (of E_3) should exist in transitioning between scientific theories. Finally, E_5 employs emergence as a metaphysical theory. "It claims that the nature of the world is such that it produces, and perhaps must produce, continually more complex realities in a process of ongoing creativity, and it is a thesis about the nature of what is produced."[62] It is important to realize that (1) only the first two meanings Clayton identifies are properly scientific; (2) that each level of meaning builds upon the previous level; and (3) that the eventual metaphysical meaning may be indicated by the previous four levels but not thereby proven.

The four approaches that Clayton identifies each use elements of the five meanings of emergence. The first approach interprets emergence as an attractor state for evolutionary processes that lifts reality to new expressions across seemingly insurmountable gaps. Clayton rightly affirms that properly scientific accounts that claim this poly-theory authority should be treated with skepticism, but the first approach continues to have efficacy as a speculative metaphysics.[63] The second approach to emergence theory is a negative interpretation. Here emergent phenomena express the limits of what science is able to accomplish in terms of its explanatory power. This approach is an epistemological model of emergence that uses the term emergence only in the sense of E_1. The third approach to emergence theory is as a mode of theorizing about the way one or more particular sciences will be able to make progress in the future. This third approach describes ontologically emergent phenomena but constrains the meaning of the term emergence to what Clayton calls E_2. Finally, the fourth approach is in many ways a reiteration of the first approach with greater specificity, and it is here that Clayton's own sympathies lie. In this approach the emphasis is on identifying a recurring pattern of emergence across various fields. It is only by

---

62. Clayton, *Mind and Emergence*, 40–42.

63. As an example, think of Broad's commitment metaphysically to an assumption about a leveled-reality. The assumption is used to construe the scientific data he marshals, but nothing implicit to the data justifies the metaphysical assumption.

careful attention to how emergent phenomena are identified in particular fields that this reiterating pattern can be explicated in terms of analogies that hold across the field-specific phenomena. Thus, despite its superficial similarity to the first approach Clayton identifies, the fourth approach explicitly identifies itself as a meta-scientific enterprise that brings to bear the analogical reasoning and constructive philosophical and theological power of emergence as it is meant in E_3, E_4, and E_5 upon the particularly and properly scientific elements of the third approach.[64]

Table 2: Clayton's Meanings and Approaches

	Five Meanings	Four Approaches
Scientific	E_1—Feature of scientific system	Approach 2—Emergence as Limits of Explanatory Power
	E_2—Connections in broader, unified scientific theory	Approach 3—Emergence as Theory for Field Specific Scientific Progress
Meta-Scientific	E_3—Common patterns across scientific theories	Approach 4—Emergence as a Reiterating Pattern across Fields
	E_4—Explanation of the existence of common patterns	
Metaphysical	E_5—Metaphysical theory about production of greater complexity	Approach 1- Emergence as Attractor State

Above, I have summarized all of the most important facets of Clayton's work in table 2. The colored rows indicate the scientific or philosophical status of the five meanings he identifies. The approaches have been lined up in order to correspond to those parts of the five meanings of which they uniquely make use. As the table makes clear, the fourth approach, which overlaps three of the five meanings and has both meta-scientific and metaphysical implications, is quite encompassing.

---

64. Clayton, *Mind and Emergence*, 47–49.

There are three important insights to be gained from Clayton's approach to emergence theory as it is theologically relevant up to this point. The first is the importance of identifying the theological value of ontological emergence as a non-reductionist approach to science. The second, related, insight is that valid ontological emergence would be identified by downward causation (top-down causality). This allows for an important distinction between emergent properties of already existent objects from emergent objects that represent a new locus of causal power in the universe.[65] The third is Clayton's insistence that the theological relevance of emergence theory lies in explicating the pattern at work in the emergence of various levels of ontologically new things. This final point is particularly important. For Clayton, the theological impetus of emergence theory lies in identifying the iterative pattern of emergence that runs itself on different substantial platforms. Emergence theory (as in approach four and definition E_5) provides the metaphysical bridge between theological and scientific reasoning about emergent phenomena.

What is interesting about all of this is to consider how Clayton's emergence typology could be used to gain some clarity about the many levels of insight at work in Deacon's proposal. For example, the three-orders of emergent dynamics that Deacon identifies could be understood as exemplars of E_2. The synergistic reciprocity establishing higher-level orthograde change by a shift to contragrade change in the component dynamics exemplifies E_3. Finally, the shift to an account of causality in terms of constraint (as it is exemplified by the synergistic reciprocity in the E_3 causal topologies) could be an example of E_4. As a result, I suggest Deacon's work on emergence theory can be interpreted in terms of the fourth approach that Clayton identifies, while the issue of how Deacon may or may not handle emergence, terminologically speaking, as an E_5 overarching metaphysics is temporarily bracketed.

My categorization of Deacon's work in terms of Clayton's typology, however, is quite different from that of Clayton's own categorization.[66] Clayton reads Deacon's proposal as a straightforward example of an E_2, third approach to emergence theory. The three dynamic orders serve as a means of explaining laws that bridge the gap between physics and chemistry on the one side and biology on the other. The primary function of Deacon's work

---

65. Clayton makes the assumption "that ontology should follow agency, then cases of emergent causal agency justify us in speaking of emergent objects (organisms, agents) in natural history" (ibid., 62). This ontological criterion is realized by instances of downward causation; emergent properties would somehow lack an authentic account in terms of downward causation.

66. On Clayton's analysis of Deacon, see ibid., 46–48.

on emergence theory, in this interpretation, is to better explain how the logic of natural selection can become operative within biological systems. Once natural selection is in place, there are no longer emergent features that develop: the iterating pattern that Clayton seeks (mutually constrained teleodynamic processes yielding a fourth class of causal topologies) is never developed in Deacon's work.

This is not to diminish the value of Clayton's analysis. First, it is only in consideration of Deacon's later writing that it becomes clear how the synergistic reciprocity and constraint account of process organization is integral to the more directly testable, or some might say properly scientific, assertions about the dynamic regimes. Second his analysis provides a key insight into the challenge and flexibility that can be used in interpreting Deacon's work.

Put bluntly, if Deacon's work is read in terms of emergent *substances* and their properties running a single, iterative law of emergence operative by downward causation, then Clayton's categorization is sufficient and it is ambiguous as to whether or not Deacon's work represents a vision of strong or weak emergence. Think about this ambiguity as follows. Consider the autogen as an emergent phenomenon. If, as with Clayton, the teleodynamics formative of the autogen is simply a heuristic tool for understanding the autogen, then the primary importance of Deacon's work is as a very specific scientific theory modeling how to bridge the divide between physics and chemistry on the one hand and a proto-biological realm on the other. If that is the focus of Deacon's emergence work, then establishing ontological efficacy is not especially relevant. Whether the autogen represents strong emergence or weak emergence is not critical to the model—the critical feature of the model is its ability to explain the means to crossing this threshold towards living things. If the autogen is something ontologically distinctive, great, if it is not, oh well; the explanatory power is not enhanced or diminished either way.

However, if Deacon's work is concerned with emergent *processes* yielding distinctive causal topologies, as I would suggest, the emergent property is a symbolic artifact of the stable organization of its causal topologies. To return to the autogen example, this would mean treating the teleodynamic as emergent and the autogen as a heuristic for the emergent dynamic. If the emphasis is placed on the architecture of the dynamic causal topology at work (i.e., teleodynamics—not the autogen model directly), then the question of whether this exemplifies weak or strong emergence is not mere adiaphora. As I already have explained above, if the emergent dynamics are primary and understood as exemplars of E_2, then Deacon's work has relevance in the E_3 and E_4 meanings Clayton identifies. It is the E_4 feature that is particularly important (the shift to an account of causality in terms of constraint) because it makes a claim about the causal efficacy of the E_2 and E_3 features Deacon identifies. While I will delve into the precise implications of what this shift from a substantial to dynamical reading of Deacon's work might mean in chapter 4, for now, let me be clear that *if Deacon's work is understood as a form of strong emergence, it must be interpreted in terms of the primacy of emergent processes, since a reading in terms of emergent properties (as in Clayton) is ambiguous about whether the work is a form of strong or weak emergence.*

This creates an interesting conundrum for theological interdisciplinary work incorporating Deacon's emergence theory. We must be clear about the difference in the mode of interdisciplinarity involving theology when dealing with E_2 versus E_3 or E_4 aspects of emergence theory. What is unique about the E_3 and E_4 aspects of my analysis of Deacon's emergence theory is that they are *integral* to the conceptualization of the E_2 phenomena as strong emergence features. Without the philosophical reconceptualization of causal efficacy establishing ontological existence in E_4, Deacon cannot avoid Kim's critique of strong emergence. The E_2 phenomena would still be relevant as descriptive, epistemic features of a weak emergence paradigm, but only this. As I engage theological topics in the second part of this work, it is important to keep in mind that the theological insights to be garnered from Deacon's analysis depend upon what typological level of material within his analysis is being considered.

The Abstential

Having outlined some of the critical features of emergence theory on its own terms and indicating what one must be aware of when interpreting Deacon's work as a form of strong emergence, I will explicate a few connections I see between the emergentist project outlined above and the conceptual history of life in chapter 1.

First, I want to draw a parallel between the contrast of weak and strong accounts of emergence theory on the one hand and the tension between the mechanical and teleological aspects of the Kantian antinomy of teleological judgment on the other hand. Notable in this regard is the idea of the epiphenomenal in weak emergence. If emergent properties are only epiphenomenal features of some type of reductive physicalist ontology, then these properties are only epistemologically significant. This parallels the way Blumenbach approached Kant's work: wherein the teleological facets of Kantian purposiveness are only heuristically valuable and ultimately decomposable to a fully mechanical explication. In both cases, there is a dispute as to the ontological efficacy of higher-order features in relation to their constitutive parts.

Of course, as I have already reviewed, Kant finds this problematic because the irreducibility of purposiveness is requisite to establishing the ontological efficacy of natural ends within the wider context of his transcendental idealism, thereby affirming that organisms are more than mere artifacts. The arrangement of parts in an organized system will never produce more than an aggregate, in the Kantian understanding, if there is no appeal to purposiveness. Purposiveness cannot be captured in mechanical explication. Similarly, the strong emergentist will insist that the emergent whole is irreducible to its constitutive parts: there is a causal power to the whole that cannot be accounted for in the parts and their organization.

I am not trying to affirm anything more than this simple parallelism in order to suggest that the debate between weak and strong emergence can be construed as a specific instantiation of the wider antinomy between mechanical and teleological reasoning: whether or not all material things can be judged as possible merely according to mechanical laws. In this way contemporary wrestling with the role of teleology in principles of life and the interpretation of the ontological efficacy of emergent features are of a common ilk. In both cases there is a persistent problem with how to conceive of the relationship between mechanical and teleological explication.

Second, if the principles of the antinomy of teleological judgment are akin to the overarching framework that informs the debate in both emergence theory and research into the principles of life, how can Deacon's work press beyond the dichotomy of the mechanical and teleological so integral to Kant's work? As to this, I have three points to emphasize: a methodological parallel between Kant's approach and Deacon's dynamics, a typological similarity in their respective work, and a conceptual distinction that expands the teleological history outlined in the previous chapter.[67]

First, a common methodological feature with regard to Kant's approach and Deacon's dynamics is that the concept of life serves as an exemplar in their respective work of the larger question of wrestling with teleological explication and phenomena. Kant deals with living things and

---

67. While the bulk of my conceptual histories have been told in terms of contrasting proof of concept arguments that oscillate between emphases on teleological and mechanical explication or strong and weak emergence, the connection I envision between Deacon and Kant is different. I would suggest there is a great deal of continuity in the principles of these thinkers. Deacon's work begins the difficult process of extricating the core insights of the Kantian perspective from their transcendental idealist framework, without making a naïve return to sublimating the teleological to the mechanical.

the principles of life only insofar as they are the example he sees of natural ends. Living things are not the primary object of his study but the primary example for his study: his focus is on those things that cannot be conceived without reference to the intentionality of the causal power of ends. Deacon's three tiered dynamical schema also provides a broader framework than a contemporary analysis focused only on the origins and principles of life. Teleodynamics, while certainly related to the distinctive dynamic of living things, is not limited to the biological realm. Instead, Deacon sees his work as a way of accounting for final causality in terms of organization and dynamics.[68] In both cases, their respective analyses are intended to describe something much broader than the principles of life themselves; however, in both cases there is also a clear realization of the potential of the analysis for establishing principles of life. The connection to principles of life derives from their common pursuit of an apt characterization of final causes.

Second, what could be characterized as similar beyond this concern for situating an explication of principles of life in the frame of an authentic conception of final causes? Is there some greater typological similarity between their approaches that might show how Deacon's work integrates to the history presented in the previous chapter? As I have affirmed repeatedly, Kant's antinomy of the teleological judgment emphasizes the tense juxtaposition that characterizes the place of purposiveness. Purposiveness stands as the necessary postulate for judging entities that cannot be conceived without reference to intention. It is always standing in tension to mechanical explication. However, as Kant suggests, the apparent contradiction between the mechanical and the teleological in such judgments *is not authentic*, but the final unity of this antinomy could only be established in a supersensible principle.

Deacon does not use the term purposiveness with any frequency, but he does use a suite of terms that at least seem related to the meaning of Kantian purposiveness. One of these terms is constraint, which I analyzed above in the explication of the dynamical orders. Constraint refers to the unrealized possible states of a system as it is restricted by its organizing features. As put in terms of Clayton's helpful typological language, I suggested that constraint was an E_4 feature that explicates the logic of the heuristically valuable E_3 feature of synergistic reciprocity at work in his dynamic regimes.

There are two other related terms still to be considered. First, Deacon introduces the term "ententional" to get around the mentalistic baggage associated with terms like "teleology" or the "intentional." Instead the ententional is intended as a general term for the wide variety of phenomena

---

68. Deacon, *Incomplete Nature*, 275.

that are fundamentally incomplete. That is to say entential phenomena are those things or processes that exist for the sake of achieving some non-intrinsic end: they are phenomena with a core inclination towards the realization of something absent.[69] This leads directly to the second term: the "abstential."[70] Closely related to the entential, the abstential denotes the features that are absent from entential phenomena. The abstential is the intrinsic incompleteness for which entential phenomena exist.[71] There is a clear metaphysical overtone to the abstential that Deacon does not pursue in his own work, being more interested in explicating the dynamics of constraint in entential phenomena.[72]

Table 3: Comparing Deacon and Kant

Emergent Typology	Deacon	Kant
E_3	Synergistic Reciprocity	Organizing and Self-Organizing
E_4	Constraint—Entential	Self-Formative Power of Natural Ends—Purposiveness
E_5	Abstential	Supersensible Unity of the Teleological and Mechanical

There is a potential parallel between Deacon's suite of concepts (i.e., synergistic reciprocity, constraint, the entential, and the abstential) and purposiveness as imagined in terms of the Kantian antinomy of teleological judgment. The parallel is not exactly a mirror-image, but I have indicated the place of key concepts and relations in table 3 above. The table is organized according to Clayton's typology of emergent features.[73]

---

69. Ibid., 26–27.

70. The term is actually "absential" not "abs*t*ential." I have made this slight change since I will be constructively developing the term. I have chosen to use abs*t*ential throughout the book to avoid confusion.

71. Deacon, *Incomplete Nature*, 2–3.

72. See especially ibid., 555n2.

73. The movements in Clayton's typology, from the material to the metaphysical, makes features of Kant's work on purposiveness seem out of order, at least as compared to their presentation in the context of *The Critique of the Power of Judgment*. Further, the comparison requires imagining Kant's account of purposiveness and organisms as emergent features, a concept that is clearly not germane to the historical time of Kant's writing and cannot be squared with his wider philosophical system in a self-evident way. However, our goal is not to remain strictly Kantian, but to examine how his work provides an important leaping-off point for subsequent exploration of the principles of life and the role of teleology therein.

First, I suggest the reciprocal structure of interrelated dynamics in Deacon's work parallels the Kantian conception of organized and self-organizing beings. Of course, the Kantian ascription of this structure to natural ends would make the parallel direct only in terms of Deacon's teleodynamics (not morphodynamics and homeodynamics specifically). However, there is also a conceptual parallel in that these E_3 features are explicitly not decomposable for either thinker.[74] I term both the organizing and self-organizing features of Kant and the principle of synergistic reciprocity in Deacon E_3 features because of the generalizability of the heuristic functions of these concepts (which ensures they are not more properly termed E_2 features). As described above, neither Kant nor Deacon are principally giving descriptions only of the origins of life. Both are offering accounts of the common patterns of naturally occurring teleological or entential phenomena, which happen also to be a potential key principle in distinguishing living and non-living things. The patterns identified in terms of synergistic reciprocity and key features of self-organization could be used as a principle of transition amidst emergent features across a wide variety of variously conceived levels.

Second, if the features of Kantian self-organization and Deacon's synergistic reciprocity can be described as poly-theory heuristic principles (to borrow language from Clayton), then the idea of a "self-formative power for natural ends" and "constraint" can be imagined to be broader theories about the nature of these heuristic principles. Thus, I categorize them as E_4 emergent features. For both thinkers, these E_4 features describe a broader pattern in nature that points towards the ontological complexity of our world. In the case of Kant the self-formative power that characterizes the existence of natural ends draws a point of radical distinction into the ontological constitution of the world: there are artifacts and there are organisms. This broader distinction in the quality of nature can be characterized in terms of Kant's notion of purposiveness. For Deacon there are entential phenomena that are of a different constitution than the standard orthograde tendencies of

---

74. In the case of Kant these two criteria of a natural end are introduced in order to explicate the separation of organism from artifact in terms of the non-decomposable features of purposiveness; in the case of Deacon, morphodynamics serves as a necessary bridge between homeodynamic and teleodynamic systems that prevents the teleological features of these higher-order systems from being decomposable into their most elementary homeodynamic behaviors. The reciprocal structuring of two lower-level processes contragrade to one another in a critical sense is required for the emergent transition to a new higher-level orthograde process. This is why the entential phenomena cannot be explicated in simple physico-reductionist means (that is they cannot be decomposed only to their material parts), the morphodynamic features are crucial to explicating the emergent teleodynamics. Deacon, *Incomplete Nature*, 319–20.

homeodynamics. These ententional phenomena represent a real distinction in the quality of nature that he characterizes in terms of the notion of constraint. By way of summary, these E_4 features each point to a real distinction in the quality of existent things that yields a theory about the heuristic E_3 patterns and can be characterized in terms of a general principle.

Third, in formulating a metaphysical, E_5, theory out of these parallel accounts, we can construct one final parallel that reveals a real difference. By Kant's account, we can postulate an unknowable supersensible principle that could dialectically account for the complementarity of mechanical and teleological explications of natural ends. In the parallel of Deacon's account, the abstential might serve as this unknowable supersensible principle and be developed into a metaphysical theory about emergence complementary to his E_3 and E_4 features.

Why does the Kantian approach mire into an unknowable supersensible while Deacon's approach yields a candidate idea that could be developed into a larger metaphysical theory about emergence? In the E_3 ascription, Kant's work and Deacon's approach are immensely similar: synergistic reciprocity and self-organization both provide heuristics for nondecomposable systems. However, in its E_4 ascription Deacon's account takes an apophatic turn that is notably distinct from Kant. The positive Kantian valuations (the self-formative power and purposiveness) are re-imagined not in terms of what is produced but what never comes to be, what is implicitly lacking (ententional phenomena and constraint). I think this apophatic turn allows for Deacon to acknowledge the unique place of the abstential.[75] The abstential does not reduce well to either mechanical or teleological explication: it resists the materialist manipulability of the mechanical and the goal-orientation of the teleological. Yet, as Deacon's account of constraint helps demonstrate, the abstential is intimately tied to the mechanical and the teleological as well.

Before running too far along this abstential road, I need to reemphasize an important point. As the analysis of Deacon's work in terms of Clayton showed, one can read Deacon's work in terms of a substantialist vision of emergence emphasizing novelty that would render it an ontologically ambiguous form of emergence: treating the dynamical orders as E_2 features divorced from any E_3, E_4, or E_5 implications of the work. I would, however, suggest that this is not Deacon's intention (or perhaps entention?) nor does it foster a primary desire indicated earlier in this chapter: if there is to be *rich* interdisciplinary dialogue between emergence theory—including

---

75. This point is especially clear if you compare Deacon's apophatic turn to the positive description of the mechanical in Kant. A clear secondary source on Kant in this regard is McLaughlin, *Kant's Critique of Teleology in Biological Explanation*, 152–56.

specifically the principles of life it might suggest—and theology, then the version of emergence theory pursued needs to be strong emergence.

Reading Kant and Deacon in parallel indicates the need for a more robust ontology to coordinate with Deacon's idea of the abstential. On the one hand, without such an ontology, the abstential risks being reduced only to its heuristic value and Deacon's account of emergence can be interpreted as a form of weak emergence seeking to reduce teleology to mechanics. On the other hand, it is clear that Deacon's dynamical explications can in no way be brought back into Kant's idealist framework to provide such an ontology (despite their many parallels). Deacon's dynamical explications propose to do much more in their explanatory power than is bounded by the epistemic limits of purposiveness: limits which allow us to assume an ontological efficacy for natural ends within an idealist framework. Further, Deacon's account of emergence by constraint creates an insurmountable tension with the positive teleology of Kant's antinomy.

3

A Phenomenology of Life

IN THE LAST CHAPTER I reviewed critical tenets of emergence theory, and I made a connection between the work of Terrence Deacon and the conceptual history of life from chapter 1, leading to two notable conclusions. First, it seemed plausible that Deacon's work could be placed in our conceptual history of life as a phase beyond the Kantian conception of purposiveness (i.e., something whose causality can only be understood *as if* it were an end or purpose—a requirement of an organism). While taking up many features of the Kantian model, Deacon's shift to thinking in terms of constraint (i.e., the mode for developing higher dynamic orders from the mutual limitation of lower orders) and the abstential (i.e., the absences characteristic of intrinsically incomplete phenomena) was a notable departure from the positive formulations of self-formative power in Kant. This departure entailed a significant difference in the ontological ramifications of their respective work.

To recap, Kant's purposiveness was a regulative idea. To understand the causality at work in an organism is to treat the organism itself as if it were the purpose of its formation. The "as if" is very important though—Kant is not saying the organism is a purpose or end caused by design, but we can only conceive of the organism as though it were so designed. Moreover, Kant's claim is more than epistemological; his account of the general purposiveness of nature indicated that purposiveness was its own sort of special *a priori*, transcendental principle. There is purposiveness to nature insofar as it is a logical necessity to establishing the unity of natural ends and is irreducible to the mechanical causality of the determining judgment (as his disagreement with Blumenbach indicates). So purposiveness is distinct and irreducible to mechanical causality, but not as a merely epistemological tool: it is a distinctive mode of causality at work in organisms as opposed to the mechanical causality of the physical universe. This led to the antinomy of teleological judgment (roughly put an irresolvable conflict between the causal efficacy of purposiveness and the mechanical).

Where Kant ends I have Deacon beginning. Deacon's dynamic regimes seek to establish a unity between mechanical and teleological principles through ententional phenomena (i.e., those phenomena that are intrinsically incomplete). That is to say, Deacon's dynamic regimes press upon the supersensible unity of the teleological and mechanical (a unity which is incomprehensible in the Kantian antinomy of teleological judgment) through the idea of incompleteness.

The challenge is that Deacon's work is ambiguous as to whether it is a form of weak emergence or strong emergence. This ambiguity reveals itself depending upon whether his work is primarily interpreted in terms of the emergent properties produced or the more primordial dynamic causal topologies. This was demonstrated by Clayton's analysis of Deacon's work. According to Clayton, Deacon's work was a bridge theory that moved from physics and chemistry to biology. The most important facet (in this interpretation) of Deacon's work is specifically the autogen model. The causal dynamics are just helpful for explaining how this threshold from physics to biology could be crossed. Read this way, the type of emergence Deacon's work represents is ambiguous: the autogen may or may not be a new causal capacity within the universe—establishing this causal capacity would be a philosophical argument subsequent to the scientific explanatory power of the autogen as a means of crossing the threshold from physics to biology.

This potential reading and its ensuing ontological ambiguity is significant for the interaction envisioned here between theology and natural science. As noted, it is only a strong emergence approach that can bear the weight of the robust theological interaction I seek. As a result, it is important for the larger purposes of this work to establish a firmer ontological grounding for reading Deacon's work (i.e., to clearly establish how and why his work ought to be interpreted as a strong emergentist account). I have already spent a great deal of energy on establishing how Deacon's work both can be and ought to be read as a strong emergentist account. In contrast to interpretations like that of Clayton, I have suggested that the primary emphasis in Deacon's work lies with his dynamic regimes and their recurrent orders of synergistic reciprocity by constraint (i.e., the formation of higher dynamic orders by the mutual limitation of lower orders reciprocally related to one another). When Deacon's work is interpreted this way, it represents a form of strong emergence by challenging the strict decomposability of mereological reasoning typically assumed to be a part of emergence.

Still, these conclusions drawn from the previous chapter lay out two sets of critical points to be developed further. First, what are the implications of Deacon's use of constraint in ententional phenomena to overcome the conflict between the mechanical and the teleological? What does it mean that incompleteness might be the site of a supersensible unity for these two principles? What is the nature of this incompleteness? Or how does something incomplete, apophatic, or absent account for something ontologically real and not just something ontologically missing? Second, what are the implications of Deacon's challenge to the decomposability of mereological reasoning? Are there consequences for the "being" of parts and wholes that need to be drawn out by Deacon's challenge? Is there a nascent ontology already implicitly at work in Deacon's formulation of this challenge that would strengthen my claim that his dynamics is a form of strong emergence?

To address the remaining questions in a satisfactory way, I will develop a more robust understanding of the abstential (i.e., the absences characteristic of ententional—intrinsically incomplete—phenomena). With this goal in mind, the work of Renaud Barbaras will be essential. Developed out of the ontological turn in Maurice Merleau-Ponty's later philosophy, Barbaras generates a constructive phenomenology of life. He seeks a primordial sense of what it means "to live" amidst the multiplicity of ways life is understood. Ultimately, he understands life as a perpetual movement that exceeds the fulfillment of its needs and can then be characterized by an essential incompleteness that is desire. As such, the fundamental character of life is made curiously present by its own absence—a feature reflective of the essentially incomplete desire driving its movement.

In what follows, I will carefully unpack the dense philosophical language and concepts that inform Barbaras's phenomenology of life and the relationship of this phenomenology to ontology. This chapter will only introduce these philosophical tools and develop some fluency with them. In the subsequent chapter, the implications of this phenomenological program will be interpreted in relation to Deacon's understanding of the abstential.

Phenomenology, Perception, and Ontology

Before delving directly into the key concepts to be drawn from Barbaras's work, let me offer an inherent challenge to making clear its ramifications for this project. Barbaras's work develops out of a deep relationship to the tradition of phenomenological philosophy—especially as found in Merleau-Ponty. Many of the ideas, terms, and theoretical constructs Barbaras employs find their origins in the earlier thinkers of this tradition. His fluency with these thinkers is so vast that one could spend a great deal of time just trying to untangle where Barbaras's constructive thought begins and the historical outlook of his sources end.[1] My focus must be on what is important for this work: the ontological resources generated by a phenomenology of life and the potential of these resources to enrich the meaning of the abstential as Deacon defines it.

Given this caveat though, I want to outline two concepts: the place of the body in phenomenology and the limitations of the concept of the living-body. These themes are essential to understanding Barbaras's phenomenology of life and connect his work particularly clearly to the philosophical aims of Merleau-Ponty. In a certain way, analyzing these concepts form a narrative. They take us through a brief history of phenomenology across different generations of its development. This is a way of journeying towards Barbaras's work; we will be following a thread of self-critique within a field of phenomenologists. As a result of this unfolding approach, the descriptions below will follow an oscillating movement between presentation and refutation: a presentation of early work and a refuting criticism that points to sites for new constructive development.

From Consciousness to the Body

First, Barbaras continues the trend of Merleau-Ponty's persistent philosophical aim—overcoming the opposition between realism and idealism through a robust account of phenomenology. This aim appears clearly in Merleau-Ponty's early work, *The Structure of Behavior*. There it is presented as the tension in understanding the relationship between consciousness and the natural order. Satisfactorily articulating the juncture and juxtaposition of the real existence of the world and the constitutive place of consciousness forms the problem-space he intends to address.[2]

However, running a fine line between these two positions is no easy task; there is a constant risk of absolutizing intellectualism (i.e., the various forms of idealism and the constitutive role of consciousness) or empiricism (i.e., the various forms of realism that do not give due credence to the constructive power of consciousness). This is nothing new for those versed in

---

1. See the translators introduction to Barbaras's *The Being of the Phenomenon*, ix–xvi. This is not a criticism of Barbaras's work, but perhaps an inevitability of his intimate treatment and use of Merleau-Ponty's final unfinished work *The Visible and the Invisible*.

2. Merleau-Ponty, *The Structure of Behavior*, 4.

philosophy of science or the development of interaction between theology and natural science. Volumes of proposals address this seesawing tension in myriad ways. However, a phenomenological approach to this issue may provide a different means of encountering this intellectualist and empiricist tension.

By intentionally pursuing the intellectualist and empiricist tension through phenomenology, Merleau-Ponty and Barbaras root themselves in a philosophical tradition steeped in the work of Edmund Husserl. This philosophical location provides an essential framework to their approach and an initial problem to be overcome. To understand this important point it is worth moving step by step from the basic outlines of Husserl's phenomenology of transcendental consciousness to Merleau-Ponty's phenomenology of perception in the lived-body.

For a phenomenological investigation, the phenomena being investigated are conceived in a different way than empiricist, rationalist, or Kantian understandings. The sensible-experience of the empiricist, the clear and distinct idea of the rationalist, nor the distinction between the thing as it appears and the corresponding thing in itself of the Kantian adequately characterizes experience for phenomenological investigation. Each of these approaches remains indebted to the Cartesian distinction between subjective consciousness and objective reality. The phenomenologist too remains indebted to the Cartesian distinction, but in contrast with these other approaches the phenomenologist seeks to overcome the *separation* between consciousness itself and the object of consciousness.[3]

To understand the way phenomenology proceeds in overcoming the separation of subject and object—self and world—means understanding the "phenomenological reduction." This reduction typically is considered in two parts: the "phenomenological epoché" and the "reduction" proper. These two moments, separate in Husserl's writings, are generally amalgamated when tacitly referring to phenomenology. In the epoché we bracket judgments of being related to the "natural attitude." This is the attitude wherein we assume the existence of an independent world. The epoché is a "parenthesizing": not a negation, but an abstention from judgments that rely upon the assumed independent existence of the world. We bracket our assumptions, experiences, and knowledge of the world as we continuously receive it every day. As Husserl writes:

---

3. See also Fink, "The Phenomenological Philosophy of Edmund Husserl and Contemporary Criticism," 88–93; and Zahavi, "Internalism, Externalism, and Transcendental Idealism," 355–74.

> We place the general thesis of the essence of the natural attitude out of consideration; with one stroke, we place anything and everything encompassed in the ontic view in brackets—that is, this entire natural world, which is continuously "there for us," "available;" and which will eternally be there as a consciously discernible "reality"—even though we may desire to keep it [the world-concept under consideration] in.
>
> If I do this, because I am perfectly free to do so, then I do not therefore negate this "World," as if I were a skeptic; but I practice an ἐποχή which for all intents and purposes has a "phenomenological" meaning. That is, I do not accept the continuously-available-to-me world, presented above, in the same way that I do the whole natural-practical life; but rather I do so more directly in the positive sciences: as a pre-existing world, and in the final view not as a universal ground of being for an awareness advancing through experience and thought. From this point on, I do not in naïve immediacy carry out any experience of the real.[4]

Of great importance is to realize the connection that Husserl makes between the natural attitude and natural science: natural science is the rationalization and better cognizance of the world of the natural attitude.[5] Natural science accepts the natural attitude without reservation, begins its investigations from the experiences of the natural attitude, and generates results that also remain within that attitude.[6] It is an empiricist investigation of the world of realism. The epoché is intended to break the stranglehold the natural attitude has upon us, and phenomenology is the science of that *new* attitude.

Thus, in the phenomenological attitude we set aside our assumptions about the world exterior to us—the world as given in the natural attitude. This is a critical step, because setting these assumptions aside frees us to realize something quite different. Not burdened by our assumptions about the exterior world, we can investigate the transcendental conditions that characterize how the world is given over to us without the added worry of accounting for what we know (in the natural attitude) that world is like. Put succinctly, by bracketing the natural attitude we are freed to do a transcendental investigation into the givenness of phenomena: how appearance comes to us.

---

4. Husserl, *Ideen II*, vol. 4, §32. On Husserl's analysis of the act of doubt that generates the epoché, see §31.

5. Ibid., vol. 4, §§2, 7, and 30.

6. Ibid., vol. 4, §§26 and 56.

Husserl frames this in a particular way. If the epoché is understood in terms of an alteration—altering our view of the world as characterized by the natural attitude (i.e., bracketing all ontic things)—then the enactment of the epoché indicates an alteration of our consciousness. This is a bit tricky though because consciousness is being used in a very specific way. Psychological consciousness remains part of the natural attitude. It is an empirical unity which, in its psychological sense, is itself bracketed in the epoché.[7] Instead, the epoché leads to a conception of consciousness that stands as the first transcendental intuition beyond the psychological. This move to a transcendental intuition is the reduction proper (the second part of the phenomenological reduction); it is the awareness of the absolute consciousness of transcendental subjectivity. The continuously-available-to-me world of the natural attitude is reduced to the more primordial concept of absolute consciousness. While I have already used this language a bit preemptively, it is this recognition of the reduction proper that inaugurates a new attitude (the phenomenological attitude). The key insight of this new attitude is the realization that the being of consciousness *is* absolutely separable from and prior to the experience of the world in the natural attitude.[8]

The epoché and the reduction proper are very closely related, and it is not surprising that they are so often amalgamated. They are like two sides of a single coin. "If the epoché is the name for whatever method we use to free ourselves from the captivity of the unquestioned acceptance of the everyday world, then the reduction is the recognition of that acceptance *as* an acceptance."[9]

To briefly recap, in bracketing the world as given to us in the natural attitude, we discover the primacy of transcendental consciousness. This transcendental consciousness is an absolute state; it is the condition before the world is given to us in the natural attitude. After this phenomenological reduction we have a new attitude, the phenomenological attitude, from which to investigate our experiences.

Now, in examining our experiences from the phenomenological attitude we find the phenomena of experience are accounted for in two senses: the phenomena as given to us and the givenness of the phenomena; phenomena both as they appear and in their appearing.[10] Still, this is not

---

7. Ibid., vol. 4, §§49 and 54.

8. Ibid., vol. 4, §54. The absoluteness of this separability characterizes Husserl's early accounts of phenomenology. As will become clear, the potentially problematic solipsistic idealism this position can be interpreted to entail, will give way to a more nuanced account. See Steinbock, *Home and Beyond*, chaps. 1 and 5.

9. Cogan, "The Phenomenological Reduction," §5a.

10. White, "Phenomenology," §2b.

a traditional subject-object divide: where the phenomenon as it appears would be the real object that in the total independence of its appearing is given over to the subject. So for an example imagine looking at a lake. In the traditional approach we would have the lake as it really is in the world and the lake as it appears in our mind: worldly-lake and consciousness-lake. But, it is precisely this traditional subject-object divide (and its account of things in terms of worldly realism and subjective experiences) that was bracketed by the epoché. Instead, to talk about the phenomenon as it appears is to account for it as it occurs to transcendental consciousness. As such, the phenomenon, or object-as-it-appears, comes to us as the lived-experience of intentional acts:[11] what Husserl calls *noesis*. Inversely, the phenomenon (the object-as-it-appears) is always given over to us in the idealization of intentionality: what Husserl calls the *noema* or object-as-it-is-intended.[12]

It is important to understand the complexity of the *noesis* and the *noema* because it is this formulation, in Husserl's account, that ought to make phenomenology neither idealist nor realist in any typical sense. The terms highlight Husserl's effort to bring consciousness and its correlative phenomena into a single complex. One way to think about this is that the phenomena given over to us in experiences, as accounted for in the phenomenological attitude, always have an "aboutness." The *noesis* is the intentional lived-experience of the *noema*. The *noema* only occurs to us through this *noesis*. The aboutness that characterizes this lived-experience of *noesis* and *noema* does not stand in its entirety on the side of the *noesis* or the *noema*; they are correlates to one another.

Understanding how the aboutness of the *noesis* and the *noema* can be correlates is best understood by what is *not* meant here. Thus, the aboutness generated by the intentional idealization of the *noesis* is *not* solely existent in consciousness. If it were, the *noesis* would be just like a category

11. This term "intentional" has a very specific meaning in the phenomenological tradition coming from Franz Brentano's work in psychology. It refers to the quality of phenomena existing in acts of consciousness, and thereby always being directed in meaning: intentional phenomena have an "aboutness." The ontological implications of this intentional consciousness are not addressed in the work of Brentano, but provide a fruitful starting point for the collapse of subject-object division in philosophical phenomenology. Most important for Husserl is to realize that the intentional quality does not indicate a relational background of references or relegate the phenomena in its givenness to being a purely mental predicate. Instead, intentionality points to the mind-transcending character of absolute consciousness as a praxis reaching out to the transcendent world. Intentional acts of consciousness give over to us things in the world. A helpful description contrasting this account to common-sense realism and representationalism can be found in Russell's *Husserl: A Guide for the Perplexed*, 80–82.

12. See Husserl, *Ideen II*, vol. 4, §§90–96 and 131. See also the very clear account of *noesis* and *noema* in Smith, "Phenomenology," §§3 and 4.

of transcendental idealism—a constitutive feature subjectivating the world. Neither is the aboutness only a feature of the *noema* as the functional or relational aspect of an object in its world. If the aboutness were conceived this way, the *noema* would only be the object of a kind of functional realism. But, we know the *noema* cannot exist in the sense of philosophical realism. Both the *noesis* and *noema* of intentional acts are realized through the epoché, which causes us to bracket the ontological assumptions of the natural attitude that underpins the account of the subject-object distinction that is epistemologically foundational to forms of realism.

So let me return to the example of seeing the lake again. We are after something different than the traditional problem of relating the worldly-lake to the consciousness-lake in our mind. The *noesis* and the *noema*, with the idea of aboutness, is the proposed way to rethink this. Put in terms of the lake, I never have a brute experience of the lake, but the lake is experienced in terms of a *noesis* as an intentional act of consciousness correlate to the *noema* or the object-as-it-is-intended. So, I do not just see a lake, but I see a lake that is a place to bathe. This experience of the lake as a place to bathe—the lake in its "aboutness"—reflects on both *noesis* and *noema*. The aboutness is not something added on to the brute notion of the lake and cannot be relegated either to the internal or external facet of a traditional account of experience. What I mean is that this experience of the lake as a place to bathe is not supposed to be just an internal feature of consciousness on Husserl's account; if that were the case then Husserl's account is just a form of idealism (i.e., the lake as a place to bathe is experienced that way because the category "bathing" shapes the constitution of the world). Nor is it supposed to be an external feature making the account a form of functional realism (i.e., the lake as a place to bathe is experienced that way because "bathing" is a fundamental functional feature coextensive to lakes). Instead, the critical point is that the aboutness is not secondary: "as a place to bathe" is not an addendum to "the lake" as a brute experience. The lake as a place to bathe is the fundamental unit of the experience and its characteristic aboutness is always simultaneously part of both the *noetic* acts and *noematic* object that make up the experience.

The *noesis* and the *noema* typologically fit neither within idealism nor realism. Instead we have "noematic objectivity": an objectivity as constituted (but not existing) in consciousness by unifying various *noetic* acts.[13] It is the objectivity of immanent lived experiences. It is objective in that, for Husserl, the *noema* of an act of intentional consciousness is not only the object-as-it-is-intended but also mediates the ideal meaning of the phenomenon. The

---

13. Ricoeur, *Husserl: An Analysis of His Phenomenology*, chap. 1.

noema is a transcendent object, not subjectively constituted; however, the shared aboutness that ties *noesis* and *noema* together highlights the inseparability of consciousness from its phenomena. Generally speaking, I have outlined from Husserl a first effort at overcoming the divide of intellectualism and empiricism—self and world—that was presented as the primary problem-space to be addressed.[14]

The real question is whether or not Husserl's work can adequately address this problem-space. Certainly, the shift to the *noema* and *noesis* represents a sustained effort to get beyond the subject-object divide that is characteristic of both idealism and realism, or intellectualism and empiricism. However, *does Husserl's turn to transcendental consciousness make it impossible for his work to get beyond the subject-centered constraints of transcendental idealism?* Does Husserl really escape the grip of idealism if what he discovers in the phenomenological reduction is consciousness? Or in terms of our example of the lake, can the lake as a place to bathe really be anything other than the lake as constituted in terms of the category "bathing"? If we follow Barbaras, we would certainly have to say Husserl cannot escape idealism. *While Husserl's project wildly succeeds in identifying what must be overcome by phenomenology, his recourse to transcendental consciousness re-inscribes the divide he seeks to overcome.*[15]

While the epoché is truly successful in realizing the intricacies of the problem in understanding how the world is given over to us, the reduction to absolute consciousness is bound to fail. Husserl is still trying to carve out a place for the transcendental reality of the world in his efforts to move beyond either empiricism or intellectualism. However, by turning to consciousness as the discovery of the phenomenological reduction, Husserl is inadvertently trapped in idealism again. Husserl's recourse to absolute consciousness cannot avoid the subjectivation of idealism. But what can we appeal to instead of transcendental consciousness, as we investigate our

---

14. To stop the analysis at this point, would make Husserl's claims subject to solipsism (of which he is well aware). He gives a robust account of intersubjectivity to allay this charge. That account however is not directly relevant to my work here. For an introduction to the way Husserl envisions moving the intentional consciousness of noematic objectivity through intersubjectivity to Objectivity, consider the following: Husserl, *Cartesianische Meditationen*, §§43, 49, 56, and 64; and *Die Krisis*, §§53–55.

15. "The subjectivation of appearance in the form of immanent lived experiences could only lead to a *subjectivation of the appearing*—in other words, to a transcendental idealism that, in regard to its ability to account for what interests us here, takes us no farther than Kant's transcendental idealism. Instead of showing how the subject is in the world (in the sense that it contributes to the manifestation of a transcending of which it forms a part), Husserl, as it were, puts the world in the subject" (Barbaras, *Desire and Distance*, 31).

experiences in terms of the phenomenological attitude, so as to avoid an inevitable recourse to idealism? When we bracket the world given to us in the natural attitude (the epoché) is there an alternative key insight we might pursue; could there be a phenomenological reduction to a transcendental intuition that is not consciousness? One possibility in this regard is to develop a phenomenology of perception: discovering perception instead of consciousness in the phenomenological reduction.

So what makes a phenomenology of perception different from a phenomenology of transcendental consciousness? The difference between these two approaches is well exemplified by Barbaras in comparing the account of perceiving a table from Husserl in the *Ideas* and Merleau-Ponty in his *The Visible and the Invisible*.[16] Imagine walking around a table. As I move around it, the table appears to me in various aspects—it never looks the same as my perspective on it continually changes. If I avert my eyes from the table it no longer appears to me, perhaps instead I see a wall, cabinet, or counter. Now both Husserl and Merleau-Ponty will emphasize the permanence of the table despite this relativity in perception from moving around the table.

The distinction between the two thinkers arises in how to locate the manifestation of the table. For Husserl, the manifestation of the table by its appearance in perception is *contrasted* to the facticity of the table as what appears through the perception. In itself, the table remains unchanged; the variations that occur happen at a different level of order: the variations occur to the table as it appears in consciousness. The table-perception is a continuity of changing perceptions; variation occurs in perception or the aspects of perception and not in the thing-itself. So what we find is that Husserl preserves a divide between the table as it appears to the conscious mind and the table as it really is in the world. The unity of living experience, the correlation of *noesis* and *noema* in the phenomenological attitude, remains subject to an initial displacement of the sense-data of appearance. As such, the distinction (i.e., the strong separation of self and world) that the living experience of *noesis* and *noema* intends to overcome *is re-inscribed* by the act of perception and the way in which Husserl preserves the facticity of the object given in appearance. In Husserl, the manifestation of the table falls to the side of the subject—to transcendental consciousness. In placing the manifestation on the side of the subject, his account of perceiving the table leaves open a site to criticize his approach: the self-world distinction he seeks to overcome remains a staple of perceptive experience.

---

16. The relevant primary texts include Husserl, *Ideen II*, vol. 4, §41; and Merleau-Ponty, *The Visible and the Invisible*, 3–14. My account is following directly on the analysis provided by Barbaras in *Desire and Distance*, 24–34.

This stands in stark contrast to Merleau-Ponty, who will assert with regard to this perceiving of the table, "I would express what takes place badly indeed in saying that here a 'subjective component' or a 'corporeal constituent' comes to cover over the things themselves; it is not a matter of another layer or a veil that would have come to pose itself between them and me."[17] The image of the "veil" or "another layer" is helpful here. The key to understanding Merleau-Ponty's account of the perception of the table is *not* to think of the perceiver as a divide between the table in the world and the perceived table. The table-itself and the table-perceived are not to be placed in separate orders of reality: world and self. Instead, Merleau-Ponty will place manifestation on the side of the world or the thing that appears in the manifestation. The act of perception itself is considered in the context of the solidity of the world—the facticity of the givenness of the table in perception. This shift means the perceptual act (with its various adumbrations) and its manifestation do not find their ultimate reference in the subject or transcendental consciousness; *instead, they find their reference in the body.* Barbaras describes this well.

> Perception assumes a body in that at least my bodily movements, indeed the very mass of my body, can hinder me from perceiving. My vision of the world is always accompanied by a perception of my body, visible at the limit and in its limits: it is covision of my body. This signifies that my vision is made from the midst of the world, always from a certain point of view, and that the manifestation of the world is relative to this worldly being. This relativity that causes me to grasp the vision as "mine" depends on the mobility of my body, both in totality and in certain of its parts. Thus the variation of manifestations, the movement that characterizes the flux of the adumbrations, refers to the strictly spatial movement of my body.[18]

Manifestation, on this account, recognizes the worldliness of the body. Perception reveals manifestation to be an intimate act of the world—the world as manifest to itself. The perceiving subject as *body*, not consciousness, emphasizes the worldly character of the perceiver and in this way the variability of perception does not need to threaten the facticity of what is given in perception. Both the table and the perceptive body belong to the world; they are of the same order. As such, perception is not veiling the thing-itself, but the act of perception grants in perspectival immediacy the

---

17. Merleau-Ponty, *The Visible and the Invisible*, 7; quoted in Barbaras, *Desire and Distance*, 25.

18. Barbaras, *Desire and Distance*, 24–25.

thing-itself. Perception gives the world-itself to us. Thus, manifestation becomes a product of the world, and not the perceiver, removing perception from its purely subjective figuring.

So Husserl gives us a critical methodological insight with his account of phenomenological reduction and the idea of the phenomenological attitude. However, his use of transcendental consciousness inadvertently entails a return to the idealism he sought to overcome. Nowhere is this made more prominent than in examining his account of perception. In the split moment before entering into the analysis by *noesis* and *noema* of the phenomenological attitude, there is a reliance on the self-world sensibility of the natural attitude to account for perceptive experience. Once this divide in perception is posited, all the tools of phenomenology are circumscribed by idealism or intellectualism. Instead, to make full use of the insights of the phenomenological reduction and the phenomenological attitude, I am following Merleau-Ponty; phenomenology must not appeal to transcendental consciousness. Instead the analysis of perception posits only one order of reality (as with our example—the table-itself was given in the manifestation to the body). This appeal to the body generated perception in the midst of the world and indicated the importance of the body as a point that needs to be investigated in pursuing phenomenology. In sum, "Merleau-Ponty relates bodily movements to the world's solidity, but at most they make the world vibrate, thus leaving the manifestation on the side of what it causes to appear; Husserl separates manifestation in the form of perception from what appears through it and thus contrasts a series of changing perceptions with an object that does not change."[19]

Why is it important to draw out these distinctions between a phenomenology of perception and a phenomenology of consciousness for this project? My goal is to use phenomenology to augment the underdeveloped ontological aspects Deacon's work hints at. I also noted that Deacon's work can serve as an extension beyond the antinomy in purposiveness and Kant's organismic model that is rooted in his wider schema of transcendental idealism. If these are twin aims in my development of Deacon's work, *then phenomenology needs to press our ontological resources beyond a variation of transcendental idealism.* Husserl provides great philosophical tools for this with the epoché and phenomenological reduction, but what he reduces to after the epoché—transcendental, absolute consciousness—ultimately yields the transcendental idealism to be overcome. A phenomenology of perception, however, seems a promising place to develop the richer ontological resources.

19. Ibid., 25.

From the Lived-Body to the Flesh

Thus far I have been playing on a difference: of placing the subject who perceives into the world or the world into the perceiving subject. Merleau-Ponty's emphasis on perception as a bodily phenomenon does the former in contrast to Husserl's emphasis on perception as a phenomenon of transcendental consciousness that does the latter. This distinction makes a vast difference in the way one characterizes how phenomenology overcomes the difference between intellectualism and empiricism—the relationship of subject and object. As I have already indicated, the turn to transcendental consciousness cannot avoid re-inscribing the same subject-object division it seeks to overcome; now, my analysis will follow the bodily trajectory of Merleau-Ponty and in a more radical way Barbaras.

Following this trajectory, though, presents a challenge; a challenge that is much the inverse of the problem we identified in Husserl. If the problem for Husserl was that his phenomenology of consciousness could not avoid placing the world in the subject and reducing itself to a type of idealism, then for Merleau-Ponty the challenge is to preserve the uniqueness of our subjectivity against a reduction to simple realism. To allow such reduction would entail the collapse of the subject into the object (i.e., the subject would be nothing more than a reactive, perceptual place in the world). Such a collapse would not allow the subject to be anything more than its physical body: a Cartesian mechanical body without even the solace of a soul. Thus, while it was clear above that Merleau-Ponty's account of perception radically placed the perceiving body in the world, in contrast to Husserl, now the focus must be on why Merleau-Ponty's turn to the body should not be interpreted as a simple recourse to the empirical body: to the body as conceived in realism. To do this, we must consider the meaning of the body as it is conceived in the phenomenological attitude: to consider the lived-experience of the body analyzed in terms of its comportment—intentional behaviors or acting—as being-in-the-world.[20]

---

20. The ideas of "comportment" and "being-in-the-world" indicate a certain continuity with Heidegger and his critique of Husserl's phenomenology. In contrast to Husserl, Heidegger uses phenomenology methodologically to describe how philosophy engages in research. This means that for Heidegger, like Husserl, phenomenology is an investigation to things themselves without the preconceptions of the natural attitude; yet, unlike Husserl this does not lead us to a conception of transcendental consciousness. Instead, Heidegger takes phenomenology to designate a hermeneutic: an artful interpretation by which we let things show themselves in themselves. For Heidegger, the importance of phenomenology is for ontology, since investigating the meaning of being requires a phenomenological approach. Thus, ontological investigation must begin from our own experience of being, which is always that of being-in-the-world. This being-in-the-world is not specifically in the sense of consciousness (per Husserl's

What do these ideas of "lived-experience" and "comportment" really mean in terms of Merleau-Ponty's thinking? Think back to the example of perceiving the table and the place of the body in Merleau-Ponty's phenomenological account of perception. When I see the table I do not have a simply blank experience. The experience of the table is somehow also uniquely mine. I do not mean uniquely mine in a subjective sense (i.e., that you experience it, I experience it, and someone else experiences it each in a peculiar way). Instead, I mean that my perceptual encounter with the table has an "aboutness": it is "intentional" as described in the earlier account of Husserl. In Husserl this "aboutness" made reference to the absolute transcendental consciousness, but with Merleau-Ponty this is not the case. Instead, the lived-experience and the intentional acts of consciousness in Husserl, now point towards the comportment, or behavior, that is characteristic of intentional acts of the body. Lived-experience manifests through the comportment of the body.

Admittedly this sense of the body is something a bit strange and ambiguous compared to our everyday thinking about the body. This is not the empirical body, which would be bracketed in the course of the phenomenological reduction. Rather, it points to a nebulous site where the traditionally conceived interiority of consciousness and the exteriority of things in the world encounter one another. The body here is standing as an alternative to the role given to transcendental consciousness in Husserl. It is the locution of primordial perception and experience uncovered in the epoché that phenomenological investigation seeks. In Merleau-Ponty, this sense where the body is between the interiority of consciousness and the exteriority of the world, belonging to neither completely, is technically speaking the lived-body. The lived-body is the site of our lived-experience; the term designating how the world is given over to us when analyzing experience in terms of the phenomenological attitude.

It is critical to understand that the lived-body has truly supplanted transcendental consciousness; the body is not a mere physical sieve for conscious intentional acts. If the body were only a sieve, then the transcendental consciousness would be the real source of my subjectivity and lived-experience always standing behind the body as its marker in the world. Merleau-Ponty is quite aware of this, and he emphasizes that the

---

transcendental reduction), but comportment. Emphasizing this shift to comportment is, however, as far as I draw this parallel between Heidegger and Merleau-Ponty. On Heidegger and Husserl, see especially Heidegger, *Sein Und Zeit*, §7 and 7c. On the connection and difference between Merleau-Ponty and Heidegger, see Barbaras, "Life and Perceptual Intentionality," 161.

lived-body is the inseparable source of subjectivity and lived-experience.[21] What does it mean though that the lived-body is an inseparable source of lived-experience? How is it that the lived-body itself, not the body as a sieve for consciousness, has a particular way of experiencing the world of which it is a part? Merleau-Ponty will claim that it is the lived-body that understands the significance of its movement in the phenomenological world. This claim is very clear in an example from Merleau-Ponty's account of habit and motility.

> We said earlier that it is the body which "understands" in the cultivation of habit. This way of putting it will appear absurd, if understanding is subsuming a sense-datum under an idea, and if the body is an object. But the phenomenon of habit is just what prompts us to revise our notion of "understand" and our notion of the body. To understand is to experience the harmony between what we aim at and what is given, between the intention and the performance—and the body is our anchorage in a world. When I put my hand to my knee, I experience at every stage of the movement the fulfillment of an intention which was not directed at my knee as an idea or even as an object, but as a present and real part of my living body, that is, finally as a stage in my perpetual movement towards a world. When the typist performs the necessary movements on the typewriter, these movements are governed by an intention, but the intention does not posit the keys as objective locations. It is literally true that the subject who learns to type incorporates the key-bank space into his bodily space.[22]

The lived-body is infused with the intended phenomena of the world through the lived-experience of enactment and movement (as our phenomenologically being-in-the-world). The incorporation of the key-bank to the typist, through habitual movement, is supposed to illustrate this. It is also important to understand what Merleau-Ponty is *not* affirming in this account of habit to better understand its meaning. The learning-curve of these habitual acts should not be intellectualized. That means in the case of the typist we should *not* think that the incorporation of the key-bank by the typist indicates the keyboard has become such a familiar tool that the typist

---

21. Merleau-Ponty develops this notion out of a careful reading of Husserl's works that, at the time, were unpublished. Critical to Merleau-Ponty's account, I believe, is his work on the apperception of the body in establishing transcendental intersubjectivity in Husserl, though a critical analysis of that connection is beyond the scope of this work. See Merleau-Ponty, *Phenomenology of Perception*, xi–xiii and 408.

22. Ibid., 144–45.

is simply no longer positing keys as individual objective locations because she is thinking in terms of what she is writing and not specific keystrokes. In this situation the keyboard would be a means to an end—an intermediary object that is glossed over with practice. I will call this "intellectualist habit" for the sake of clarity. I want to suggest, Merleau-Ponty is after something different that another example without so many linguistic and intellectual components may be able to make clearer.

Imagine yourself learning to ride a bike. You struggle at first. You have to start by going downhill to get enough speed to find your balance. Your feet fumble with the pedals when you start trying to ride on flat ground and you fall over. Eventually, however, you get the hang of this exercise and riding a bike becomes natural to you—something that with an instant back in the saddle you can do immediately much later. Now that you know how to ride a bike, you can ride it any number of places—the grocery store, the park, school, etc. Now let us interpret what is going on in learning to ride a bike. From the perspective of "intellectualist habit" we initially have to focus directly on the activity of riding the bike in learning this skill. Eventually when we no longer have to direct our attention directly to the process of riding, the intention of riding a bike can be directed towards other things: riding the bike becomes a means to the end of getting to school. The act of riding is habitualized so as to streamline our pursuit of a different end; the riding becomes a nearly unconscious intermediary. This is analogous to the interpretation of the key-bank in intellectualist habit: it becomes a means to the end of our writing that becomes increasingly less obtrusive with practice.

What I would suggest, and what I think Merleau-Ponty's account points to, is that there is something missing in understanding the habitual act this way. As one who commutes by bike a great deal, in the process of commuting the bike never becomes a means to an end; even when used for another purpose, the act of riding remains a distinctive intentional act. While in typing it may be easy for the keys to abscond themselves form our interpretation because their use for writing is so immediate, in riding a bike the habitual act is not so easily hidden from our attention—you have a few miles to notice this if you try it.

So if the habitual act that incorporates to the lived-body is *not* akin to making the habitual act into an unconscious means to a greater end, what is happening? What is this incorporation to the lived-body? Again, I think riding the bicycle is a very helpful example. Initially, as I learn to ride the bike I do not have a great sense of balance and I fumble with the pedals, brakes, and handlebars. The bike and I are at odds with each other. The bike resists my direction and instruction. With practice and time this resistance lessens and there is a certain symbiosis I share with the bike. No longer at odds with each other the bike becomes a ready partner, even an extension of my own body as my way of being-in-the-world: it is incorporated to my lived-body. As I become more adept I even use technologies to deepen this connection that incorporates the bike. I ride with pedals that hook my feet to the bike so they cannot easily be removed, and I use brakes that integrate my shifters so I do not have to change my position while riding and fumble around when needing an easier gear.

Even without these technological extensions of my incorporation of the bike, the habitual practice of riding is not well described by being something that falls away in the face of the goal of getting to a place. The habitual act of riding does make my movements fluid—the bike no longer stands as an obstacle towards my experience of moving in the world—by becoming more and more incorporated to the movement of my body. It is the same with the incorporation of the key-bank. It is not that the keyboard falls away in light of my thinking being governed by my more pressing interest in what is being written. Instead, the habitual practice of typing makes the key-bank less at odds to my movements in the world—with practice it no longer stands as something foreign over and against my hands but it is incorporated into the space of my hands, it is a part of my lived-body. In the habitual act these two parts of the world become unified.

I have dedicated so much space to this example because it is important not to interpret Merleau-Ponty in terms of intellectualist habit. The reason it is important is because of the implications of intellectualist habit for the body. If, as with intellectualist habit, the habitual use of the bike or the key-bank is described by its being excised from our conscious attention, *what is to prevent the body from being the most excised tool of all*? If habit has its real reference in conscious attention (i.e., the development of habitual movement, as with the intellectualist understanding, is designed to streamline the process towards a greater end), then the body is really serving as the greatest habit maker for our consciousness—the body becomes a sieve for conscious acts that are the real location of our lived-experience. This is explicitly what Merleau-Ponty is trying to avoid. The aim of Merleau-Ponty's account must be to incorporate or extend the lived-body in the midst of its world.

That being said, the intellectualist interpretation is not without merit; it does seem like a potentially reasonable interpretation of what Merleau-Ponty might mean by habit. In fact, it is fairly difficult to understand what Merleau-Ponty means without presenting this opposed position. This ambiguity is a significant problem for his account of the lived-body—a problem that Barbaras draws to our attention repeatedly. Put succinctly, the problem is that Merleau-Ponty's analysis of the lived-experience garnered through the lived-body (as with our examples above) remains tethered to the language of transcendental consciousness via Husserl. Being thus tethered, it is also yoked to the account of the subject-object divide Husserl's language re-inscribes. The lived-body can never seem to get beyond the subject-object distinction it seeks to overcome because it primarily constitutes itself by what it denies: namely the efficacy of the intellectualist or empiricist approach.

Think of the lived-body riding a bicycle again. Here the bicycle is incorporated to the body in a symbiotic harmony; the lived-body is what we call the site of this connection. As such, we can say that the lived-body is the point in the world from which we garner our lived-experience of the world. However, beyond this fairly minimal claim not much is said, in a positive way, about what the lived-body *is*. Largely, the understanding of the lived-body is established in contrast to the empirical body or consciousness. So while it is clear the bicycle is infused into the lived-body, *the quality of this infusion is never described in terms that get beyond the conceptual ground that the lived-body is intended to overcome*. That is to say the lived-body disabuses us of any recourse to typical intellectualist or empiricist descriptions of lived-experience, but it continues to rely on a divide between a subjective consciousness and an objective world to describe how it is to be understood. As a result it can never really get beyond either intellectualism or empiricism; it limits itself by relying on the ontological suppositions and categories of these approaches. If the lived-body were to come to a full and adequate expression it would need a new, positive ontological language not beholden to the traditional subject-object delineation, which could allow us to be more explicit about what the lived-body is and what it means that its mode of lived-experience is to incorporate its world.[23]

Such a positive articulation, one which presses the lived-body beyond intellectualism and empiricism, awaits the development of Merleau-Ponty's interpretation of the chiasmic flesh. The idea of a chiasm is in itself not difficult to grasp; though the interpretation of the meaning of a chiasm is more opaque. Chiasm refers to the simultaneity and reflexivity of an event. It is most often described in terms of the sensation of touching and being-touched that occurs in pressing your right hand to your left hand. In touching my right hand to my left hand, the left is initially a physical object given to the right hand in its tactility. However, if I grant the left hand some sentiment of priority the right hand becomes the physical object given to the left in its tactility. The role of sensing-subject and physical object are continually exchanged so that they nearly simultaneously become both touching and

---

23. Barbaras, *The Being of the Phenomenon*, 7–8.

touched. This sensation of touching and touched can be generalized beyond two sentient hands to our touching other things in the world. For instance, in touching a table my hand touches the table and is touched by the table: I feel the table and in such touching I am made aware of my own corporeality as the table presses against me. This reflexivity of sensibility indicates the insoluble correlation of sensing and being-sensed: to sense is to be susceptible to being sensed.[24]

Why is this account of the chiasmic quality of sensibility important? The chiasm presses beyond the account of the living-body to the notion of the flesh. The limitation of the concept of the lived-body, its lack of a positive description, begins to be overcome by an understanding of chiasmic flesh that mutually institutes the sensing-body and its world. The key to understanding this slight, though immensely significant, shift is to take radically seriously the necessity of the correlation between being-sensed and sensing. Without being-sensed there can be no sensing; as such, sentience is not the product of a pure consciousness that has a body as an object in the world creating a divide between consciousness and the body. Instead the body is the incarnation of this sensibility that can be sensed—it actualizes the immanence of sensing and being sensed. Perhaps, we might more properly say that sensibility is itself incarnation; sensibility is nothing other than its body. Far from such sentience relying on consciousness, consciousness can only open itself to the world through the incarnation of sentience.

This is a critical juncture. In examining our lived-experience from the phenomenological attitude, there can be no primordial place for transcendental consciousness. There is only sentience from which consciousness arises. This also means that there is no longer an interior and an exterior: appearances given to a conscious self separated from the things themselves in the world. This is because to sense entails being sensed. Sensibility's incarnation makes it indistinguishably part of the world it perceives. Our sensibility does not stand over and against the world; sensing or perceiving is bodily and is of the world. Our perceiving institutes, not constitutes (i.e., makes appear instead of creates), the sensed world; this act of perception is the world, through us, becoming manifest to itself.

This makes for what Barbaras calls an "ontological kinship" between our perception and the world. The manifestations of perception are not given to consciousness as some other ontological order that stands against the things themselves of the world which it receives—constantly struggling to overcome the body's intermediary role between world and consciousness.

24. The chiasm is not limited to the sensation of touch. Vision is well accounted for in the phenomenological literature as chiasmic as well (i.e., to see is necessarily to be susceptible to being seen)

Instead, our perception—with its incarnated sensibility—is of the same ontological plane as the world. The manifestations of this perception are also on par to this ontological plane. Thus, the thing as it appears and in its appearing, manifestation of a phenomenon and facticity of the phenomenon coalesce. On this approach there is not a difference between the phenomenality of our lived-experiences and the things themselves given to us in these lived-experiences.

Finally, since the incarnation of sensibility is only reflexively produced as its being sensed, the reflexivity of touching and being touched, seeing and being seen, sensing and being sensed all point to an irreducible adventing[25] of body and sensed world that mutually inhere. Without the incarnation of sensibility there could be no sensed world, and without a sensed world there is no way for the facticity of the world to be reached. Body and world advent, come to being, together.[26] This always unified complex of incarnated sensibility and sensed world is, or more properly is the visible occurrence of the otherwise invisible, flesh of the world. This flesh of the world designates the inseparable, mutual inhering ground that institutes being-in-the-world as manifesting world-in-the-being.[27]

What I have found is in contrast to Husserl's appeal to transcendental consciousness in the phenomenological attitude, in Merleau-Ponty there is

---

25. I am using the term "adventing" intentionally here, even though we rarely see it this way anymore. My intent is to emphasize that the body and the world cannot be conceptualized in independence from one another at all. They come to be or arrive always together—an event of each anticipating the other.

26. "[T]he thickness of the body does not impose a distance between sensibility and the world. On the contrary, the very possibility of a sensible experience requires this thickness. It is by virtue of this ontological kinship with the world, a kinship conferred on it by the body, that 'consciousness' can open itself to the world itself. A consciousness that would not be *of* the world would be consciousness of nothing, since it would fail to have this ontological complicity. Deeper, therefore, than the opposition of consciousness and object or consciousness and its body there is the irreducible advent of the world—and, strictly speaking, there is only the world. Because sensibility is synonymous with its incarnation, its being-world, it finds fulfillment as the world's presence" (Barbaras, *The Being of the Phenomenon*, 155–6). See also Barbaras, "Life and Perceptual Intentionality," 158–59.

27. For the sake of clarity, I have written large portions of this section without much citation to avoid distracting the reader. In my analysis I have relied heavily on four key sources: Husserl, *Ideen II*, vol. 4, §§37 and 45; Derrida, *Le Toucher—Jean-Luc Nancy*, 184–203.; Lawlor, *The Implications of Immanence*, 21–29; and Merleau-Ponty, *The Visible and the Invisible*, 130–55. I have appealed to these sources because Husserl introduces a concept of chiasmic touch, Derridas provides an immensely helpful critique of these sections of Husserl, Derrida's text and its relation to Husserl is indispensably elucidated by Lawlor, and Merleau-Ponty's account of chiasm seems to be a positive parallel to the critique of Derrida.

an appeal to the lived-body as the site of our lived-experience. This lived-body is not simply the empirical body, but is a complex that incorporates its world to itself (as exemplified by the typist and the cyclist above). The lived-body is a first attempt to overcome a strict separation of subject and object, of self and world, in order to overcome the separate ontological spheres of consciousness and the world as assumed in intellectualism or empiricism. The problem for the lived-body was that it remains bound to the ontological or metaphysical language of the intellectualism and empiricism it seeks to overcome. As a result the lived-body cannot seem to get past being only an intermediary to a subjectivity that is truly of consciousness and a world that remains always external to the subject. In response to this problem, I have introduced the turn in Merleau-Ponty's late writings to chiasmic flesh—an immensely important concept for understanding Barbaras's own writing. The reciprocity of sensing and being-sensed in the chiasm provided a ground for imagining new ontological language and recognizing the primacy of the incarnation of sensibility as before consciousness. The idea of the flesh places our incarnated sensibility into the same ontological plane as the sensed world and insinuated how these two structures always emerge in tandem to one another. This mutually inhering complex whereby through our bodies we, as part of the world, manifest the world to itself was termed the flesh of the world. The flesh of the world provides an ontological ground for recognizing the mutuality and inseparable intimacy of self and world that is a part of our lived-experience; it is a term that confounds and cannot be contained by traditional philosophical categories.

Life as Movement and Desire

What I have thus far outlined is a vision of phenomenology that issues into an ontology alternative to either subjectively constituted idealism or the world of an empiricist realism. The flesh indicates this institutive site that goes beyond the neither/nor characterization of the lived-body (i.e., the lived-body is characterized by being neither of intellectualism nor empiricism, without offering an alternative positive characterization). In the flesh, self and world are always coming-to-be, adventing, in an intimate reciprocity to one another. The flesh represents the chiasmic ambiguity of touching and touched that gives a deeper ontological sensibility to the incorporating motility of the lived-body, bridging the divide between subject and object (as in the examples of the typist and the key-bank or the cyclist and the bicycle). With this basic understanding of the workings of phenomenology and the meaning of the flesh, I will follow Barbaras in applying the phenomenological attitude to the vexing question that has occupied us thus far: what is life?

A Phenomenology of Life ~ Movement

As we now shift more directly into an analysis of the phenomenology of life, we find that life is characterized by a tension between its intransitive and transitive senses. Simply put, this means that "to live" indicates both physically being alive (i.e., I live) and the experience or feeling of living (i.e., I lived the horror of that war). In terms of the human way of being, I have already begun examining this tension: the lived-body brought together lived-experience with the empirical body. Now the same tensions between intellectualism and empiricism that we have considered in the lived-body are brought to a more primordial level. The very human way of being inculcated by our examples of the lived-body has to give way to an analysis adequate for describing all kinds of living things (especially non-conscious living things). In sum, a phenomenology of life is charged with the difficult task of bringing these two moments (the intransitive and the transitive, being alive and the feeling of living) implicit to what it means to live into a unity. This unity must recognize the tensive quality of the intransitive and transitive sense of what it means "to live" while stopping short of polarizing this tension into absolutes that tear asunder the original unity.[28]

It is tempting to simply turn directly to biology in order to circumscribe what it means to live in biological terms. However, such an effort will necessarily fail by Barbaras's account. Why would this be? The answer is that biology analyzes the functioning of organisms that are already implicitly recognized as living; identifying what constitutes the living per se is not the object of biology. So biology first must distinguish the living and the non-living, and only subsequent to this distinction begin an inquiry into how a living thing functions. However, this distinguishing experience of a living thing evades the objectification of the biological analysis—it cannot be assimilated to an analysis of the modes of functioning in living things.[29]

---

28. Barbaras, "Life and Perceptual Intentionality," 160; Barbaras, *Desire and Distance*, 87; Barbaras, "A Phenomenology of Life," 207; and Barbaras, "Life, Movement, and Desire," 3–4.

29. Barbaras, *Desire and Distance*, 88; and Barbaras, "Life, Movement, and Desire," 5. It is worth noting that this course of argument is markedly similar to the Kantian contention reviewed in chapter 1: that the distinguishing quality of living things is irreducible to mechanical explication. For this reason, in terms of the teleological history of principles of life we offered in that chapter, I would suggest Barbaras is adding yet another layer of complexity to that story.

By not running headlong into biology to understand what it means to live, Barbaras is enacting a certain kind of *epoché* and making a phenomenological reduction. There is an *epoché* of our natural attitude towards life and the study of life in biology. We bracket the inclination to define life by emphasizing the critical functions that make life a property of a certain class of things (i.e., we bracket the intransitive sense of living). There is a phenomenological reduction in the realization of the implications that this assumption entails. Notably, that in going directly to biology we take for granted the criticality of the experience of living. Instead, approaching life from the phenomenological attitude, we find that the identification of the living thing must rely inescapably on the feeling of living (i.e., we discover the primordial quality of the transitive sense of living). "I know myself as living insofar as I feel myself, and it is on this condition that I can recognize living beings."[30]

It is immensely important, however, to realize that this recognition of myself as living through my feeling (by which I am also able to recognize other living things) is not purely auto-affective (i.e., feeling myself). Feeling, used here, is not a purely internal principle by which I analogically account for the affective quality of other things; it is not just that I feel myself, see others behave in ways analogous to me, and thereby assume they also can feel. This would make the feeling of living purely interior. Instead, the lived-experience we are after must be present in exteriority as well—the feeling of living is always expressive.[31]

Technically speaking, the auto-affection of lived-experience (interior feeling) must also manifest some hetero-affectivity (indicative expression of the feeling) that makes my lived-experience manifest in my objective body. This sounds more complicated than it really is. Think back to the idea of the flesh and chiasm above to understand the relation of auto-affection and hetero-affection. Auto-affection and hetero-affection are analogous to sensing and being sensed. Just as to sense required the possibility of being sensed, the auto-affective feeling of living requires the hetero-affective possibility of being felt as alive in some manifest way.[32]

What is most important is to understand that life represents a unique mode of being that is *not* sufficiently characterized in terms of the schism of internal consciousness and external world. Whether this schism is

30. Barbaras, "Life, Movement, and Desire," 5.

31. Barbaras, *Desire and Distance*, 89.

32. In sum, "if life does not coincide with the functioning of the living being, because the recognition of life refers to my life, then my life also does not reside in the invisible of pure auto-affection but rather contains a relation to exteriority" (Barbaras, "Life, Movement, and Desire," 7).

represented in terms of the intransitive and the transitive, the feeling of living and the organismic functions, auto-affection and hetero-affection, or in the general phenomenological tension between empiricism and intellectualism, the same problem arises. *We fail to understand the phenomenon "life" if we cannot account for the unity of its physico-chemical and psychic features.*[33] How can this schism be overcome? In what way do we characterize the phenomena of life such that physico-chemical and psychic features are in unity? What does the intransitive and transitive sense of "to live," organismic life and lived-experience, really mean? How are the exteriority of life and the interiority of lived-experience to be brought back together?

These are all ways of asking the same question that demands a phenomenological answer, with a further consideration of its ontological implications. Let me state baldly that *movement* is the fundamental phenomenological feature of living. Barbaras finds this movement well expressed, at least initially, in the work of Hans Jonas and his account of metabolism. For Jonas, metabolism is conceived widely as those processes that perpetuate a form across the total replacement of the material parts. This is metabolism conceived as the independence of form in relation to its matter. To make a claim about the independence of form does not mean it is immaterial: the form relies on new material parts to replace the old parts. Instead, it indicates that the form is not dependent on any single *particular* part to be maintained.

In Jonas's work, metabolism's form provides the means for an *act of self-preservation*: it fulfills the need of the living thing to incorporate new material parts. The form that is metabolism is also a *movement* in that it drives the living thing to seek out the needed material from outside itself.[34] In sum, the metabolic movement of living beings appropriates features of the external world in satisfaction of specific material needs, which institute a minimal sense of formal independence to metabolism. I will call this action of metabolism self-preserving movement.

The self-preserving movement of metabolism coincides to a minimally emergent sense of self and world by the fulfillment of needs. The self persists despite a total replacement of material parts and is distinguished from the world as that which is the aim of the metabolism's sustenance in contrast to that which is exterior to this aim from which it draws this sustenance.[35]

---

33. "This in no way means that we must embark upon a reductive path, but on the contrary, this means that an adequate determination of life must also be able to account for its highest forms and, notably, for the dimension of knowledge peculiar to the human order" (ibid., 8). See also Barbaras, "A Phenomenology of Life," 212–14.

34. Jonas, *The Phenomenon of Life*, 83–84.

35. Barbaras, "Life and Perceptual Intentionality," 163.

However, such an account is always circumscribed by death. Self-preserving movement only yields a sense of life itself as preservation; however, to understand life in terms of its own preservation indicates circularity. *Life itself is presupposed* in understanding life as the preservation of life. The appeal to self-preserving movement presupposes what it intends to define.

Part of the reason for this limitation is that this appeal to movement via self-preservation will *always* only be characterized in terms of that which it resists: death as the extinction of life. Self-preservation is always a struggle against the disintegration of that which is being preserved. When we understand the living self in terms of this ability to fulfill its needs, our understanding is implicitly always reliant on what it is intended to overcome. The needs of metabolism's movement are a response to the continuing degradation of its material parts. This is life understood as resistance to death. The account of living beings given in terms of self-preserving movement fulfilling needs must always be circumscribed by death as that which is being resisted in this movement.[36]

Despite this limitation, what the self-preserving movement of metabolism highlights is a primordial emergence of an interior self and an exterior world. The exterior world is the place one searches out what is missing from the interior self. This co-extensive occurrence of self and world in movement hints at a visceral, corporeal way to imagine the ontological insights we have already developed through an idea of the flesh of the world: the ontological place from which self and world ecstatically appear. In sum, movement is a critical feature in offering a phenomenology of life providing a key site for making the ontological insights of the flesh of the world tangible.

However, this must be pressed further. The characterization of movement thus far has been in terms of self-preservation. But could we unhinge movement from the limitations identified with accounts of life made in terms of self-preservation? What makes movement itself possible? Why is it that movement satisfies need and works so well for self-preservation? Why not appropriate some other mode for the satisfaction of needs? These questions press the understanding of movement deeper, getting beyond the correlation of movement to satisfaction of needs and self-preservation. I am searching for how movement reveals itself when decoupled from need: movement as a creative accomplishment not confined to preservation and needs.[37]

---

36. Barbaras, *Desire and Distance*, 106–7; and Barbaras, "Life, Movement, and Desire," 9–11.

37. Barbaras, "Life, Movement, and Desire," 11.

Technically speaking, this is a call for a positive phenomenological characterization of movement (i.e., movement understood in a more fundamental sense than as it functions in self-preservation). Movement conceived beyond self-preservation is a third kind of being. By this I mean that movement is a kind of being in addition to the intransitive and transitive sense of a living being with which I began. Now there is the extrinsic living thing, the intrinsic lived-experience, and movement. Moreover, movement is what advents these transitive and intransitive senses of living being. So in this positive phenomenological characterization of movement it is no longer only the *property* of a subject or constituted being—now movement constitutes, it accomplishes life. With this characterization of movement, the living thing can be understood in terms of its life. That is to say, through movement life is not just understood as a constituted being *as* living (i.e., living added as a property to being) but a *living* being (i.e., life as the mode of movement's distinct kind of being irreducible to either its intransitive or transitive sensibility). Barbaras outlines this clearly.

> The only authentic thought of life is that which recognizes its movement as the "third" fundamental and irreducible kind of being, so that far from movement being an expression of life, it is instead life that is a modality or a category of movement. It is clear to us that this movement escapes the separation of interior and exterior of lived experience and the living being. Movement is neither consciousness nor matter but another mode of being on the basis of which a fragment of matter present to itself, that is, a flesh, can probably constitute itself. This is why life can be equally grasped from the interior and from the exterior. The act of the living being manifests its life insofar as it is the moment of an accomplishment, and my movement of accomplishment passes into exteriority because it is only realized through concrete movements.[38]

This is a good point at which to recap. I began with a phenomenological reduction of life. In the epoché of this reduction biological explications of life that only approach life in terms of its functioning were bracketed. In approaching life through this phenomenological attitude, it became evident that the biological emphasis on understanding the *functioning* of life initially presupposes an understanding of what is alive; the strictly biological approach has to assume what is alive in order to determine its object of study. Having bracketed the biological explications, I treated life in terms of the phenomenological attitude and attempted to let life reveal

---

38. Ibid., 13–14.

its meaning by considering our own experience of living or feeling of living. In this way, life reveals an intransitive and transitive sense—an extrinsic, worldly living sense and an intrinsic, subjective sense of lived-experience. A thoroughgoing account of what it means to live must hold these two senses of life in unity. In attempting to hold this intransitive and transitive sensibility together, I posited that movement is the meaning of life as pursued in the phenomenological attitude. Initially, metabolism (as understood by Jonas) was suggested as an exemplar of this movement. What this account of self-preserving metabolic movement helpfully revealed was the coextensive emergence of an interior and exterior, a primordial sense of self and world. However, the self-preserving aspect of this movement indicated that I needed to press the understanding of movement as the meaning of life beyond this metabolic analogy; self-preserving movement was not a *positive* characterization of movement, but one whose meaning was always bound by its own contradiction. In this case, the self-preserving movement of life could only be fully understood in terms of how it provides resistance to death. What was needed was a more robust, positive characterization of movement as the phenomenological meaning of life: a characterization of movement not as a means to the greater end of preservation, but movement itself. In treating movement beyond self-preservation I suggested that it was a third kind of being that advents the intransitive and transitive sense of being characteristic of living. Such a conception of movement made it akin to the idea of "flesh" (from which self and world arise in reciprocity to one another) described in the previous section. Movement is the primordial sense of being from which the exterior being of the living thing and the interior being of the lived-experience arise. Life is, in a phenomenological sense, a mode of movement's distinctive being, because it is through movement that the unity of the intransitive and transitive sense of life advent and can be held together. As such, life is irreducible to the intransitive or the transitive, the exterior or interior, the empiricist or intellectualist alone; life as movement is a distinctive kind of being from which these polarizations take flight.

An Ontology of Movement ~ Desire

It is fine to say that this robust sense of movement characterizes the phenomenological account of life, but what does this mean? What does it mean that movement is a third kind of being? To gain some clarity in this regard requires examining the ontological meaning of movement. To that end, I would claim that movement as a third kind of being exhibits an excess. The constancy of living motion always exceeds the satisfaction of needs and indicates there is incompleteness at the heart of living being. "Life's unceasing mobility refers to an absence that cannot be filled in and to a lack of being that is like the very definition of the living being."[39] This incompleteness, lack, or absence is insatiable. In order to adequately characterize this insatiable absence, Barbaras employs the term "desire" in an ontological sense. Living being as movement is desire.

As might be traditionally assumed, desire is not here subordinate to need (this is why I have emphasized desire is being used in a specifically ontological sense). The ontological sense of desire points to the insatiable absence of life's movement as its mode of being. The subordinate, or psychological, sense of desire points to what I grew up calling lagniappe—a little something extra. We should pause and examine the contrast between these newly introduced ideas: subordinate desire and ontological desire.

Desire is subordinate when it is excessive or extra. For example, I am hungry. I eat an apple and fulfill my need, but I still desire chocolate cake to round out my healthy snack. Here, desire is treated as something added on to the fulfillment of needs. It implies a certain frivolousness or excessive longing. I prefer to call this subordinate desire in that the desire is subordinate to needs or less essential than needs.[40]

Subordinate desire is very different from the ontological sense of desire. Ontological desire is an insatiable absence. In this mode attaining a desired object only yields a limited satisfaction. Simultaneous to this limited satisfaction, desire is carried forward to new desire.[41] Why would desire be carried forward at this point and not satiated? What is critical to understand is that the *real* object of desire is *not* what has momentarily satisfied it. This momentary, or direct, satisfaction is a function of need. Instead, in desire there is a dynamic at work that exceeds the circularity of needs. So let us return to eating the apple. I am hungry; I eat an apple to fulfill my need. The need is the ingesting of the apple—it fulfills a specific lacking (i.e., material for my stomach to digest). The hunger I feel is desire. My hunger concerns an object and the fulfillment of a need (the apple and its digestion); however, what the hunger is aiming at is of a different order. Hunger manifests as *a felt presence only characterized by absence*. So even when we say to ourselves, "I am hungry for an apple," in this moment we consciously transmute the primordial presence of absence that is hunger into a definite lacking that can be fulfilled.

---

39. Ibid., 14.
40. Sometimes this is called psychological desire.
41. Barbaras, *Desire and Distance*, 110–11.

Whereas need begets satisfaction that is always locked to the interest of self-preservation, thereby entailing new needs; *desire desires desiring* as an excessive dynamic.[42] In the ontological use, needs are only a specific species of the wider genus of desire; or, needs are only the ontic facet of living beings whose ontological mode is desire as insatiably pursued in movement.[43] In short, the lacking we feel with a need has a definite object that can be made present, and the need ceases to be; the absence manifested by desire has only intermediate objects (or we might say provisional objects—objects not fully engaged—objects as means to a deeper sensibility of desire), desire leads us towards these objects but only in the mode of absence, and the satiation provided by the object only inflames desire highlighting the mode of absence it manifests.

Now comes the key turn in this argument. Life is phenomenologically characterized by movement. This movement is not the self-preservation of metabolism, but an always excessive movement (a movement constantly driving the living thing outside itself) that I have called a third kind of being. Life is no longer being characterized by survival and the self-preservation of metabolism, which is a satisfaction of needs or the definite fulfillment of something lacking. Instead, life is understood in terms of the phenomenological excess of movement and the ontological mode of insatiable desire. In light of this shift, for what does life aim? If survival was the teleological aim of life characterized by self-preservation and needs, what is the aim of life characterized by movement and desire?

Three conclusions to be drawn regarding this question will recap what has been discovered about movement and desire in the analysis thus far. First, life as ontologically characterized by desire continues to entail a fundamental relation between the living being and its world—as was emphasized in the account of movement. Even in the metabolic account of movement this feature developed, and it is a feature that persists as the account of movement is given in terms of desire. Simply put, my claim is that *life entails the mutual arising of a self and a world.* In this sense, living being is (quite concretely) the actualization of the flesh of the world explored in the analysis of Merleau-Ponty's work. It is the actualization of the chiasmic quality that is essential to the flesh of the world moving beyond intellectualism or empiricism. Just as sensing entailed being sensed, the movement of living being entails the mutual adventing of self and world as an analogous

---

42. The insatiability of desire and its wider ontological implication in relation to need is not unique to Barbaras, though its application to a phenomenology of life does seem quite distinctive. For instance, this insatiable instance of desire (developed quite differently) is also in Levinas, *Totality and Infinity*, 258.

43. Barbaras, "Life, Movement, and Desire," 15.

chiasm. The ontological ramifications of the phenomenology of perception are evidenced in the movement of living being. Life is flesh of the world.

Second, the chiasmic relation in the movement of living being is given in the mode of absence, when understood in terms of ontological desire. This "mode of absence" reveals something very distinctive about the chiasmic quality of the movement of living being. We need to understand this mode of absence as it relates to both parts of the chiasm: both the self and the world that mutually advent in movement.

How is it that the world toward which life's movement is always directed is present only in the mode of absence? It is essential to understand that the world, as used here, is an expansive horizon. The world is not simply the sum of all other beings in the world (though I am not suggesting that it appears apart from these beings). Instead, it designates the common element unifying all beings but is never manifest in itself. As such, the contours of the world can never be completely elucidated. The important consequence here is that the world can never be totalized. So absence indicates that the totality of a world present to us is a fiction; the world given over to living being has an unending surplus of meaning. The world itself then is always elusively beyond our grasp and absent from us. Moreover, we can assuredly say that this absence of the world is not just a lack that is the inverse of a positive presence—something missing. Rather, the world gives itself to the living being as absence that is a fundamental incompleteness.

The mode of absence as related to the world correlates to the mode of absence as related to the self. How is the self from which life's movement is perpetually issued present only in the mode of absence? To answer this question requires remembering what I have already rehearsed concerning ontological desire. The intermediate objects, or not fully engaged objects, of desire constantly drive living being beyond itself. The fulfillment proffered by an intermediate object only further enflames new desire. This "enflaming" is crucial to understand. The enflaming of desire by intermediate objects indicates a dispossession at work in desire itself. Though it may sound a bit cryptic and paradoxical at first, in possessing the desired intermediate object, desire is immediately dispossessed from itself.[44] In fulfilling a need with a particular desired object, the lacking of that need is fulfilled; but because the desired object was only partially engaged desire is immediately dispossessed from that particular object at the moment it provides fulfillment. Desire incessantly moves through this process; it is a continuous experience of dispossession. This dispossession is the mode of absence at

44. "The life of the living being lives on [*se nourrir de*] a fundamental lack of being, but this lack of being roots itself in an original relation to what is necessarily lacking. Life is not the satisfaction of needs but the experience of dispossession" (ibid).

the heart of desire at work in the movement of living being that institutes a sense of self. Moreover, this kind of dispossession educes an irreducible alterity in living being. In this alterity the desiring self cannot be exclusively autonomous: the absence at the heart of desire entails openness to things other than the self. This dispossession means that living being is never its own. In sum, the absence in the desire of living movement is generated as an experience of dispossession in desire itself that indicates a point of irreducible alterity at the heart of living being.

First I emphasized the chiasmic relation of self and world adventing from the movement of living being, and second I claimed that this is only adequately described in terms of the mode of absence. Bearing these two claims in mind allows me to draw one more conclusion for a final question: what is the aim of life as characterized by movement and desire? I already noted that this aim can no longer be thought of as self-preservation, since thinking of movement this way is limited to need and its fulfillment. Self-preservation is not adequate for characterizing the insatiable absence correlate to the constancy of movement in living being. Desire does get at the ontological meaning of this insatiable absence, but what then is the aim of desire (i.e., if the aim of movement fulfilling needs is self-preservation, what is the aim of movement toward desire's insatiable absence)? When understood in terms of desire, the movement of living being is aimed towards *manifestation*.

There is reciprocity in the absence that institutes the chiasmic sense of self and world arising from the movement of living being understood as desire, fostering a kind of "ontological curiosity." In the mode of absence for the self-side of this chiasm, there is the dispossession characteristic of desire. The dispossession constantly presses the movement of the living being beyond its needs in an exploration of the contours of its ever-widening world. Conversely, this dispossession can continue indefinitely because it correlates to the mode of absence in the world-side of this chiasm. There is an infinite surplus of meaning to the world that makes its totalization impossible. The world is absent as an ever-receding horizon. Understood in terms of desire, living being is world manifestation as unceasingly presented through movement, driven by dispossession, and directed to a world so far beyond our grasping it is perpetually absent to us. In sum, self and world are co-institutive (they always appear together); they are constituted by life as desire and movement (both self and world are best characterized in terms of the incessant absence that drives the continuous movement of living being); and life, understood this way, is the realization of the chiasmic flesh that a phenomenology of perception pursues (living things are the distinctive mode of being that is the flesh of the world). Succinctly, the world's abyss of absence could not appear without the manifesting movement of desire in living being, instituted as dispossession that is its own insatiable absence generated in the face of the world's persistent withdraw.[45]

---

45. Ibid., 15–16.

4

Abstential Desire

Having laid out these variegated concepts, it is time to begin weaving them together. The goal here is twofold. First, I will briefly recount the main themes of the material covered so far, in an effort to help the reader make connections between my account of principles of life, Deacon's dynamical emergence, and Barbaras's phenomenology of life. Examining the principles of life has taken us across a vast sweep of philosophical and scientific approaches, and it behooves us before venturing into the theological portion of our task to take stock of what has been discovered. It is a moment to regain our vision of the forest and not just the trees.

Second, I noted in the introduction to the previous chapter that the phenomenological resources, especially through Barbaras, were being developed to enrich the ontology nascent in Deacon's dynamics of emergence—especially his idea of the abstential (i.e., the fundamental incompleteness of phenomena). With that aim in mind, I suggest there are two questions to consider. (1) How, if at all, does Barbaras's account of movement and desire aid the ontological deepening of Deacon's use of the abstential? (2) What are the ramifications of such an analysis for a constructive theological project concerned with the religious symbol "God is living"? To answer these questions, I will move through three crucial steps I take in linking Deacon's abstential and Barbaras's desire. As the title of the chapter indicates I will refer to this union of approaches as "abstential desire." I will conclude by offering four statements that will help guide the subsequent theological analysis.

A Brief Review

I began by outlining three major philosophers with regard to their thinking about the principles of life: Aristotle, Descartes, and Kant. Further, I examined how each responded to the challenges set forth by his predecessor. Aristotle begins by articulating a means by which to distinguish living things from non-living things: living things are those that have a soul as their form. The Cartesian perspective was given in contrast to this Aristotelian affirmation (or at least opposed to the scholastic appropriation of the Aristotelian affirmation). The soul was exiled from living things in Descartes's account and he strove to give an account of life in pure mechanical terms without recourse to teleology. The Cartesian approach radically brought to the fore the importance of organization in giving an account of living things. Finally, Kant sought a space for living things beyond the mechanical. In contrast to Descartes, Kant envisioned an irreducible principle of purposiveness in the organized and self-organizing features of living things. The idea is that one can only understand (or even recognize) an organism by treating it *as if* it had been created purposefully. As a result, this purposiveness was essential to establishing normative laws of living things that maintain a certain contingency regarding basic natural laws.

While establishing the ontological efficacy of purposiveness relied on situating the concept within the wider approach of his transcendental idealism, what proves especially important is to understand purposiveness in the context of the antinomy of teleological judgment. Simply put, the purposiveness of organisms (or technically "natural ends") presents an insoluble tension between giving an account of their causality in terms of the mechanical and the teleological. Ultimately these mechanical and teleological accounts describe two sides of the same causal structure for Kant, but that unity could only be established by a "supersensible principle" that would be impossible for human understanding. In various ways this tension between the principles of life imbued by the Cartesian mechanical account and the Kantian organismic account continue to shape contemporary scientific research into principles and origins of life. The crux of my assessment was that it is crucial to examine how the teleological facets of Kantian purposiveness are employed and extended in the conceptual suppositions of scientific research concerned with principles of life.

For this reason, I examined emergence theory—with its traditional concern for major transitions in the fabric of the universe (such as the occurrence of life and mind). However, the brief review of historical accounts of emergence demonstrated just how difficult it is to set down principles for what qualifies as "emergent" and what the respective ontological or epistemological status of that emergent might be. After establishing three principles that need to be considered for any contemporary account of emergence (monism, leveled ontology, and clarity with regard to the critical feature demonstrated by emergent transitions), I limited the scope of the treatment offered here to strong or ontological emergence, wherein an emergence is identified by the generation of new causal capacities of a whole irreducible to the causal capacities of its parts. By contrast weak emergence maintains causal power remains at microphysical levels and emergent features are only descriptive of increased complexity. This strong form of emergence was particularly important because it provides a more robust partner for interdisciplinary work with theology. Notably, it is difficult to envision how one reckons a theological account that maintains divine action in the world with weak emergence theory. If we are to preserve an account of divine action and have interdisciplinary engagement with emergence theory, the account of emergence theory used must be strong emergence.

Subsequently, I focused on the work of Deacon and establishing it as a form of strong emergence. Deacon's work is particularly appealing amidst the various emergentist thinkers I could use because of the unique way it de-emphasizes traditional facets of mereological reasoning (i.e., part-whole reasoning) and novelty as critical features of emergent transitions. Instead, he develops an account whereby emergent transitions indicate changes to the dynamic causal topology operative at particular levels of complexity. The emergence of distinctive causal topologies occurs by constraint: where two or more lower-level dynamics reciprocally constrain one another to generate a more complex higher-level dynamic. Across the spectrum of increasing complexity that Deacon's dynamic account of emergence proposes, there is a special place for two concepts that point towards the ontological and meta-scientific resources at work in his theory: the entential (i.e., phenomena that are intrinsically incomplete) and the abstential (i.e., the intrinsic incompleteness towards which an entential phenomenon exists). I suggested that in light of critiques like that of Clayton, which emphasizes emergent substances instead of emergent dynamics, it is critical to establish the ontological robustness of these crucial concepts. Without a more robust account of constraint and the abstential, Deacon's work can be read as either strong or weak emergence—and my interest is in strong emergence.

Lest this investigation of Deacon's emergence theory seem disconnected from our account of the principles of life, I also showed specifically how Deacon's account could be interpreted as an extension of the paradox that the Kantian antinomy of teleological judgment (as it relates to purposiveness) puts forward. As such, I suggested that the abstential could represent the supersensible unity between the accounts of mechanical and teleological logic at work in purposiveness, which Kant affirms cannot be realized. Said another way, Deacon provides a new way around the tension in Kant's work by entering into its tension from a negative approach (i.e., constraint and absence). In sum, a strong emergence interpretation of Deacon's work could represent a major conceptual gain in regard to the history of the principles of life I traced from Aristotle through Descartes to Kant. Deacon's work could provide a way beyond the tension between a Cartesian mechanical approach and the Kantian organismic approach that is still dominant in the contemporary scientific imagination. Still, this conceptual gain can only be realized with a strong emergence interpretation of Deacon's work; an interpretation that could be contested if the ontological resources informing his approach are not enriched.

To bolster these resources, I turned to the phenomenological work of Barbaras. He is rooted in the tradition of a phenomenology of perception as developed by Merleau-Ponty. A crucial feature of Merleau-Ponty's work was its effort to overcome the bifurcation between an empiricist and an intellectualist approach to reality. Instead of this split, there was a culmination of his work towards a chiasmic concept: the flesh of the world. This "flesh" represents a chiasm of sensibility (i.e., to sense requires being-sensed) that provides an alternative concept of reality: constrained neither to the predominance of the exterior world, as with the empiricist approach, nor the predominance of the interior self, as with the intellectualist approach.

Barbaras insists on probing deeper into the insights of this phenomenology of perception. The phenomenology of perception and the flesh of the world must be transmuted into a phenomenology of life that tries to get beyond a negative description of the flesh to a positive articulation of its meaning. In short, Barbaras wants to say in a more specific way what the flesh *is* rather than what it *is not* (as with the more typical assertion that the flesh is neither empiricist nor intellectualist). He begins this process by providing a rich investigation into the meaning of life, in both its intransitive and transitive senses: the living thing and the feeling of living. Resisting the urge to turn directly to biology for an understanding of living via an analysis of the functioning of living things (an *epoché*), Barbaras is able to take stock of the importance of the feeling of living in understanding life. In an effort to account for both the feeling of living and the functioning of the living thing in constant union with one another, Barbaras turns to the work of Hans Jonas on metabolism as a kind of self-preserving movement. While movement provided a promising phenomenological account of life, its restriction to self-preservation was a hindrance. To emphasize self-preservation inscribed the meaning of life in an ontology of death (i.e., presupposed in self-preservation was an understanding of life as resistance to death; such an understanding tautologically presupposes knowing what is purportedly being investigated—the meaning of living).

Thus, while movement is a crucial feature of the phenomenological account of life, a correlate ontological meaning of life as more than self-preservation had to be described. In Barbaras's writings he proposes that desire is the ontological meaning of life's movement. Desire is a concept wider than the needs characteristic of self-preservation because it is insatiable: the fulfillment of the object of desire only inflames desire's longing. This means the object of desire is only partially engaged (i.e., attaining the object provides limited satisfaction) and correlatively that desire is dispossessed from itself (i.e., desire moves to something new in the moment a particular need is fulfilled). This dispossession is at work in the continual movement of living being understood as desire. The result is that at the heart of the living being there is a fundamental incompleteness or absence. If the ontological mode of living being is desire, then Barbaras indicates that its aim is not self-preservation but manifestation of the world of the living being. This manifestation is a perpetual process wherein desire dispossesses itself in the face of an absent world (i.e., the world as a horizon with an infinite surplus of meaning that is absent insofar as it is non-totalizable).

Three Critical Ideas

With all of the critical threads gathered up from the previous chapters we are better equipped to connect Deacon's concept of the abstential and his dynamics of emergence to Barbaras's concepts of movement and desire. To this end, I will examine three crucial concepts: teleodynamic desire, abstential desire, and the potential unity of the mechanical and the teleological in living things.

Teleodynamic Desire

To begin, I suggest correlating Deacon's morphodynamics and teleodynamics to Barbaras's distinction between need and desire as in table 4 below. The gain of this correlation lies with Barbaras's reversal of the commonsense relation between needs and desire. Initially, desire may appear as an aspiration superfluous to the satisfaction of needs; however, Barbaras asserts the opposite. "Need refers to a definite lacking; it aims at restoring vital completion which is why it is always a need for something determinate. Desire, on the other hand, is not based on a lacking and strictly speaking it does not lack anything. The aspiration that animates it is not the reverse side of an absence."[1] Desire is not just a lacking; the being of desire is not defined in terms of a lack to be fulfilled. Instead, the key is recognizing that desire cannot be fulfilled. Desire is originary incompleteness not a definite lacking. To be clear, in the commonsense approach need is the fundamental category while desire is superfluously added to need; however, in Barbaras's approach desire is the more fundamental category representing originary incompleteness of which need is a definite or specific incompleteness. Need is the lack of some object's presence; desire is the presence of absence itself.

This schema can help illustrate the real disjunction between teleodynamics and morphodynamics. Morphodynamics has a simple recurrent causal structure that relies on homeodynamics. This causal structure was well exemplified in the description of Bénard cells (i.e., hexagonal cells formed by continually heating a thin layer of oil): without a continuous input of heat the cells broke down. The heat had to continuously be put in so that the molecules would rise and fall as they dissipated excess heat from the bottom of the oil to the top; then the molecules would begin bumping into each other as they tried to more rapidly convey the heat and eventually form convection cycles to achieve maximum efficiency. Now, in combining Deacon's and Barbaras's approaches, we might say the Bénard cell has heat as its "need." The heat would be the definite object to the cell that if lacking causes the convection cycles to break down and the cell to disintegrate. Now we can generalize from our example: morphodynamics (the organization of the Bénard cell) has homeodynamics (the heat) as a "need." It is a need, not a desire, in Barbaras's language because the morphodynamic will disintegrate without the presence of the homeodynamic. The homeodynamic, as the needed part of the morphodynamic, is fully engaged: its absence threatens the stability of the morphodynamic.

Table 4: Correlation of Dynamics to Need and Desire

Barbaras's Account	Deacon's Dynamics
Need	Morphodynamics
Desire	Teleodynamics

The case of teleodynamics is quite different. Teleodynamics has a hyper-recurrent causal topology reliant on morphodynamics. This causal topology was exemplified by the autogen and its very basic sense of "memory"

1. Barbaras, *Desire and Distance*, 111. The language here can be a bit confusing because of how I have used the term "absence" technically (i.e., as in Deacon's absential) in contrast to Barbaras's use here. He uses "lack" and "absence" interchangeably. In the interest of clarity I will attempt to use absence more specifically in its association with desire and lack in its association with need.

to a reference state: as when the autogen would break open (in a substrate rich environment) and reform a new complete cell. This represents a substantial degree of stability not realized in morphodynamics. There is greater stability because the component dynamics can cease (or we might say be in a dormancy) without the teleodynamic system disintegrating. I am suggesting this stability reveals the primordial incompleteness characteristic of Barbaras's desire.[2]

How could this animating force of desire be described in terms of teleodynamics? Let us think about the autogen again, but in a little more specific way. I outlined in detail how the autogen consists of autocatalysis (i.e., where chemicals A and B make C, D and E make F, C catalyzes the reaction of D and E, and F catalyzes the reaction of A and B) and self-containment (i.e., where the product F not only was a catalyst for A and B but also formed containers). Now, imagine an autogen that is broken open. Using Barbaras's language, the product F, which forms the autogen container, is the broken open autogen's object of desire. Assuming the autogen had enough substrate materials from within it and its immediate environment, the autocatalytic process will go to work, creating more substrate F, and satisfy the autogen's desire. However, in the moment of satisfying the object of desire there is a simultaneous dissatisfaction. This is because the object of desire (substrate F) was not fully engaged. In the autogen, getting more substrate F was the aim, but in the moment this aim is fulfilled the desire of the autogen has been enflamed towards something else; at that moment, it can be better said that the autogen's object of desire is to find substrate to restart its autocatalytic cycle. Put concisely and technically, in the autogen satiation of the desired object by the presence of substrate F immediately retreats behind the wider desire that is the potency of the teleodynamic to reinstantiate itself upon future disruption through the production of its autocatalytic cycle.

In the account of the autogen's desire, it might be helpful to augment it with the term need. Substrate F, which I have been calling the object of desire, is a need. Like the need of the Bénard cell for constantly inputted heat, the ruptured autogen needs substrate F. Or, to be more specific, it is the autogen's morphodynamic component process of self-containment that needs the substrate. In either case, substrate F is a definite object lacking from the ruptured autogen, whose presence can fulfill this need. Yet, at the heart

---

2. While the conjunction of Barbaras's and Deacon's terms is my own, I believe Deacon affirms a distinction between morphodynamics and teleodynamics that is not significantly different from what I am offering here. He describes the difference in terms of constraint: morphodynamics amplify constraints generating the metastability of self-organization while teleodynamics reproduce the formative system of constraints and can self-reconstitute. See Deacon, *Incomplete Nature*, 261, 270, and fig. 9.1.

of satiating this need, getting more substrate F, is the deeper teleodynamic desire of the autogen that can never itself be fulfilled. The hyper-recurrent causal structure of teleodynamics is important in this regard. In the simple recurrence of morphodynamics there was a need for constant input from its constitutive dynamics (i.e., Bénard cells constantly needing heat), but the hyper-recurrent structure of teleodynamics does not need this constant input (i.e., the autogen does not need the autocatalytic cycle to continuously run to make sufficient levels of substrate F to keep its cell closed). In teleodynamics, there is desire that drives beyond satiation by any definite object or dynamic.

This correlation of Barbaras's need and desire to Deacon's morphodynamics and teleodynamics might be little more than an interesting language-game without remembering Barbaras's insight about the relation between need and desire. "[D]esire would not be a capricious and optional aspiration that is added to the necessities of need, but rather this originary overflowing, which runs deeper than any incompleteness, of which need would only be the deficient and finite form."[3] Desire is a more primordial ontological structure than need. Need is for something specific, fulfilled, and then finished. Desire can consist of many needs, but desire itself points to a deeper, more primordial ontological insight in which need participates. Drawing the insights outlined here towards a conclusion I would claim the following:

1. Teleodynamics relies on morphodynamics for its formation and is a more complex causal topology.
2. The idea of a definite lacking and its fulfillment in Barbaras's need can be correlated with Deacon's morphodynamics.
3. Barbaras's need is not sufficient to characterize Deacon's teleodynamics.
4. Instead, Deacon's teleodynamics more aptly correlates to Barbaras's desire.
5. If this is the case, then even though Deacon's teleodynamics is a more complex causal topology than morphodynamics, the desire correlate to teleodynamics reveals an ontological insight that is more primordial.

There is a more fundamental ontological structure revealed in a vastly more complex dynamical system. In such a schema, crossing the threshold from morphodynamics to teleodynamics is a truly critical juncture ontologically speaking because it takes us beyond the immediacy of needs: it takes

---

3. Barbaras, *Desire and Distance*, 111.

us beyond a definite lacking being essential to the dynamic, to (perhaps for the first time) a dynamic that reveals absence itself.

Abstential Desire

While I have discussed the place of lacking in relation to need and morphodynamics above, I did not address the role of absence in desire (which is so much a part of Barbaras's understanding) as it relates to teleodynamics. The challenge is parsing apart three terms that each draw on the theme "absence." There is Barbaras's use of absence in terms of desire; Deacon's concept of the abstential as it relates to strong emergence; and Deacon's use of absence in what he calls ententional phenomena. Before delving into the potentially constructive interplay between these terms, let us remember what each term means.

Barbaras used absence to denote the quality of desire that is different from a need: the quality of desire is absence and the quality of need is lacking. In need, the lacking is the inverse of something present; in desire, the absence is fundamental—it is *not just the inverse* of something present. In interpreting Deacon, I asserted that ententional phenomena are those that are intrinsically incomplete and the abstential is the intrinsic incompleteness itself: the incompleteness towards which ententional phenomena exist.

I want to press the distinction between Deacon's two concepts (the ententional and the abstential) further than he himself does by correlating them with Barbaras's work (in terms of needs and desire).[4] Ententional phenomena will correlate to needs. The abstential will correlate to desire. This correlation of the ententional to need and the abstential to desire allows us to extend our previous conceptual table, as depicted in table 5 below.

Table 5: Correlation Extended to Emergence Language

Barbaras's Account	Deacon's Dynamics	Deacon's Emergence Language
Need	Morphodynamics	Ententional
Desire	Teleodynamics	Abstential

4. As indicated in chapter 2, Deacon's use of the abstential is a mirror-term to the ententional: it designates the absence constitutive of ententional phenomena. My own reading of the term "abstential" is broader—it drives its meaning into the metaphysical "abstentialism" that Deacon resists pursuing insofar as such a metaphysical paradigm is beyond his goal of explicating the dynamics of the emergence of ententional phenomena. My reading makes the ententional a narrower concept and the abstential a wider concept than in his use.

Let me be very clear that this table does not directly follow Deacon's usage. For instance, Deacon would call the autogen—as our prime example of teleodynamics—entential. In the account I have proposed in the table, the autogen could be called abstential but not entential. This separation of the abstential from the entential does not occur in Deacon's text. Still, I do not think connecting need to the entential and desire to the abstential is without warrant. As Deacon indicates various entential phenomena are characterized by their orientation to something specific that they lack.[5] To understand these phenomena is to understand what they are without. Think back to the Bénard cells again: what is it that these cells lack? The Bénard cell lacks the tendency of its molecules to be evenly dispersed. The consistent input of heat disrupts this tendency by forcing the molecules to convey heat from the bottom of the oil to the top. This lack of molecular freedom of movement is critical to formulating this phenomenon.

With that in mind, I can bring need, morphodynamics, and the entential together in a coherent way. A need is the lack of something particular that when present fulfills the need. In making the connection between morphodynamics and need I gave the example that the Bénard cell has heat as its need: no heat, no cells. To call the Bénard cell entential it should be oriented to something specifically lacking. What lacked in the cells was the free tendency of the molecules to be evenly dispersed. The lack (i.e., the tendency of the free moving molecules) that makes the Bénard cells entential is complementary to the need of the Bénard cells (i.e., the heat, which provides the constraint to the free movement of the molecules). To generalize, the need of a morphodynamic (i.e., the heat for a Bénard cell) provides the constraint generating the characteristic lack that makes the morphodynamic entential (i.e., the heat constrains the free moving molecules into convection cycles). Without the continued presence of the morphodynamic need (i.e., the continued heat input to the Bénard cells) the characteristic lack of this entential phenomenon dissipates (i.e., the tendency of the free moving molecules resumes).

The idea of the abstential I have in mind is something quite different from this characterization of the entential. I am reading the abstential as synonymous to the originary incompleteness of Barbaras's desire. This incompleteness always exceeds any object that might satisfy it because the object of desire is only partially engaged. Resultantly, dispossession is at the heart of desire: desire is dispossessed upon fulfillment by a particular desired object. Dispossession was crucial to understanding the absence or originary incompleteness characteristic of desire in Barbaras's account,

---

5. Deacon, *Incomplete Nature*, 27.

and it is this feature that I think can correlate to my expanded reading of the abstential.

To get a sense of what this might mean, I will bring together desire, teleodynamics, and the abstential in terms of my oft used teleodynamic exemplar—the autogen. In the previous section, I already described how the autogen can be understood in terms of desire. Notably, the stability afforded by the causal topology of the autogen (i.e., that there is not *continuous* input from its autocatalysis or self-containment processes—it is hyper-recurrent) meant it was better characterized by desire than need. I demonstrated this in terms of the autogen that has been broken open. The desired object of the ruptured autogen was more substrate F, but the moment this particular need for substrate F is fulfilled the desire of the autogen is dispossessed: no longer needing substrate F, its desire is dispossessed toward restarting its autocatalytic cycle. It is this moment of dispossession in desire, the feature that makes desire intrinsically incomplete—or that makes desire manifest absence itself—which I want to correlate to the abstential.

As such, abstential phenomena (characterized by desire) are more fundamentally incomplete than entential phenomena (characterized by need). *The satisfaction of objects of desire for abstential phenomena only fans the flame of its desire whereas satisfying the need of entential phenomena leads to satiation without this recursive action.* Teleodynamics (as with the autogen) and morphodynamics (as with the Bénard cells), respectively account for the dynamical interaction institutive of abstential desire and entential need.

Finally, in the previous section I noted that the correlation of teleodynamics to desire indicates that teleodynamics reveals a more primordial ontological form than morphodynamics and need, even though morphodynamics is conceptually and functionally less complex than teleodynamics. I could make a similar claim in terms of the abstential and the entential. There is an ontologically primordial character of the abstential even as the abstential's manifestation would be reliant upon particular instantiations of the entential.

Uniting the Mechanical and the Teleological

Finally, I proposed that Deacon's negative approach (i.e., his use of constraint and the abstential) might provide us with something like the unrealizable supersensible unity of the mechanical and the teleological in Kant's antinomy. Having indicated the correlation between the abstential and desire, I can be more explicit about how to envision this unity.

To review, what Barbaras's work gives us is a means to thinking about the intransitive and transitive quality of living. Life is both organismic being and being as lived-experience. The phenomenological and ontological implications of this fundamental sensibility have already been addressed in terms of movement, desire, and manifestation. Namely, living being is phenomenologically best understood in terms of movement. This movement is more than self-preservation (i.e., the movement of metabolism), but movement conceived as a distinctive kind of being—a third kind of being (in addition to organismic being and being as lived-experience). Movement as a distinctive kind of being is ontologically understood as desire (i.e., the meaning of this type of movement is well described by desire). Here desire is not a capricious addition to needs, but a primordial absence. The absence drives desire beyond itself to explore the horizons of its world, and in so doing desire is driving the living thing to make evermore manifest its world. Living-being is desiring movement that manifests the sensible world.

This account alters some traditional ontological presuppositions. In an oblique way I have already hinted at this, but let me try to make the alteration clearer. Life, as movement and desire, is an insatiable absence because the object of desire is only partially engaged and always inflames desire itself. This is desire's dispossession. *This structure of desire indicates the absence of life's essence to itself.* Perhaps it will be clearer to make this argument stepwise. If (1) life's ontological mode is desire and (2) desire is only present as absent (i.e., desire cannot be apart from the object of desire but is never given over in its totality in the object of desire), then (3) the essence of life—its ontological meaning—is fundamentally characterized by this absence. I have correlated this feature of desire to Deacon's term "abstential" and the causal topology of teleodynamics. I called this complex of ideas abstential desire (i.e., the correlation of desire, teleodynamics, and the abstential).

All of this is of course review of where the previous section left off. However, Barbaras presses this connection I have made further along; he articulates this assertion about life and absence in mereological language (i.e., part-whole reasoning) in order to demonstrate its importance.[6] If life,

6. Readers may note that a problem seems to arise at this point. While Barbaras is employing mereology here, I chose to follow Deacon's work (as explained in chapter 2) because its rejection of mereology provided a way around Jaegwon Kim's critique of strong emergence. This would seem like a significant conflict for integrating these two approaches. However, as will become clearer in describing Barbaras's use of mereology, I would suggest that Barbaras's work provides the philosophical legwork for the rejection of mereology that Deacon employs. Notably, Barbaras's account of absence and life in terms of part-whole language reveals how the whole is not decomposable to the parts, which is precisely the reason for Deacon's rejection of mereology.

as a whole, is nothing more than its parts—while not being reducible to the parts and the organization of the parts themselves—then the nothingness or absence characteristic of the whole has a certain reality. An example is helpful to imagine what this means. Think of this reality of nothingness or absence on analogy to playing a theme and variations in music. Music of this form introduces a theme that is played simply the first time and is replayed in a variety of different styles after the initial theme presentation. Barbaras imagines life in terms of theme and variations music, but without the initial theme ever being directly presented.

> The organism is thus like a musical theme that is never played as such and so only appears in its variations. On the one hand, the theme determines each variation and is in this sense effective: there would be no variations if they did not refer to this theme. On the other hand, the theme is absent from the variations because each variation is not itself the theme, but precisely a modification of it. In this example, the theme is present as absent, as that of which the variations are manifestations. In the same way, the organism is that unity without which the parts and the events would have no meaning but that is never present as such: the organism is present as absent, that is, as hidden in the events it governs.[7]

Here, the musical theme is absent but present in its variations by manifestations. The theme is effective as absent; or, the theme is effective like the mereological whole mentioned above—it is absent to the parts that make up the whole, but it is effective as the global structure without which there would not be parts per se. What this mereological language and the musical example help make clear is that nothingness need not be absolutely opposed to the positivity of being. This is important because it serves as a concrete way of thinking about absence in desire. In these examples, absence or nothingness is not a lack: it is not a space empty of being, pure non-being; however, it is also different from being positively present: it is not something. Absence is neither some-thing nor no-thing.

The absence of desire or the nothingness of the whole, which characterizes the essential quality of living things, indicates there is a *reality* to nothingness and absence. The whole is both real and absent. The same thing could be said for living being: living being, as desiring movement, is real as an absence. Living is not some-thing added to matter baldly conceived; rather, living is the insatiable absence driving this distinctive type of being.

---

7. Barbaras, "A Phenomenology of Life," 227.

These insights into absence press us to bracket a staple assumption of our thinking: we must let go of the sense of being that makes a radical binary between being and the nothingness of non-being. Living things as a distinctive form of being, as *living being* characterized as movement and desire, requires us to press beyond a strictly positive ontology (i.e., where to be must mean to be something). It presses us beyond a positive ontology because the whole that living being represents is nothing more than its parts. The whole represented by living being is real, but its reality is that of an absence that is not any positively conceived addition to its parts.

How is the reality of a whole that is a no-thing to be characterized? Barbaras has an important insight in this regard. He finds that if the whole is nothing more than the parts, nothing positively added, then the best way to characterize the whole is to explain how there is a fundamental change in the parts. This change is in the spatiotemporal quality of the parts. The parts, in the context of the absent whole, cannot be just point-like spatiotemporal events; rather, the parts have to be understood in terms of their possibilities and the relation of these possibilities to the possibilities of other parts. In other words, we must understand the absent whole in terms of the transversal communication amidst its parts; in this context, the parts of the whole have to be understood as "they communicate with their own future and their own past."[8]

Understanding the communication of the parts with their own future and their own past—parts as more than point-like spatiotemporal parts—is the most critical piece for my purposes. The ramifications are twofold. First, if the parts of the absent whole have a transtemporal and transspatial quality, we must take radically seriously their potential encroaching upon other parts. To understand this difference between the part itself and the part as within the absent whole, imagine the part along a timeline. The part itself can be adequately accounted for just in terms of its present state, but the part being within the absent whole is only sufficiently accounted for when it stretches into its past and future. Instead of a point along the timeline (the part itself) you have a dash (the part being within the absent whole). Second, the whole is not something added to the parts in anyway. There is no appeal to an essential whole apart from the entangling of the parts as they encroach upon one another. The whole "must therefore be defined as the transversal dimension that links all spatiotemporal events, as the axis along which the events are equivalent, like a melody, which is nothing more than the notes, but precisely as they communicate with one another."[9]

8. Ibid., 228–29.
9. Ibid., 229.

Abstential Desire 119

Still, how do we characterize the transversal dimension that links these events? Can we be more specific about what this transversal dimension is and how it is formed by the communication of its parts? What is the nature of this communication? Barbaras's other writings would certainly suggest that the characterization must be in terms of desire, but what does this really mean? How does desire characterize the "encroaching" or "communication" betwixt the parts of the whole?

Deacon's text can help fill in this gap. Following our correlation of desire, the abstential, and teleodynamics, the relationship amidst the parts must be one of reciprocal constraint[10] that mutually narrows free future states of the parts themselves. In simplest terms, if Barbaras realized that the adequate account of parts in an absent whole cannot just be point-like but has to include the past and future states of the part, what Deacon's work makes clear is that the past and future states are not just the total free possibilities of the part itself, but the part as it is directed by the other parts in a very specific way. It might be helpful to think back to the autogen and its component dynamics, autocatalysis and self-assembly, once again as an example for this. These component dynamics with a free reign of possible future states would not form an autogen: autocatalysis would run itself out of substrate materials and self-assembly would never come to pass because there would not be enough substrate present in a sufficiently small space to form a container. By constraining the possible future states of each of these component parts a more complex dynamic, the teleodynamic autogen, is formed. In the description of Deacon's work, I noted that when the component dynamics come into reciprocal relation there is a shift in the possible future states of the component dynamics: from orthograde (the standard tendency) to contragrade (a constrained tendency). *This shift in the future state of the component dynamic, from orthograde to contragrade, gives a specific meaning to the "encroaching" of parts upon one another that Barbaras describes.*

Now a way beyond the antinomy between the teleological and the mechanical is beginning to appear, which also deepens our understanding of what it means to be living being. On the one hand, Barbaras and Deacon lead us around the teleological prong of the antinomy by eliminating the positive characterization of teleology. Abstential desire is not a simple entelechy or some positively conceived teleological lure. Instead, with abstential desire the whole or living being is present as absent. Nothing is added to the parts. Abstential desire arises entirely from the interrelation of the parts.

---

10. Technically speaking what I am after is the constraint typical of teleodynamics: the synergistic reciprocity of contragrade morphodynamic processes in a hyper-recurrent causal topology.

Though arising entirely from the parts, the absence of abstential desire constrains the parts—specifically the possible future states of the parts. Let us call this apophatic teleology—teleology realized by the exclusion of other possibilities.

On the other hand, Barbaras and Deacon lead us around the strictly mechanical prong of the antinomy by emphasizing the transmogrification of the parts of living being. *The part of a living being is not the same as a part in its own accord.*[11] This is well described by the shift from orthograde to contragrade tendencies. The orthograde tendencies of lower-level dynamics with their wide possibility spaces are constrained into mutually reinforcing contragrade tendencies with narrow possibility spaces in higher-level dynamics. With regard to living being, if the parts (morphodynamics) of a whole (teleodynamics) are no longer conceived only in terms of the specific spatial and temporal locality but also in terms of their transversal communication (i.e., understanding the part in terms of its constraint and contragrade tendency), then the shift from orthograde to contragrade tendency represents a real change in the parts formative of the whole. The shift in causal topology characteristic of Deacon's model of dynamical emergence, when read in terms of the widened characterization of the ontological constitution of parts and wholes in Barbaras, undercuts the mechanical logic of living things. *Parts cannot be substituted in for other parts in the living being, because at the moment of their substitution the part in the midst of the whole becomes something different from the part as given in its own right.*

Granting non-mechanical parts and an apophatic teleology, the logic of living being is neither strictly mechanical nor teleological. Instead, the mechanical and teleological explications mutually inform one another. The mechanical explication of the interacting parts of a whole living being requires a consideration of the ontologically and teleologically significant future possibilities of the parts; the teleological explication of the pull of the whole living being over its parts requires the mechanically significant constraint of the parts. The reality and efficacy of living being as abstential desire incorporates the teleological into the mechanical explication and the mechanical into the teleological explication of living things; abstential desire provides a vantage point whereby the two modes of explication with regard to living being are integral to one another.

---

11. In contrast, consider McLaughlin, *Kant's Critique of Teleology in Biological Explanation*, 150.

God as Living—What is Relevant?

My goal has been to identify what it means that something is alive, which has led us to consider a wide swatch of material covering diverse concepts. As I am about to move into a more squarely theological analysis of what it means to talk about God as living, let me offer four important conclusions from the preceding discussion that take the form "Life is . . ." These conclusions need to be kept in mind as we think about the significant contribution these insights make to understanding "life" in the twenty-first century—insights that cannot and should not be ignored in constructive theological work today. I will use these four concepts to guide the theological considerations developed in the next part.

Life is dynamic flesh

The characterization of life I have offered here cannot be called static in any sense. With Deacon, we found a dynamic account of living beings through and through. Teleodynamics relied on components that were also dynamic, morphodynamics. Even more traditionally conceived emergent properties that arose from stable dynamics were described as akin to symbols that point toward and participate in that which they symbolize: properties as traces of their constitutive dynamics. In Barbaras's account of living being we also saw a dynamic approach being developed. Life was phenomenologically understood as movement and ontologically understood as desire. Succinctly, the very appearance of life itself is given in terms of desiring movement. Throughout the accounts I have offered here, living being is always moving being.

However, when I claim that life is dynamic, I also mean something more than understanding living being as moving being. Living being is moving being in particular ways. It is an incessant movement of living being into its world. This incessant movement is what gives rise to the more traditional ways of thinking of life in terms of the functioning living thing and its lived-experience—the intransitive and transitive senses of living. I call life dynamic flesh, because it is life that is a primordial instance of the flesh of the world that Merleau-Ponty described or a "third kind of being" as Barbaras put it. Life is an initial instance of the chiasmic encounter, sensing and being sensed, that gives rise to the interior and exterior sensibility that governs our everyday encounter with the world.

There are two consequences that need to be highlighted in stressing this point. First, this is an account of being that roots itself in movement.

Life is an immensely important form of that movement in that it advents the ontological sensibility of self and world. Consequently, despite how counterintuitive this might seem, the conclusion to draw is that though a living thing is not the most basic structure in terms of its dynamic complexity, it is ontologically fundamental. I have tried to indicate this schematically in table 6 below.

Table 6: Depicting Dynamics and Ontology

Barbaras's Ontology	Deacon's Dynamics	Deacon's Emergence Language	Dynamical Complexity	Ontological Insight
Need	Morphodynamics	Entential	Fundamental	Derivative
Desire	Teleodynamics	Abstential	Derivative	Fundamental

Life is radically dependent

This claim about dependence can occur in either the ontological or the dynamical register. In terms of the ontological register, the movement that gives us a sense of the functioning living thing and the lived-experience of that thing causes these two facets to always arise together. As they arise together there is an insoluble interdependence between the sense of self and sense of world generated by the movement of living being.[12] In terms of the dynamical register, life is a self-organizing process that entails a specific form of reciprocity to generate the complexity required to form a minimally stable sense of self. It relies on more complex dynamics being formed by lower level dynamics achieving increased stability through their mutual dependence on one another.[13] Both the ontological and dynamical register reveal different aspects of irreducible dependence critical to the formation of a living self: in the ontological there is the dependence between self and world; in the dynamical there is the dependence of reciprocal processes to generate sufficient complexity for something to be called a self.

This primacy of place for dependency in giving an account of life urges us to be very careful about how we articulate the autonomy of living

12. Technically, in the ontological register living being as dynamic flesh advents the intransitive and transitive sense of living simultaneously, indicating a chiasmic dependence between these two senses.

13. Technically, the orthograde self-reconstitution of teleodynamics relies upon the synergistic reciprocity of contragrade morphodynamic components.

being, which is traditionally an important concept. While I have not discussed autonomy in any detail, I did introduce the typical strong emergentist paradigm wherein novel causal power characterizes ontologically emergent phenomena. This affirmation of novel causal power is indicative of the self-government and self-directedness typically used to characterize life's autonomy. While the term "novel causal power" is in vogue for those working in the field of emergence, the idea encapsulated by that phrase is not significantly different from the affirmation of "top-down causality" so often employed in theology and science dialogue (wherein a whole effects the behavior of its component parts in an unprecedented way such that the whole can be conceived of as an ontologically distinctive thing irreducible to the causal powers of the parts).

In any case, I emphasized in my recounting of Deacon's work that the role of novel causal power as the characteristic distinctive of strong emergence has to be deeply rethought in light of dynamics and causal topology.[14] Notably, the central problem was to imagine how the organization of a dynamic is not just a descriptive property; how does organization have causal force? Deacon's promising answer to this question involved reconceiving organization in terms of constraint, instead of understanding it merely as a descriptive global property. Thus, ontologically significant emergences could be identified not directly by novel causal power but by the occurrence of reciprocally constraining dynamics. That change is significant, because instead of using organization to describe the differences in complexity of various systems exemplifying an emergent causal power, the very specific nature of the constraints that make up the organizational topology of the dynamic are given causal force. As such, it is not the novelty of the causal power that makes it emergent, but the organization of the constraining dynamics that are themselves the new causal power allowing for emergent properties to arise.

What I want to emphasize is the implication that this rethinking has in light of my affirmation of radical dependency in the constitution of living things. To account for living being as autonomous and ontologically significant (i.e., to treat life as an ontological emergence), we must closely examine the constraining dependence formative of the "memory" characterizing the transition from morphodynamics to teleodynamics. Here I use the term memory to indicate "memory to a reference state." This memory to a reference state, distinctive of teleodynamics, is generated by the interdependence of morphodynamic processes (i.e., in a substrate rich environment the reciprocally dependent morphodynamics will persist and reform in relation

---

14. See Deacon, *Incomplete Nature*, 364–70.

to one another). This interdependence or memory is also a means of individuation (or as Deacon technically uses "reflective individuation"). This means that the interdependence of the component morphodynamic processes is so strong and distinct that they exemplify a dynamical boundedness by which this system can distinctively be thought of as a self apart from the dynamics at work in the rest of its environment. In brief, the synergistic state of interdependent dynamical systems is so distinct and persistent that they can be bracketed off from the rest of their environment. This describes the process by which a teleodynamic whole is defined in and through its morphodynamic parts, revealing just how inextricably entangled the parts are to the whole.

The implication here is important. *If the individuation of teleodynamics is best characterized by identifying dynamical boundedness and life emerges as a function of teleodynamics, then living being is never, even in its inception, its own.* Instead, living being will always be most adequately articulated in terms of the interdependency characteristic of its dynamical boundedness. The autonomy of living being—that is so crucial a feature of typical scientific investigations into the principles of life—is not violated by my affirmation of life's radical dependency. On the contrary, the autonomy of living being is always arising from a primordial synergistic dependency.

There is a real and important consequence to this way of thinking about living being. The subsequent development of new teleodynamic forms as the work of homeodynamics, morphodynamics, and teleodynamics endlessly runs its course complicates this dependency of the self even further.[15] *The dynamical boundedness of the selfhood of living being (instead of a material or energetic boundedness) allows for a widely distributed sense of selfhood.* Deacon offers a description of mitochondria in a host eukaryotic cell as an example of this.

> In the case of mitochondria and their "host" eukaryotic cell, for example, both the nuclear genome and the mitochondrial genome are partially "reciprocally" degraded, so that neither can persist without the other, but for most functions they remain relatively modular and individuated in their functions. *This tendency for modularity, implicit in the nature of teleodynamics, is what makes complex multi-leveled selves possible.* Without it, a complexity catastrophe would be inevitable—too many components, needing to interact in a highly constrained manner in a

---

15. Ibid., 468–74; and Haag, Deacon, and Ogilvy, "The Emergence of Self," 329–30.

finite time, despite vast possible degrees of freedom—setting an upper limit on the complexity of self. [Emphasis mine].[16]

What this example demonstrates is that teleogens can be composed of other teleogens that degrade certain features of their individuation in a *modular* synergistic reciprocity. This capacity of teleogens for modular synergistic reciprocity, and the accompanying complexity it creates for dynamical self-boundedness, reflects the fundamental and inextricable dependency in the individuation of living things: modular synergistic reciprocity is a complexification of the basic "memory" institutive of the individuated teleogen. The result of Deacon's model is the possibility, and perhaps even the inevitability, of multi-leveled selves—selves as parts within more complex selves. If, as indicated above, the autonomy of living being is always based in a primordial synergistic reciprocity, modular synergistic reciprocity demonstrates that the component parts of a living being can be complex, dynamic selves in their own right. Just as there can be multi-leveled selves we should be sensitive to the possibility of multi-leveled life: living beings reciprocally degraded so as to persist within the context of a larger teleodynamic whole with its own sense of living selfhood.

Thus, both the memory to a reference state and the modular synergistic reciprocity described above reflect the radical dependency of life. The memory to a reference state indicates the lower-level synergistic interdependence institutive of emergent entities; the modular synergistic reciprocity of teleogens indicates the dependence of an irreducible connection of the teleogen to its conditioning environment. The teleogen is dependent in both interiority and exteriority—in its constitution and its environing existence. This irreducible dependency of the teleogen's dynamical boundedness, as revealed in its inceptive emergence and subsequent development, builds on my conclusion that life is dynamic flesh. The radical dependence exemplified by the teleogen models the chiasmic touch of the flesh of the world: where the interpenetration of self and world, subject and object are co-instituted. The teleogen's individuation must always be instantiated and understood in conjunction with its world or horizon; the autonomy of a self relies on the synergistic reciprocity of dynamics in its world. Across the spectrum of the complexity of life this radical dependency will occur.

---

16. Deacon, *Incomplete Nature*, 473.

Life is always manifesting

The radical dependency of the teleogen is not arbitrary. It reflects something expected if desire is characteristic of teleodynamics. Remember I used desire to characterize the insatiability at the heart of teleodynamics. Desire points to the fulfillment of particular morphodynamic needs within the teleodynamic as they arise, but these needs are only partially engaged as the desired object of the teleodynamic. The partial engagement allows for the fundamental dispossession at work in desire to be exemplified by teleodynamics (i.e., the desire of the teleodynamic is in a perpetual process of dispossession demonstrated in moments when particular morphodynamic needs are fulfilled). The radical dependency in the component dynamics of a teleogen is what makes the dispossession of desire possible: there must be at least two alternating needs in order for there to be sufficient complexity for desiring being to arise.

In reviewing Barbaras's work, I also emphasized that desire was connected to manifestation. The movement of living being—whose ontological meaning is desire—represented a constant process of manifestation. There was an incessant widening of the horizon that constituted a living being's world because the dispossession of desire constantly drives living being beyond a satisfaction with the fulfillment of its needs. If (1) living being is characterized as desiring being through dispossession (where dispossession is concomitant to sufficient complexity generated by the dependency of synergistic reciprocity) and (2) it is the dispossession of desire that drives living being towards manifestation, then it is reasonable to expect that the dependency of living being is related to manifestation.

Above, I claimed that there was radical dependency in the teleogen in two senses: internal and external; memory to a reference state and modular synergistic reciprocity. Can both of these modes of dependency correlate to some sense of manifestation? Yes, which is why I would say life is always manifesting. Key to this claim is establishing the initial act of manifestation (i.e., that there is an act of manifestation at work in generating memory to a reference state).[17]

---

17. This is the key for two reasons. First, it is not all that difficult to imagine how complex instances of modular synergistic reciprocity inherently involve some act of manifestation. This more complex sense of selfhood already arises from more primordial senses of self, which I am suggesting can be engaged in acts of manifestation. Second, the modular synergistic reciprocity as external dependency is an analogous complexification of the basic memory to a reference state as internal dependency. Just as this interior and exterior dependency is analogous, I would claim that the act of manifestation across these dependencies is also analogous.

What then is the act of manifestation coextensive to establishing the memory to a reference state? In terms of the memory to a reference state, or the internal dependency of the teleogen, *the teleodynamic at work is itself a manifestation of its world.* The teleodynamic is formed from harnessing morphodynamic components of its environment by using them to mutually constrain one another into a stable reference state. These morphodynamics are a part of the conditioning environment in which the teleogen is formed. Formed from these morphodynamics, the desire of the teleodynamic will express itself in terms of the specific morphodynamic needs constituting it: the desire of the teleodynamic will reflect the formative needs of its morphodynamic environment. As such, the constitution of the teleodynamic is itself an initial act of manifestation revealing a morphodynamic world to the teleodynamic self. The teleogen is always manifesting its world and we might assume the same for living being insofar as it is teleogenic.

Life is abstential desire

I have already rehearsed the details of this claim above. Let it suffice that to say "life is abstential desire" indicates that the ontological meaning of life's movement towards manifestation is abstential desire. This abstential desire shows life to be dispossessed from itself: something present as absent, an effective absence. The ontological implication is two-fold. First, living being challenges the strict divide between being and nothingness as an instance of the ontological reality of nothingness. Second, the parts that make up the absent whole of living being are only sufficiently characterized in terms of their transversal communication with past and future states as the parts encroach upon one another. The reconceptualization of part and whole in the living being provides a vantage point for overcoming the antinomy between mechanical and teleological logic at work in Kantian purposiveness. The absent whole as a teleological aim and the non-point-like parts of the living whole are indicative of a logic that brings together teleological and mechanical facets but cannot be adequately characterized by either teleological or mechanical reasoning alone.

I want to make clear two important implications of this point. First, though I have addressed it last, there is a sense in which the claim that life is abstential desire is the most critical. In some sense my claims that "life is dynamic flesh, radically dependent, and always manifesting" are implications of the insight that "life is abstential desire."

Second, in the discussion of Barbaras, I emphasized that giving a definition of life that includes its intransitive and transitive senses entails pressing beyond a materialist biological account: it requires a phenomenological investigation of our intuitive capacity to identify something as alive. Resultantly, I have sought out an understanding of life beyond self-preservation and the resultant descriptive understanding of life that limited its meaning to resistance to death (i.e., life inscribed by an ontology of death). The shift away from inscribing life in death represents an important widening of the philosophical bounds of biology as the discipline that studies living things. Perhaps, this can be clarified in terms of Deacon's own placement of teleodynamics in general biology.

In concluding that "life is radically dependent," I reviewed how teleodynamics generates an end-directed organizational form with a persistent identity. Think of the autogen, wherein the correlated morphodynamic processes of containment and autocatalysis reciprocally depend upon one another. The synergistic reciprocity of morphodynamics in the autogen forms a teleodynamic system that self-maintains and displays the dynamical-boundedness of selfhood. The organizational form of the autogen's dynamical boundedness is a representation of its environment that allows us to evaluate surrounding environments as beneficial or detrimental to the autogen's continued maintenance.[18]

This quality, the intrinsic identity of teleodynamic processes, warrants the inclusion of Deacon's work on emergence theory within that group of approaches seeking to explicate the emergence of life in terms of complex systems dynamics.[19] Deacon goes further than most in this field by formulating a new taxonomy of general biology based on principles to be drawn from the autogen model and teleodynamic emergence. He proposes that the functional affinity between autogens (as an example of teleodynamic phenomena) and life, insofar as both self-repair and self-propagate, suggest a functional classification he calls *Autea*. However, there is a distinct difference between autogens and life as well. Autogen reproduction relies upon stereochemical effects, while organisms traditionally considered alive rely on template-based, coded reproduction (a genetic medium separated from phenotypic variation). Thus, Deacon suggests distinguishing between *Semeota* as those *Autea* that use molecular coding for reproduction and *Morphota* as those *Autea* that are constrained to molecular morphology for reproduction.[20] As Bruce Weber rightly notes, the implication of this

---

18. Deacon, *Incomplete Nature*, 309–11.
19. Weber, "On the Emergence of Living Systems," 350–52.
20. Deacon, "Reciprocal Linkage," 146–47; and *Incomplete Nature*, 447–57.

taxonomy is that "life did not arise as an event that transformed dead matter, but rather as a process of emergence from rich chemical dynamical systems."[21]

However, *if life is abstential desire, which is to say if life is attributable where the ontological mode of abstential desire appears, then teleodynamics indicates the presence of living being.* We can continue to follow the taxonomy and take heed of Weber's assertion (life arises as a process of emergence from dynamical systems morphodynamic systems particularly), but there *is* a moment of transformation. *Autea* are not on their way towards living things; *Autea* are the fundamental class of things that actualize abstential desire. The moment where a present as absent whole of desiring, that is living being, can be said to transmogrify the free play of the transversal communication of its parts in a relationship of synergistic, constraining reciprocity, there is a fundamental change in the structure of the universe: life advents.

---

21. Weber, "On the Emergence of Living Systems," 352.

5

Who is this Living God?

THERE IS UNANIMITY IN the theological tradition in affirming a connection between God and life. Whether one emphasizes the oath formulas of the Hebrew Bible, the prophetic vision of Jeremiah, the poetic attributions of the Psalms, the explicit correlation in the Gospel of John, or the various connections of God to life via Christ and the Holy Spirit in the Epistles, the Christian tradition has a deep religious sensibility that our God is a living God. In theologically explicating this religious sensibility, "God is living," theologians face an immediate challenge. On the one hand, we might first treat God in a more general sense and then ascribe life to God as an attribute. On the other hand, we might first treat life in a more general sense and propose that God's living gives meaning to "life" well beyond our finite comprehension. Or, we might make various uses of both of these approaches, since they certainly do not represent a watertight distinction. Whether we treat God primarily or life primarily, it is clear that our theological explications can begin from quite different suppositions that need to be made explicit, for they can produce a variety of positions with regard to what it means to claim "God is living."

I bring up this initial conundrum not to divide the discussion of this religious symbol into opposing camps before even beginning, but to highlight a challenge that arises in the face of theologically explicating this concept. This religious symbol appears smattered across loci if I were to trace its theological development. Since there is a fundamental openness about the primary referent to be theologically considered (i.e., "*God*, who is living" or "the *Living* God"), its theological dimensions have been widely construed. It can be an attribute of God, a statement about eternal life, an indication of similarity between God and creation, or a means to indicating the connection between God and Christ to name a few perspectives. Its theological relevance is attributed to developing notions of creation, salvation, Christology, and even eschatology. There is no way that I can treat the entirety of the theological array of meanings produced by this symbol or account for the ways it bleeds across traditionally conceived loci in a single chapter, perhaps even in a single book.

As such, I am choosing to focus specifically on the use of life as an attribute of God: to treat the symbol "God is living" in terms of the doctrine of God. Who is this living God? What does it mean about God to claim God lives? With this structure in mind, I want to offer a kind of conceptual history to give a shape to the various ways God's living can be understood. I am shaping this history in terms of the four conclusions I offered in the previous chapter: life is dynamic flesh, radically dependent, always manifesting, and abstential desire. With these four statements in mind, I will treat two theological thinkers, Karl Barth and Jürgen Moltmann, who explicate the theological meaning of God's living in a way that helps recognize some of the same phenomenological insights about life that we discovered from Barbaras, but never brings God's living to a point that it is directly accountable to any of the four conclusions garnered from the previous chapter. Next, I will consider two theologians, John Zizioulas and Sallie McFague, who in two very different ways each treat God's living in terms of the statement that life is radically dependent. Finally, I will consider one theologian, Paul Tillich, who could be interpreted as treating God's living in terms of the statement that life is dynamic flesh. It is this final approach, with its potential correlation to the concept of dynamic flesh that I believe has room for the most radical theological development. The insights garnered from this approach will be used in the subsequent chapter to constructively develop the meaning of God's living in terms of abstential desire.

God's Living as Aseity and Promise

Many theologians who have asked the question that I am concerned with here (i.e., what does it mean about God to claim that God lives) correlate the meaning of the religious insight to a theological explication of the relation between God's being and act. *For these thinkers to affirm that God is living is to affirm the aseity of God's being.* Amidst the thinkers that treat God's living in this way there is not a great deal of divergence in the logical reasoning. Certainly different conceptual schemes and philosophical languages are employed by various theologians reflecting their socio-cultural and historical location. Still, the minutiae of these subtle distinctions need not trouble us here. These distinctions are most often reflective of differences between the wider metaphysical resources being employed by the respective theologians, rather than reflective of crucial distinctions in their interpretation of this religious sensibility.

Let me offer a brief example of what I mean. Certainly the respective understandings of God as living in Augustine's *Confessions* and Aquinas's *Summa Theologiae* are quite different in their ramifications. In Augustine, God's living is made synonymous to God's being in terms of two implications: (1) it is contrasted to our dependency for life and being on God and (2) it leads to his concern for the immutability and simultaneity of God's eternity.[1] Moreover, the connection between God's living and God's being is formed in the vein of Neo-Platonism.[2] In Aquinas God's living is made synonymous to God being life itself. This is in turn explicated in more formal Aristotelian language. It indicates that God's living as life itself is distinct from other living things which are a union of matter and form (per traditional hylomorphism) where the matter is the individualizing feature correlated to the defining form. God being life itself is its own individualized form apart from any matter.[3] Here the distinctiveness of God's life demonstrates the distinctiveness of God's being in terms of an Aristotelian framework. Certainly, there are very different systematic implications of adopting a neo-Platonic versus Aristotelian metaphysical language for articulating the meaning of God's being. However, for my work *the key is to recognize that while there are differences regarding the implications of what it means to say that God is God's own being, there is no question that to affirm God is living is to affirm that God is God's own being.* Here God's living indicates the aseity implied by the theological term *actus purus*.

Perhaps more than any other thinker, Karl Barth is a 20th century exemplar of this approach.[4] He crystalizes the theological implications of the

---

1. Augustine, *Confessions* 1.6.10.

2. For instance, see Kenney, "Augustine's Inner Self," 79–90; Corrigan, "Love of God, Love of Self, and Love of Neighbor," 97–106; and Matthews, "Anselm, Augustine, and Platonism," 61–83.

3. Aquinas, *Summa Theologiae*, 1a.3.3sc and c.

4. My choice to follow Barth on this concept is not arbitrary. As will become clear in the course of my recounting, it is critical to recognize that the pure, naked power implied in correlating God's living to God's being cannot be sustained. Content has to be given to this establishing event of God's free, aseitic action; content that comes from interpreting the religious symbol that God is love. Recognizing how tight this correlation must always be, for many thinkers God's life and love nearly collapse into one another, because it is by the revealed omnipotence of God's love that we are able to enter into the wider meaning of God's omnipotence (the traditional loci wherein God's living is coordinated to God's being). Using Barth as an exemplar is helpful because

actus purus into an *actus purissimus*.⁵ In particular we will focus on Barth's treatment of this concept in one section of his *Church Dogmatics*.

Barth treats this insight that God is living in his first section detailing the reality of God after his lengthy treatment of the knowledge of God. It stands as an investigation into the meaning of the claim "God is" in light of the possibility and limits Barth establishes for knowledge of God.⁶ For Barth, to investigate the meaning of God's being, the claim that "God is," is always an investigation into God's works. God is not another than revealed in these works: the works truly reveal who God is. This is not to claim that God is not more than these works, for as Barth emphasizes, "They [God's works] are bound to Him, but He is not bound to them."⁷ The important point here is that if God is made known in these works and these works are true expressions of who God is, then our investigation into the meaning of the claim "God is" must always be guided by what God does; to know who God is, is to know God as revealed to us in act.⁸

As such, it should be clear that for Barth an investigation into the doctrine of God cannot be an investigation into the general doctrine of being. God's being and act are always held together for Barth. In fact, if there is to be an investigation into being generally conceived at all it must reflect God's action, since the reality of God that is God's being in act is not only the inner reality of God but the source of our reality.⁹

---

there are already such clear delineations between life and love (freedom as the mode of God's life and love) in his text. A contemporary example of how life and love remain distinct but are expressed in terms of the depth of their intertwining might be Wolfhart Pannenberg, where the life of God is tightly correlated to Trinitarian dynamics characterized in terms of the ecstatic movement of the Logos as an expression of omnipotent love. See Pannenberg, *Systematic Theology*, 411–22, esp. 412.

Of course, Aquinas could be the exemplar for this approach. Perhaps, it is most odd that in developing the *actus purus*, he will not receive an extended treatment. Nonetheless, I have chosen to follow Barth because the deference to Aristotelian metaphysical language in Aquinas's account risks making this section less understandable to those not initiated to the contours of this dense way of thinking. Simply put, I feel that Barth provides a more manageable conversation partner for the twenty-first-century reader. On the connection between Aquinas and Barth on this topic, see the indispensable work by Franks, "The Simplicity of the Living God," 275–300.

5. Karl Barth, *Church Dogmatics*, 2/1:263. Henceforth references to the *Church Dogmatics* will appear as *CD*.

6. Ibid., 2/1:257.

7. Ibid., 2/1:260.

8. See also Stratis, "Speculating About Divinity?," 23; Franks, "The Simplicity of the Living God," 294; and Malysz, "From Divine Sovereignty to Divine Conversation," 32–34.

9. Barth, *CD*, 2/1:262.

To deal, first and foremost, with God's act is to deal with an event; however, this is an event of a peculiar quality. Barth makes this clear in terms of a temporal distinction. The event that is God's acting is not conceived on analogy to an event of our acting, wherein we might plan, act, and remember the act as something past. Rather, the event of God's acting is historically complete, fully contemporaneous to the present, and still to come upon us in the future. This distinction indicates the transcendent quality of the event of God's acting. While our action is temporally bounded, God's acting cannot be transcended in any way—not even by time. The event of God's acting is a moment of transcendence beyond which we cannot go. Since God's being and act are held together so tightly for Barth, it is nonsensical to seek any transcendent moment beyond this event of God's acting. That is to say there is no more transcendent feature to be pursued beyond God's acting (i.e., a notion of God's being which directs such acting), for in God's acting we are given God's own being. We could also call this event, where God's acting happens upon us in a way that cannot be made more transcendent in any way, an instance of revelation.[10]

Barth connects this account of God's acting and event to the biblical assertions about God as living: God's being is life. "We recall in this connexion the emphatic Old and New Testament description of God as 'the living God.' *This is no metaphor.* Nor is it a mere description of God's relation to the world and to ourselves. But while it is that, it also describes God Himself as the One He is [emphasis mine]."[11] It is important to dwell on this non-metaphorical connection of event, act, and life to God's being. Just as Barth asserts that the transcendent quality of the event of God's acting makes it impossible to deduce its structure from our own temporally bound sensibilities concerning acting, Barth affirms something similar regarding life. God really lives, but this does not imply a metaphor to our sense of living. For Barth, just as God's act completely surpasses what we know as acting since all of our acts can be transcended, God's living completely surpasses what we know as living since all things we know to live die. For Barth, the implication here is clear; we cannot know what event, act, or life is, as it might be generally conceived, apart from God as event, act, and life.[12]

---

10. Ibid., 2/1:262–63.

11. Ibid., 2/1:263.

12. "We can never expect to know generally what event or act or life is, in order from that point to conclude and assert that God is He to whom this is all proper in an unimaginable and incomprehensible fullness and completeness. When we know God as event, act and life, we have to admit that generally and apart from Him we do not know what this is" (ibid., 2/1:264). See also Franks, "The Simplicity of the Living God," 296–97.

Since the general happening of event and act are distinct from the event and act that are the meaning of God's living, it is fair to also claim that God's life in its event and act is something quite different from our own. Notably, while the events and acts of God's living (revelation) are particular and take place within the general course of other events, they stand out against this generality: they are a part of and a contradiction to this generality.[13] It is this contradiction to the generality of life that Barth is emphasizing here in understanding God's being. This contradiction is more than God's differentiation from all other life as its essential source; instead, Barth is pursuing a radical kind of transcendence that entails no immanent connection to the general course of living—*a way of conceiving God's life completely beyond life's general happening.*

In pursuit of this end, Barth calls the being of God, which is God's living, free life. God's life bears no dependence upon its relationship to that which is outside of itself. God's free life represents the singularity of a pure act.[14] It is actuality without reference to potentiality, not even reference to potentiality as the essential manifestation of the dialectical tension of actuality and potentiality. God's free life is pure aseity.

Barth can also claim that this free life of God is personal. The freedom of God's aseity does not have the character of fatality or necessity. The "I" that is the locus of the happening of God's personal, free life is a self sufficient omnipotence. In total, this is to claim that the motivation of the movement entailed by God's life is always self-movement, never generated from something outside of it—a self-directing pure actuality.[15]

I will conclude with what might be call "Barth's Rule on Living" for any theological explication of the living God.

> If we have life on the basis of His creation and hope on the ground of the resurrection of Jesus Christ, *our quality of life can never be confused with His*, or compared or contrasted with it as a commensurate. The validity of every further statement about God, as a statement about the living God depends on the avoidance of this confusion, or this comparison and contrast, between His life and ours [emphasis mine].[16]

---

13. Generally, I refer to God's life, rather than God's event, act, and life. Though Barth continues to do the latter—and the reader should continue to assume the unity of all three of these facets in my writing on Barth—the phrase becomes cumbersome and more obfuscating than helpful here.

14. Barth, *CD*, 2/1:264–65.

15. Ibid., 2/1:267–68.

16. Ibid., 2/1:272.

What Barth's rule reveals is an expectation concerning principles of life for any theologian who would emphasize the *actus purus* as the way to understand what it means that God is living. Succinctly put, the expectation is that the properly construed conceptual principles regarding life will not violate the conception of God's living. The living of creatures would always be in an asymmetric analogy to the revealed principles of life manifest in God's eternity and omnipotence. It is an asymmetric analogy because while we could (perhaps) work down from the principles of God's living to our own, we could not work up from the principles of life established in creation to those in God's living.

While the aseity of God is traditionally very important for understanding God's living if a theologian emphasizes the *actus purus*, I want to highlight that a theologian can reach a similar conclusion to the asymmetric analogy of Barth's rule without emphasizing a classic account of God's omnipotence. For this I turn to the work of Moltmann. His treatment of life and God as living is scattered in bits throughout his works. However, in a general sense, we can anticipate the major themes that will influence his treatment of the theological meaning of life and the living God: promise, anticipation, hope, and eschatology.

> For our knowledge and comprehension of reality, and our reflections on it, that means at least this: that in the medium of hope our theological concepts become not judgments which nail reality down to what it is, but anticipations which show reality its prospects and its future possibilities. Theological concepts do not give a fixed from to reality, but they are expanded by hope and anticipate future being. They do not limp after reality and gaze on it with the night eyes of Minerva's owl, but they illuminate reality by displaying its future.[17]

Life and God's living, in Moltmann will be conceived in terms of the anticipation of hope and eschatology. His is an examination of the future of life and the future of God's living, which are inextricably bound together. To treat Moltmann's theological approach to life is to consider what the meaning of God's living holds for life's future.

Bearing this in mind let us begin with life. Its theological meaning from an eschatological perspective resides less in the present features of living things or their past coming to be, but their future possibilities. As such, Moltmann's theological treatment of life is always also a treatment of resurrection. The key to this correlation is that life, for Moltmann, can only be understood in light of the life-creating power of God. This life-creating

---

17. Moltmann, *Theology of Hope*, 35–36.

power is most potently manifest in the resurrection hope of life beyond/after death, because it is only in resurrection that life overcomes its greatest, and seemingly inevitable, hindrance.

Lest we move too quickly to the central place that Christ's resurrection will have in understanding this connection between life-creating power and resurrection, I must emphasize that this correlation is not an exclusively New Testament conception. Moltmann finds this correlation of the meaning and fulfillment of life to a powerful promise exceeding death in the prophetic books of the Hebrew Bible. In these works the life-giving creative power of God must overcome death as the boundary of life; if it does not then death threatens to exclude creation from the promises of God's fullness. Without such an overcoming, the promises of God could not fully be realized—they would always be limited by the bounds of death. In such a case, the power and promise of God would not reach to the new ultimate reality of an eschatological realization and the power of God's promise would always be limited.[18]

This point appeals to a key insight within the Judeo-Christian tradition: *our understanding of life can never be bound by death*. While theologically this point certainly does not emphasize anything new, it brings to our attention that a Christian understanding of life, interpreted within a framework emphasizing the power of God's promise, can never define life in terms of its relation to death (which I have repeatedly noted to be quite common in biological accounts). To define life in terms of processes that resist death would inadvertently limit the life-creating power of God. For its full eschatological realization, life must always exceed its seeming boundary in death. The key here is that Moltmann's supposition, that a Christian commitment to God's life-creating power effects our suppositions about the natural world (i.e., our understanding of life must be more than resistance to death), is an expression of the asymmetric analogy we found in Barth's rule above. The Christian expectation would be that the principles of life we affirm ought not violate the meaning of God's living. I think it is fair to claim that Moltmann, by putting the language of life and death in the context of God's life-creating power, is starkly drawing out the implications of a Barthian supposition. These are implications with real efficacy; to affirm that it is insufficient to understand life as being bounded by death is to disagree with the oft used biological principle of understanding life in terms of self-preservation (for we have already argued in chapter 3 that to understand life in terms of self-preservation circumscribes life in an ontology of death).

18. "Only when the horizon of expectation extends beyond what is felt to be the final boundary of existence, i.e. beyond the bounds of death, does it reach an *eschaton*, a *non plus ultra*, a *novum ultimum*" (ibid., 132; see also 130–33).

If this insight about limiting the fullness of God by limiting our understanding of life as resistance to death appears in the prophetic literature, Moltmann finds that it is in the apocalyptic literature that the power of this promise of life receives its fullest articulation amidst the writers of the Hebrew Bible. In the hands of the apocalyptic writers, the promise of God's life-creating power takes on a universal tone that is a compliment to the initial act of creation where God brings forth all of the created order. Resurrection hope is here not a hope of reanimation; it is not a hope of resuscitating life after death. The emptiness and horror of death is preserved. Instead, it is *through* death where the hope of life has vanished that a new act of God's life-creating power can take place. If such an act of God were limited only to believers or a specific people, then we would inadvertently limit God's fullness, but in the apocalyptic writers there is recognition of this potential limitation and a concomitant focus on the vastness of this illimitable life-creating power.[19]

It is from this relationship central to the prophetic and apocalyptic imagination between the promise of life and the overcoming of the boundary of death that the resurrection of the Christ and the Christian eschatological vision of life must be understood. For Moltmann, Christian resurrection hope speaks to the prophetic expectations of a theology of promise. Given this theological location, Moltmann still emphasizes that the confession of the church, namely that Jesus is the Christ, can never be separated from the work of God who raises Jesus from the dead, pressing upon the limits of a theology of promise.

Emphasizing the connection between resurrection hope and the work of God in the life-creating power of resurrection, Christ's passion reveals more than what would be traditionally ascribed to Christology alone. The passion event provides a critical insight into God's suffering and grief at the death of Christ.[20] Since the passion event reveals a profound insight about God, this moment of Christ's death and resurrection becomes a critical point for understanding the general eschatological hope shaping a theological interpretation of created life and God's living.

In terms of the promise of life, Christ's resurrection is "a conquest of the deadliness of death."[21] It is an overturning of the finality of power in death by revealing the promise of life in and through the deadliness of death. In Moltmann, this aspect of the promise of life is an extension of

---

19. Ibid., 209–10.

20. Ibid., 166; Moltmann, *The Crucified God*, 243; and *The Trinity and the Kingdom*, 21.

21. Moltmann, *Theology of Hope*, 211.

the general logic that he applies to the event of the cross: God is revealed in God's suffering over the death of Christ in the crucifixion. God reveals God's own self in this moment of Godless abandonment.[22] In an analogous way life (and eternal life) reveals its meaning through the moment of its negation. Yet, like the resurrection relates to the suffering of the crucifixion, the meaning of life is not bounded by death but passes through the deadliness of death into a more powerful meaning—eternal life.

The event of crucifixion and resurrection points in an expectant way to the future of life: to the promise of eternal life that passes through death as a negation of the negative. Further, it is the Spirit that points to this expected hope arising from the event of the resurrection.[23] In this way the Spirit is both a reminder of Christ and the promise of Christ's future. It reminds us of the suffering of Christ's death by leading us into fellowship with this suffering through conformity to Christ's death. It leads into the future of Christ's glorious resurrection and through that resurrection to the promised glorification of all creation. This leading of the Spirit is not empty hope for Moltmann; instead, he suggests that this leading "subjects man to the tendency of the things which are latent in the resurrection."[24] Thus, the claim is that in obedience to the leading of the Spirit all of creation is shaped towards the promise of God manifest in the crucifixion and resurrection of the Christ—a promise whereby life overcomes its seeming boundary in death. The Spirit leads us through the "progression of grace" that proleptically brings the anticipated kingdom of God into the present; the Spirit brings the resurrection hope in the life-creating power of God from the eschatological future to the present.[25]

Given this anticipatory power of the Holy Spirit, Moltmann most substantially develops what it means to understand that God is living in terms

---

22. Moltmann's position entails the classically untenable notion of patripassionism. On this point, however, Moltmann takes some issue. He asserts that the axiom preserving God's apathy in the Christian tradition stems from a desire to avoid making a comparison between created suffering and the divine. What is *not* excluded, by his account, is any and all ascriptions of pathos to God; what is placed out of bounds by the affirmation of the apathetic axiom is a comparison of creaturely suffering to divine suffering. Moltmann affirms God's suffering fervently, and affirms it as what he calls "active suffering." This is the suffering necessarily associated with passionate love—a suffering that comes with a love that lays oneself open to the other. Insofar as God passionately loves then God also necessarily suffers. See Moltmann, *The Crucified God*, 27 and 72; *The Trinity and the Kingdom*, 23, 47–52, and 80–83; and Müller-Fahrenholz, *The Kingdom and the Power*, 72–73.

23. Moltmann, *Theology of Hope*, 211–12.

24. Ibid., 212.

25. Ibid., 216.

of this Trinitarian person. Let us consider this connection Moltmann makes between life and the Spirit—connections between our thinking about the eschatological meaning of created life and God's life—in two steps. First, the Spirit points to the expected hope arising from Christ's resurrection: a hope leading to glory through the revelatory suffering of God and Christ manifest in this event. This indicates that created life must be understood in terms of the anticipatory hope of eternal, eschatological life that overcomes death by moving through death. This hope is not unrealized in our present life, despite that we have not passed through death. For Moltmann, our present life can manifest this anticipation of eternal life in experiences of unconditioned and unconditional love. Put slightly differently, eternal life is experienced here and now through instantiations of the life-giving Spirit as unconditional love.[26] The importance of this insight for created life is that life that does *not* open itself to the risk of experiencing the potential loss and suffering *correlate* to this unconditional love (as exemplified in the crucifixion) is life that dies before it begins. It is life that is not-yet-living—a life unlived.[27] God as *living* must also experience the risk of loss and subjection to death that comes with authentic living that exposes itself to the other in unconditional love.

What would this risk of loss and death look like in God? On the one hand, the passion of Christ gives one means of imagining this as I have already reviewed. However, to understand God as living, *still living*, entails also expecting that God must not only experience the risk of loss and death in one historical moment alone but continue to feel its threat in conjunction with creation as God *continues* to offer God's self to the creation in unconditional love. This brings us to the second point. What Moltmann offers is a vision of the Holy Spirit, who continually gives God over to us as the spirit of creation and resurrection (the sanctifying source and hope of our renewal), as the Trinitarian person that continually manifests the powerful way in which God lives in our midst.[28] The Spirit is the source and giver of life that indwells with the creation and connects God to life. In this connection of indwelling with creation there is a *kenosis* of the Spirit[29]

---

26. Moltmann, *God in Creation*, 270.
27. Ibid., 269.
28. Moltmann, *The Source of Life*, 53–54.
29. Traditionally the term *kenosis* is applied in the context of Christology to describe the self-humiliation or self-emptying of God in the act of incarnation. Moltmann uses the term for the Spirit as well noting a parallel between the traditional Trinitarian terminology of Christ's incarnation and the Spirit's indwelling. In both cases there is a self-emptying of God in a commitment to be with creation. Moltmann, *God in Creation*, 102.

that brings the history of suffering into God's own self. By choosing the self-limitation of living in the midst of creation, the Spirit—as God's own self—suffers with creation through its vicissitudes. In sharing in this suffering God remains always open to the risk of suffering and loss that is a part of the unconditional loving of life.[30] In the self-limitation of the Spirit whereby the suffering of creation can be taken up to God, God's living can be shown to be a present reality.

It is crucial to understand that Moltmann's work is methodologically akin to Barth. In both cases asymmetric analogy is the key to their argument for understanding God as living. While Barth employs a more explicitly classic vision of God's omnipotence and aseity, Moltmann's argument is nearly identical methodologically; where it most fervently differs is in its privileging of eschatological promise as the content of God's omnipotence. Certainly this is not an insignificant distinction in its ramifications, but it is insignificant regarding the structure of each argument. Here, the meaning of God's living is not discovered by any analogy to our own living; the meaning of God's living comes to us as a revelatory (and in the case of Moltmann eschatological) event.

Both theologians provide an expectation to guide the formulation of principles of life: a Christian vision of life cannot be inscribed within an ontology of death. Moltmann helps make this point especially clear. If, as with Moltmann, resurrection hope is a critical feature of understanding life and God as living, then theologians should have a vested interest in how the principles of life—from the natural scientific standpoint—are articulated. Notably to define life in its resistance to death, or to articulate the principles of life in such a way that they remain inscribed to an ontology of death, is a diminishment of the Christian understanding of life as it limits the fullness of God. Moltmann's connection of resurrection hope to the prophetic and apocalyptic witness emphasizes this point most clearly. If life is understood as resistance to death, then we inherently also limit the life-creating power of God.

In terms of the four concluding statements about life that I offered in the previous chapter (life is dynamic flesh, radically dependent, always manifesting, and abstential desire), neither Barth nor Moltmann provide an understanding of God as living that interacts with these statements in a significant way. Instead, their theologically driven argument is most akin to the critique that Barbaras made of Jonas. Notably, Barbaras rejected Jonas'

Through this chapter and the next, I too will use the idea of kenosis in a much wider sense. The details of my use of kenosis will be addressed in the subsequent chapter and are quite similar to that of Moltmann, though I more explicitly follow Simone Weil.

30. Ibid.

position, regarding the self-repair of metabolism, as sufficient for describing life because it inscribed life to an ontology of death. While Barbaras's reasoning on this point was phenomenological, Barth and Moltmann are offering a similar rejection that is instead rooted in a theological affirmation.

Certainly, Barth and Moltmann represent one way of pursuing what it means to understand that God is living. However, for my own project I will pursue a different angle. My interest is in a robust interaction between theology and natural science that will, methodologically speaking, both allow and encourage the development of our understanding of God as living in terms of the principles of life.

God's Living as Relationality and Dependence

Understanding what it means that God is living directly in terms of principles of life has until very recently seemed a bit foolish, and this is with good reason. If life is understood *primarily* in its resistance to death, then created life is axiomatically dissimilar to the eternity of God's living. It has not been until very recently that this feature of life, resistance to death, has been unmoored as a foundational principle of what life is. The understanding of life in terms of abstential desire that I have elaborated in the previous chapters builds on this recent trend. I have strictly sought to conceive of life beyond its circumscription to an ontology of death: life's resistance of death is not a fundamental principle of living.

If this is the case, then we can more easily imagine how principles of life might directly bear on our theological imagination as we try to understand what it means that God is living. In sum, if death is not a principle of creaturely life, then we need not make distinguishing God's living and creaturely living a vital concern just because living things die, which stands in sharp contrast to God's living as eternal. In the absence of this problem, the variations in understanding what "living" entails can have direct relevance to interpreting the affirmation that God is living. Thus, distinctions in various understandings of what constitutes living being can entail distinctions in the theological affirmation "God is living." Bluntly, if resisting death is not the primary principle of life, what we instead choose to emphasize as this primary principle can have a direct bearing on understanding what it means that "God is living"; however, we might choose to emphasize different principles and this will (potentially) result in quite divergent models for understanding God's living. In the following two sections I will consider three theologians with three different understandings of what it means that God is living. In this section, I will treat Zizioulas and McFague. Both of these thinkers are constructing a model of God's living that emphasizes the second conclusion I offered about life in the previous chapter: life is radically dependent. Though their conclusions are quite different, both of these theologians offer a way of imagining how the living God is a dependent God.

The primary concern of John Zizioulas may be to generate a robust account of ecclesiology, but this ecclesiology is tied to a thorough understanding of the being of God. In his work, there is a strong resistance to a monistic vision of being; instead, he posits a relational approach to being. He roots this relational approach in the work of the bishops and pastoral theologians of the patristic period—for whom the focus on understanding God's being through the ecclesial life of the church provided a distinctive insight as compared to the apologists and catechetical theologians who focus on revelation.[31]

Life is treated by Zizioulas in the context of being and the relational quality of communion. "Being means life, and life means *communion*."[32] This formulation is immensely important. It indicates that the being of God is known through personal relationship and love; authentic life manifests the communion characteristic of this intimacy in relationship. But there is something more in Zizioulas' formulation as well. For his account, being means life, but we can also say this indicates being is life. The quality of being is always to live.[33] In this sense, life has a key place in Zizioulas' work even if it is not the object of his work per se. Insofar as communion is a primordial ontological structure, communion is also a primordial vital structure because of the tight correlation between being and life.

To better understand this complex of terms, being-life-communion, it is important to have a sense of why Zizioulas finds the patristic approach to these ideas so unique. Indispensable to that end is his development of the "person" as given in the Greco-Roman thought world. In the Greek philosophical conception there is a reliance on an ontological monism that treats the authentic being of all existent things in terms of a harmonious unity that is the cosmos. Differentiation and individuation against, or apart, from this harmonious unity is a tendency towards non-being. The meaning of person

---

31. Zizioulas, *Being as Communion*, 15–16.

32. Ibid., 16. Of course we have to acknowledge that the "life" Zizioulas has in mind is personal, human life. However, the way he is tying his conception of life to being more generally, I believe, allows us to gloss over the obvious anthropocentrism.

33. This could be akin to the way in which, as we will soon see, Tillich decouples life from a prototypically biological understanding by treating it ontologically in his multidimensional unity. Here, life is treated not only in terms of the functioning of life, but in terms of a way of living that is distinctive of being.

(πρόσωπον also meaning the mask of an actor) develops against the background of this unifying monism and out of its usage in Greek tragedy. In these tragedies, the human being strives against the fatalism that is a part of the prevailing monistic ontology; she tastes freedom in an ultimately futile bid to cast off the necessity of cosmic harmony. Still, this ultimate futility prevails and the freedom of the person to challenge the necessity entailed by the ontological monism proves insufficient. Though there is a taste of ontological distinctiveness in this radical freedom, the freedom is shown to be "circumscribed" to the harmony of the cosmos. The human way of being remains, ultimately, for the sake of and in the harmony of the cosmos; the ontological distinctiveness of the person—manifested by this free act against the cosmos—is not authentic. Personhood is not representative of true being in this monistic ontology; like a mask, the person is something added onto being.[34]

The Roman idea of *persona* extends the implications of the Greek πρόσωπον. Here too personhood is "adjunct to concrete ontological being."[35] Instead of this adjunct status arising in the face of the harmony of cosmic unity, in the Roman *persona* personhood is adjunct to the freedom of the state that defines the boundaries of personhood and equips the person with the possibility of action. Personhood delineates the social ability of the citizen and is ultimately always subject to the ontological reality imbued by the freedom of the state.

Two related conclusions need to be highlighted from Zizioulas' account of personhood and ontology in the Greco-Roman thought world. First, while the Greco-Roman thought world revealed the concept of the freedom of personhood, this freedom remains additional to a human essence that is always constituted within the wider scope of its cosmological or sociological framework. Human being is shown to be personal, but this personal quality is not ontologically constitutive.[36]

Second, Zizioulas implicitly makes a connection between ontological content and freedom. The ontological yardstick, so to speak, for Zizioulas is the presence of a freedom sufficient to affect one's essence. Think back to Zizioulas' problem with the circumscribed freedom of Greek tragedy: the problem is that the freedom of personhood never bears on the essence of human *being*. Zizioulas' measure of ontological efficacy is freedom with regard to essence.

---

34. Ibid., 32; see esp. 27–33.
35. Ibid., 34.
36. Ibid., 35.

Who is this Living God? 145

This turn to freedom as the marker of ontological content is not accidental. It is a consequence, according to Zizioulas, of the revolutionary shift introduced into Greek philosophy by patristic Trinitarian thinking: the identification of hypostasis with person. The complex history of the development of this association is not directly of interest to us (nor is it to Zizioulas). Following Zizioulas, my concern will be for (1) two shifts in the appraisal of Greek philosophical ontology that must take place in the patristic approach in order for this identification to be tenable and (2) a twofold thesis resultant from this identification.

As to the first shift in appraisal, the identification of hypostasis with person relies on questioning the ontological necessity of the cosmos. As outlined above, the constitutive element of ontology for an individual was being located within the unified harmony of the cosmos in the Greek account. However, the biblical theology of the patristic authors—with its conception of *creatio ex nihilo*—made the cosmos contingent. Whereas in the Greek philosophical approach the cosmos was an absolute constitutive ground, for the patristic writers this was simply not the case because the world itself must trace back to a deeper ontological source: God. Instead of having "being" associated to the necessity and harmony of the cosmos, it is now more closely tied to the freedom expressed in the act of creation.[37]

As to the second shift in appraisal, the identification of hypostasis with person relies on identifying the being of God with the concept of the person. Of course, this leads directly into the winding history of the early church's development of the doctrine of the Trinity, into which we need not delve. What is critical is the interpretation of the final formulation of the doctrine as "one substance, three persons." If the "one substance" is the ontological principle of God (God first as God and subsequently Trinity), then we have something very akin to Greek philosophical ontology: the person becomes subsistent to the unity of substance in which it finds itself. Instead, Zizioulas fervently affirms that this is a misunderstanding of the patristic writings on the Trinity. The ontological principle of God consists in the person of the Father, since the one substance cannot be apart from some mode of existence. Personhood constitutes substance.[38]

As these two shifts (i.e., the emphasis on freedom in ontology given the contingency of the world in *creatio ex nihilo* and the identification of the being of God with the Trinitarian person of the Father) are moved to their logical conclusion, the patristic authors develop an ontological schema alternative to that of the Greek philosophical approach. Zizioulas identifies

37. Ibid., 39.
38. Ibid., 41.

a twofold thesis that expresses the radicalness of the shift from the Greek philosophical approach to this alternative patristic ontology. First, person is not a category added to an existent being otherwise ontologically constituted. Instead, personhood itself becomes associated with (or is) the substance of being, akin to the Trinitarian formulation whereby the person of Father is ontologically constitutive. Second, if personhood is connected to the substance of being, then it is to the person that we must turn to understand that which constitutes being. In this turn to the person, instead of the harmony of the cosmos, the biblical theology of the patristic writers with its *creatio ex nihilo* provides a model for being's constitutive element: God's free act of creation.[39] As these two points are more systematically tied together, the patristic writers bring about a dramatic shift in ontological principles from cosmological harmony to personal freedom.

With personal freedom as an ontological principle, an existential question arises for humankind: how as created can we enact this absolute freedom of genuine personhood? Being created entails a necessity to our existence. The importance and implications of transcending this necessity and our existentially realizing personhood is well summarized by Zizioulas.

> The person, consequently, cannot be realized as an intramundal or fully human reality. Philosophy can arrive at the confirmation of the reality of the person, but only theology can treat of the genuine, the authentic person, because the authentic person, as absolute ontological freedom, must be "uncreated," that is unbounded by any "necessity," including its own existence. If such a person does not exist in reality, the concept of the person is a presumptuous daydream. If God does not exist, the person does not exist.[40]

For Zizioulas, the key is that the ontological principle of God's freedom lies in the Trinitarian person of the Father (*not* in a naked essence or substance). Let me explain, if the absolute freedom of God is understood in terms of God being uncreated by nature, in contrast to our being created, then there is no hope that we can become persons. On this interpretation, the ontological freedom of personhood is a consequence of a nature we can never possess. Instead, if this ontological freedom lies not in nature or substance baldly conceived but in the person of God as Father, then the ontological freedom is enacted through the very mode of the Father's personal existence: by begetting the Son and bringing forth the Spirit. These acts of begetting and bringing forth are acts of communion: they establish a loving

39. Ibid., 39.
40. Ibid., 43.

relationship. Thus, to exercise an ontological act of freedom is an act of communion or love—love and ontological freedom are the same. This gives hope to created life that we too can become persons; just as the ontological freedom of God is constituted through the personal mode of the Father's existence as loving acts, so too created being realizes personhood through loving acts.[41]

Of course, there seems to be another option that Zizioulas acknowledges: humankind might also enact the absolute freedom of the personal, control over her existence, through a radical negation—suicide and death. He notes that in existential philosophy this negative power over one's own existence leads to an ontologizing of death that is untenable to the Christian outlook. Its impossibility for the Christian outlook stems from the insight that "God constitutes the affirmation of being as *life* [emphasis mine]."[42] In a short passage, immensely important to our purposes, Zizioulas outlines what life here means.

> The life of God is eternal because it is personal, that is to say, it is realized as an expression of free communion, as love. *Life and love are identified in the person*: the person does not die only because it is love and loves; outside the communion of love the person loses its uniqueness and becomes a being like other beings, a "thing" without absolute "identity" and "name," without a face. Death for a person means ceasing to be loved, ceasing to be unique and unrepeatable, whereas *life for the person means the survival of the uniqueness of its hypostasis*, which is affirmed and maintained by love [emphases mine].[43]

Life, love, and freedom indwell to one another in Zizioulas' approach to the person. All are expressions of the ontological principle that is the person. The importance, for my purpose, is that in this text our life and God's life are akin to one another. Being is realized through the personal freedom of love that is communion—both for God and for us. Life in Zizioulas' sense points to the uniqueness and unrepeatability of the person through enacting this ontological principle. Here, to claim "God is living" and "we are living" is identical—it is ontological uniqueness realized in the love of free communion constitutive of the person.

---

41. Ibid., 44–46. Zizioulas emphasizes more strongly than I that love is not a secondary property of God's otherwise constituted substance; this view would represent a return to the ontological necessity of the Greek ontology.

42. Ibid., 48.

43. Ibid., 49.

Strangely, there is a distinct connection between the ontological freedom of Zizioulas and the quality of life as radically dependent I outlined. For Zizioulas the ontological power of freedom broke the stranglehold of necessity imbued by the power of harmony in the older Greek tradition. Affirming freedom, instead, meant authentic life was an ontological expression of uniqueness that was maintained by being a locus of love in communion to others. Zizioulas' approach to life and being institutes a dialectic that establishes a unique living self *always* in the context of its beloved—a dialectic modeled on the immanent life of the Trinity, wherein the substance of the Trinity becomes from the person of the Father. The critical feature of life, both for God's living and created life, is being this distinctive locus of loving action that brings about the subsequent relationality and harmony of the living being's world.

The dialectic involved in Zizioulas' account of God's living and human living is analogous to the earlier affirmation that life is radically dependent—especially as in the idea of modular synergistic reciprocity (i.e., where teleogens can be composed of other teleogens by degrading certain features of individuation). In modular synergistic reciprocity something of the radical autonomy of the self is given over into a more complex dynamical boundedness that generates inextricable dependency and solidifies the individuated features through its reciprocity. (The example borrowed from Deacon was of the nuclear and mitochondrial genomes in a eukaryotic cell). The ontological freedom to love, constitutive of Zizioulas' understanding of life, seems to show analogous features to this modular synergy. The continuing uniqueness of the person of the Father can only be solidified in the loss of radical autonomy that comes in begetting Christ and bringing forth the Spirit; and, the continuing uniqueness of living things is able to persist through forming relationships of inextricable dependency that preserve uniqueness through reciprocity and dependence. In both Zizioulas' approach to life as ontological freedom in love and in my claim that life is radically dependent, there is a common thread in the affirmation that a living self gives itself over to its world in specific ways making them interdependent.

If Zizioulas provides an account of dependency in God's living that emphasizes the communal relations of the immanent Trinity, the dependency of God's living in McFague's work is something very different. However, before delving into McFague's work it is important to note that feminist theology, and ecofeminist theology in particular, has made great strides in imagining what it might mean that God is living; strides that go well beyond the texts I am examining here. Still, there is a sense in which McFague's work stands as a classic in that corpus. Her image of the world as God's body and the interdependence it emphasizes has been tremendously influential. As a metaphor, it has something important to contribute to our understanding of life and the living God.

To understand the implications of McFague's claim that the world is God's body, I need to review the technical and very specific way she treats metaphorical language. In *Metaphorical Theology*, Sally McFague accounts for the process by which theologians move from first-order religious language to second-order theological language. This movement from the expressive, imagistic quality of language to the conceptual quality is complicated by two serious threats: idolatry and irrelevance. Idolatry occurs when imaginative religious language becomes reified in its theological conceptualization (literalism). Irrelevance occurs when the imagery of religious language becomes meaningless to the contemporary interpreter.

McFague uses feminist theological critique to illustrate the irrelevance that threatens religious language—particularly three points of the feminist critique. First, since "feminists generally agree that whoever names the world owns the world,"[44] these theologians claim that the thought world of western religion has been named by men and excludes women. Second, feminist theologians assert that the patriarchal character of religious language has, in western usage, become an idol; this concretizing literalism makes religious language irrelevant to women. McFague examines this point in depth through her an analysis of the model "God the Father," which some feminist theologians claim to be an idol.[45] Third, feminist theologians claim that religious language is not only about the divine but also about us. By choosing to "divinize" a particular religious image, it becomes exalted—excluded images are not so honored. The paucity of feminine images for the divine in Western religion simultaneously indicates a lowering of self-image for women in these traditions.[46]

McFague argues the threat of idolatry and irrelevance in religious/theological language today can be addressed by understanding this language in terms of metaphors and models. She sees religious language as largely metaphorical, which she contrasts to the traditional mode of viewing religious language as *symbolic*. The symbolic rests on the analogy of being; it understands religious language in terms of the profound similarity that permeates all reality creating a sacramental participation in the transcendent. McFague is not demonizing the symbolic (it is still very important as her reference to David Tracy's *Analogical Imagination* demonstrates), but

---

44. McFague, *Metaphorical Theology*, 8.
45. Ibid., 147–52.
46. Ibid., 9–10.

she believes theology today must understand religious language in terms of metaphor.[47]

Unlike symbols, metaphors operate in terms of the "is and is not" tension expressed by Paul Ricoeur. *Metaphor consists of two active concepts in interacting tension with one another.* This means that two concepts, both active in the mind, are made equivalent: an equivalence that highlights the "is and is not" metaphorical tension of their similarity and dissimilarity. This is different from a *simile*. Simile offers a comparison of two concepts, softening the dissimilarity through its use of "like" or "as."

A model is simply a dominant metaphor.[48] McFague draws heavily upon work in theology and philosophy of science to elucidate how a model functions.[49] What is critical is to understand that a model serves to gently press the metaphorical, imagistic, first-order language of religion into a conceptual schema—second-order theological language. Most often the formation of a model is facilitated through the use of a root-metaphor, a concept much akin to David Tracy's or Hans Georg Gadamer's notion of the "classic."[50] The root-metaphor provides a conceptualizing schema that gives order and meaning to subordinate metaphors in the model, thereby ordering a network of loosely connected religious metaphors into a theological tradition. The tensive, *partial* quality of any metaphor (even a root-metaphor), inculcates the need for many metaphors to stymie the threat of idolatry. Respecting this tensive quality prevents the root-metaphor from becoming hegemonic.[51]

This method informs McFague's theological models—such as the world being the body of God. In particular, I cannot overstate the importance of the root-metaphor at work in her models: relationship. Not only is this root-metaphor central to her theological construction, she also sees relationship and interdependence as key themes for a contemporary view of reality. She argues that our world today is best characterized by a sensibility that acknowledges the interdependence of all life.[52] The ecosystem provides not only a scientific vantage point on this interdependence but a poetic

---

47. Ibid., 13–14.
48. Ibid., 14–19, 32–42, and 82–86.
49. Ibid., chaps. 3 and 4; and Barbour, *Myths, Models and Paradigms*, chaps. 3 and 4.
50. See Gadamer, *Truth And Method*; and Tracy, *The Analogical Imagination*.
51. McFague, *Metaphorical Theology*, 138–40.
52. McFague, *Models of God*, 8. There is an exegetical component influencing McFague's choice of relationality as a root-metaphor: Jesus' parables, and here also understanding Jesus as a parable of God, are central to understanding the work and person of Jesus as the Christ. An in depth analysis of her exegetical work is beyond the scope of my focus. See McFague, *Metaphorical Theology*, 42–54 and 108–11.

vision of the shift in our perspective on reality. Reality is no longer best characterized by the model of a machine, but by a mutualistic or organic model. Living things themselves become the most appropriate model for interpreting all of reality.[53]

Contrasting this ecological sensibility, and the interdependency it envisions, is the nuclear. The nuclear sensibility indicates the vast power human beings possess through nuclear power—especially weaponry. It makes us keenly aware of the power we possess to destroy not only ourselves, but nearly all forms of existent life on the planet. For McFague, what is critical is "the acceptance of this knowledge and of the responsibilities that come with it."[54]

The ecological and the nuclear (as the subtitle for *Models of God* suggests) are twin prongs for a sensible view of reality today. These terms, ecological and nuclear, are really equivalent to life and death. Not life and death baldly conceived, but life as wondrously interdependent complexity and death as our vast human power to wipe out this creative order.[55] The ecological and the nuclear emphasize our very human power to foster the prevalence of life or death on this planet. Of course, McFague has shifted her language with regard to the "nuclear." Instead of the immediate threat in the nuclear, she has more recently emphasized ecological deterioration as a subtle power that human beings hold to wipe out life on this planet.[56] Whether emphasizing the nuclear or ecological deterioration, her primary concern is for our power to foster life or death on the planet. McFague's models of God need to be relevant to this human power to make life or

53. McFague, *Models of God*, 10. I am glossing over the argument that McFague makes in the interest of relevance to the wider scope of this work. McFague sees a key shift in scientific thinking towards the interdependency of systems thinking, gradually overturning the standard reliance on mechanical models. Thereby, she is highlighting themes that often are emphasized in emergence approaches (i.e., novelty, chance, and interdependence). The organismic model she proposes reflects this distinctive change in how we conceptualize the world across various fields.

54. Ibid., 15.

55. That life and death are not baldly conceived, as I have put it, is an indispensable point. The nuclear is a power of human beings. This is important to McFague because it relates her account to political and social oppression, bolstering her claim that ecological theology is liberation theology in its concern for the use of dominating power. Ibid., 16.

56. McFague, *The Body of God*, 2. McFague clearly lines out three differences between the nuclear and ecological deterioration: speed and subtlety of the destruction; effects along the lines of class, race, and gender; and the complexity of the problem in the face of our capacity to repair it. These themes are immensely important, but do not radically change the emphasis she is making about the human power to wipe life out from the planet.

death prevail. "What understanding of the relationship between God and the world can address *that* situation?"[57]

For McFague this relation is addressed by Jesus' appearance stories in the Gospels. The meaning of these accounts does not lie in assuring our own bodily resurrection: Christ's resurrection and subsequent appearances are not, as with Paul's interpretation,[58] the first instance of the general resurrection. Instead, "[t]he resurrection is a way of speaking about an awareness that the presence of God in Jesus is a permanent presence in our present."[59] If this is the theological meaning of the resurrection, McFague's contention is that we need new models and metaphors to emphasize God's palpable presence to us in all times and places. In deference to this need, she proposes the world is the body of God.[60]

This model is powerful because of its flexibility and its prohibition of spiritualizing. In terms of flexibility, the diversity of ways the body can be used metaphorically is almost endless. We can speak of our own bodies, the bodies of atoms, our ecological body, or the universe as a body. An understanding of body can potentially include all forms of matter in the universe.[61] Given this is the case, to imagine God in terms of the body is an apt metaphor for emphasizing the palpable presence of God in all times and places. In terms of prohibiting spiritualizing, the primary means by which we can understand the model of the body of God is in terms of the bodies of those closest to us. Imagining the world as God's body means that we cannot spiritualize away pain, suffering, and hunger of other human bodies or the ecological degradation done by us to the ecological body. If the world is the body of God, then salvation must entail the well-being and care for that body.[62]

I want to emphasize two points about McFague's model of the body of God that are most relevant to my investigation of life. First, the centrality of this metaphor for McFague is tied to how the body uniquely represents the matters of life and death that condition our encounter with reality.[63] She expresses the poetic sensibility of this insight very well. "Everything else that we cherish depends upon it [the body]—appreciating the first leaves on

---

57. McFague, *Models of God*, 29.
58. 1 Cor 15:12–34.
59. McFague, *Models of God*, 59.
60. Ibid., 60–61.
61. McFague, *The Body of God*, 17.
62. Ibid., 18.
63. In fact, McFague claims that the positive characteristics of this model are epitomized by the phrase "a matter of life and death" (ibid., 23).

a tree in spring, a child's smile, or a favorite piece of music: the body is the bottom line. The shock of the death of a loved one is precisely the blankness, the void, that replaces that person's rich complexity and special uniqueness, which are housed in the body."[64]

Second, McFague's body of God advocates an immanental transcendence. While the immanent implications of imagining the world as God's body are self-evident (i.e., it necessarily entails a form of panentheism), the transcendence of God that is so important to our classic conception can seem lost. However, McFague emphasizes that the transcendence of God is still operative as the enlivening spirit of the universe that is the source and aim of all creation. "As we are inspirited bodies—living, loving, thinking bodies—so, imagining God in our image (for how else *can* we model God?), we speak of her as *the* inspirited body of the entire universe, the animating, living spirit that produces, guides, and saves all that is."[65]

I would suggest that through this emphasis McFague, like Zizioulas, forces us to be critically aware of the implications of what I identified as the second key feature of life—radical dependency. McFague's model of the body of God, in a theological register, metaphorically conveys a complexity analogous to the dynamical boundedness of modular synergistic reciprocity. To review, in modular synergistic reciprocity two teleogens remain largely independent for most functions but are reciprocally degraded so that one cannot persist without the other. I think it would be fair to say that this reciprocity that is a critical feature of the development and increasing complexity of life is akin to the way McFague is relating created life (especially human created life) to God as living. By having a nuclear and an ecological sensibility, we realize the responsibility we have for sustaining the world. If we can understand the world to be God's body, it seems appropriate to claim that the consequence of McFague's view is that there is a real sense in which a living God cannot persist without a realization concerning our ecological responsibilities. God's living, on this approach, is a life dynamically bound to the well-being of creation.

What I find in Zizioulas and McFague are two theological approaches to understanding God as living that highlight the relationality and dependence of life. What is quite different between the two, however, is the relation itself. For Zizioulas, the relationship at stake is one of communal love between the Trinitarian person God the Father and the Son and Spirit. The loving acts of begetting and proceeding are formative of God's being, inculcating a dependence of God's being on these immanent Trinitarian

---

64. Ibid.
65. Ibid., 20.

relations. For McFague, by contrast, the relationship is established between God and the world. The world serves as the body of God forming interdependence between God and the created order.

God's Living as Dynamic Flesh

Zizioulas and McFague each model one way to think about God's living in terms of the radical dependency of life, but neither theologian offers a sustained consideration of what such dependency indicates for the classic sense of selfhood in relation to the world. My worry over this is similar to the worry Barbaras expresses over Merleau-Ponty's notion of the lived-body in chapter 3. There Barbaras thought the lived-body, with a few notable exceptions, remained inscribed to the intellectualist and empiricist language it tried to overcome. The lived-body defined itself in the negative (i.e., the lived-body understood as neither empiricist nor intellectualist) without offering a positive characterization. By contrast, the idea of the flesh represented a first effort beyond the lived-body to give this positive characterization of the relation of self and world. In both Zizioulas and McFague, there is a fantastic sense of the role relationship and dependency might play in understanding God's living, but this is given in classic self-other language; a language put in question by my first and fourth affirmation about life—life is dynamic flesh and abstential desire.[66] How might the dependency and relationality of God's living stretch this classic ontological language to a breaking point? Or how might the dependency and relationality of God's living relate to life as dynamic flesh?

To understand how life as dynamic flesh might have implications for God's living, I will turn to the work of Tillich. In looking at his *Systematic Theology*, we find that his treatment of life comes largely in two parts from the first and the third volume. In the first, Tillich treats God as living; in the third Tillich treats the multidimensional quality of life across the created order. I will intersperse insights from both of these critical sections of Tillich's work to get a more robust sense of what it means for Tillich that God is living.[67]

---

66. This may be an overstatement against Zizioulas's position. He does describe in great detail how communion and love are the primordial ground from which being arises. The problem that remains for my work, even in the context of a more charitable reading, is the anthropocentric character of the analysis. God's living is akin to *human* living in these communal acts, but what about the life at work in the rest of creation? My aim is to relate God's living to life in a wider sense than what Zizioulas would intend.

67. Pieces of this section come from two previous articles: Pryor, "Tillichian Teleodynamics"; and Pryor, "God as Still Living," 14–20.

Tillich seeks an ontological conception of life that he defines as the "actuality of being." It is a concept derived from the phenomenological characterization of those existing things that we deem living in a quotidian sense. What he discovers is that living things are those which emphatically include their own negation: living beings are always dying beings.[68]

By Tillich's account his approach has two distinct advantages. First, "[t]he ontological concept of life liberates the word 'life' from its bondage to the organic realm and elevates it to the level of a basic term that can be used within the theological system only if interpreted in existential terms."[69] Tillich's definition of life makes it a "structural condition" for all being. Second, this ontological definition of life fits very well within the dialectical tension of the essential and existential characteristic of his larger systematic project as a whole. As actualized being life incurs the conditions of estrangement and represents a mixture of essential and existential elements in all its manifestations.

His concept of the multidimensional unity of life is intended to represent the essential quality of life; it is an idealistic precursor to his existential analysis of the ambiguities of actualization. When describing these essential dimensions of life, Tillich intentionally avoids the hierarchical concept of level.[70] In this way, his approach remains distinct from a minimalist interpretation of Aquinas' great chain of being.[71] Instead of levels, Tillich proposes the suite of technical terms dimension, realm, and grade. The problem caused by the mutual independence of levels, namely how to characterize the relationship *between* levels of life, disappears when our vision of the actuality of being is characterized in terms of dimensions. Dimensions (unlike levels) can cross one another without being in conflict; dimensionality is introduced as a metaphor to emphasize the continuity of all life. If conflict exists between dimensions, it is a result of the ambiguity of existential actualization that is inherent to all life processes. Still in need of some taxonomic means of distinguishing the variety of living things, Tillich introduces the term "realm." He identifies fives realms: inorganic, organic, psychological, spirited, and historical. It is used in a social sense (as in a kingdom) that preserves the discontinuity and uniqueness that the

---

68. Tillich, *Systematic Theology*, 3:11. Henceforth references to Tillich's *Systematic Theology* will be made as *ST*.

69. Ibid., 3:12.

70. Ibid., 3:12–15.

71. Tillich makes a more nuanced case against the conception of levels than I briefly mention here. At the heart of his critique is his concern for the inadequacy of expressing the relationship between levels when this metaphor is used to characterize distinctions in life. Ibid., 3:14.

metaphor of levels previously indicated. It represents those strata of living things under the rule of a particular determining dimension. However, in any realm, all of the dimensions are present, even if they are only potential. For instance, in the organic realm one of the determining dimensions is the presence of self-preserving forms; living things in this realm are under the rule of the actualization of this dimension. Simultaneously though, a determining dimension of the psychological realm (self-awareness) is already present as a latent potentiality.

There is interplay between the terms dimension and realm. This interplay leads us directly to Tillich's third concept: gradation. There exists a gradation amidst living things so that those dimensions which characterize higher realms rely upon the actualized dimensions of lower realms (a new dimension does not replace a previous dimension). Further, "in the realm which is characterized by the already actualized dimension particular constellations occur which make possible the actualization of a new dimension."[72] To use the organic and the psychological as examples again, the actualization of the psychological relies on the complexification of self-preserving forms in the organic realm. This relationship between dimensions makes a classificatory schema of realms different from levels (there is no ontological break between realms as with levels) and allows for an ontological gradation of value amidst living things: where the criterion of such a value judgment is the maximization of actualized dimensions.[73]

Tillich is careful, however, to note that the five realms he identifies are not final: as the phenomenological analysis of living things yields new dimensional categorizations, this set of realms may expand or contract. New dimensions are identified by their modification of the finite structures of being and thinking that make up the fourth-fold of Tillich's ontology.[74] Each of these dimensional distinctions represents a modification (phenomenologically) of time, space, causality, or substance that characterizes the dimensional predominance for that realm.

72. Ibid., 3:16.

73. Ibid., 3:15–17; and Roesler, "Reconstructing Paul Tillich's Anthropology," 70–71.

74. A full account of Tillich's fourfold ontology is beyond the scope of this project. Let it suffice to remind readers that Tillich develops a four-fold ontology that outlines many of the themes treated in the *Systematic Theology*. These folds are (1) a fundamental distinction between self and world; (2) the three polar tensions characteristic of the self/world distinction—freedom/destiny, dynamics/form, and individuation/participation; (3) a distinction between essence and existence that allows for the imbalance of the polar tensions we experience in our existential reality; and (4) the categories that make up our experience of existential reality—time, space, causality, and substance. See Tillich, *ST*, 1:161–81.

The details of each of these realms are not critical for this project; however, I will highlight features of the inorganic and the organic realms, which are most relevant. The characterizing dimension of the inorganic realm is fundamentally necessary for the actualization of every other dimension: it is the substantial actualization of a living thing that makes possible "spatial-temporal-causal relations."[75] The inorganic signifies a fundamental phenomenon by which there is something rather than nothing, and its actualization is of fundamental importance to Tillich's rejection of process philosophy.[76] As such, it is the dimension symbolizing God's originating creativity.

The organic realm might also be called the vegetative, and it is characterized by "self-related, self-preserving, self-increasing, and self-continuing *Gestalten* ('living wholes')."[77] The emphasis on the development of self in these dimensions is clear. It seems to echo the formulation that Tillich rehearses in the first facet of his four-fold ontology—where a self is formed in contrast to its world when "the reaction to a stimulus is dependent on a structural whole."[78] We might summarize by suggesting that the dimensions of the organic realm perpetuate an identifiable self composed of constellations of inorganic substance, which through the use of spatial-temporal-causal relations interacts with its environment.

As we begin to examine what it might mean that God is living, it is important that much like his account of "life" Tillich begins his discussion of the meaning of God through a phenomenological description: God is humankind's ultimate concern—the answering correlate to the implied question of our finite being. There is, though, a tension between what is "ultimate" and what is "of concern" that Tillich identifies; it is "an inescapable inner tension in the idea of God."[79] Our ability to be concerned is in direct correlation to the concreteness of the object of our concern. For a universal concept to be of concern at all requires that it be represented through finite, concrete experiences. In contrast, for something to be truly ultimate it must transcend everything finite and concrete. As this transcendence occurs, though, that which is ultimate becomes increasingly abstract. Thus the inner tension of our being ultimately concerned: if God is what concerns humankind ultimately, then as God is identified with and through finite, concrete experiences our concern is increasingly engaged, diminishing our appreciation of the ultimacy of God; vice versa, as the finite is transcended

75. Ibid., 3:19.
76. Ibid., 1:197; and *ST*, 3:25–26 and 297–99.
77. Ibid., 3:20.
78. Ibid., 1:169.
79. Ibid., 1:211.

in realizing the ultimacy of God, the concreteness that fosters our concern is diminished. By the logic of Tillich's account, this is the basic problem of the doctrine of God and emphasizes the existential quality of humankind's relation to God's ultimacy.

I suggest that Tillich's description of "God as living" points to a unique position with regard to this tension between ultimacy and concern. To call God living is to take the first step in overcoming the unapproachable ultimacy of God as being-itself. This develops naturally out of Tillich's own affirmations. First, Tillich asserts that God is the ground of the very structure of being. However, to approach God in terms of our concrete concern, we cannot baldly encounter God as being-itself or the structure of being; we must encounter God through the structures for which God is the ground. To call God living affirms that our encounter with God through concrete concern is reflective of the reality of God.[80] Thus, I would suggest by Tillich's account that to affirm God is living (i.e., that God is symbolically manifest in the ontological elements) is a symbol that posits a real ground for further symbolization. *A living God is the first move towards concreteness beyond the abyss of ultimacy.* Without a "living" God there would be no sense of a creative ground that is simultaneous to abysmal transcendence. This can become clearer by investigating more thoroughly what Tillich means by God as living.

For Tillich, to understand this symbol is to understand life as the actualization of the polar elements of his ontology: life is the process in which potential being becomes actual being and can be symbolically applied to God as the ground of life. This ties in tightly with the characterization of the multidimensional unity of life outlined above. In the multidimensional unity of life it is the phenomenological modifications of the fourth-fold of Tillich's ontology (space, time, causality, and substance) that characterize increasing complexity across various realms, while the "actuality of being" characteristic of life generally is demarcated in terms of the second-fold of his ontology (the polar elements freedom/destiny, dynamics/form, and individuation/participation). While the polar elements stand in constant tension in their existential reality, God's ultimacy as the ground of being unites these polarities. Where *God* is conceived in individuation, dynamism, and freedom, these subjective elements are seen in symbolic unity with their objective counterparts, participation, form, and destiny.[81]

There is an important caveat to be made in this characterization. For Tillich the polar elements apply to symbolizing God as living because they

80. Ibid., 1:238.
81. Ibid., 1:241–44.

point to *qualities* of being not *kinds* of being.[82] The fundamental self-world structure of Tillich's fourfold ontology (the first-fold) represents kinds of being. They are rooted in the divine life, but to make these kinds of being symbolic for God risks positing God as *a being and not being-itself*. The divine life is a unity of subject and object that cannot be adequately thematized by a symbolic instantiation of this structure. The polar elements, as qualities of being can be symbolically applied to God without risking making God into a being instead of being-itself.

Moreover, Tillich makes a distinction between the "proper" and the "symbolic" sense of the elements as qualities of being. The proper sense always refers to the existential situation between humankind and God that gives rise to the polar elements themselves. Vast stretches of theological error arise from directly constructing the proper sense of the polar elements in an account of the doctrine of God. Since God is not subject to the distinction in kinds of being (self and world) that structure the elements in Tillich's construction of ontology, the "proper" use of the elements applied to God will inevitably result in subjecting God to the distinction in kinds of being that God as being-itself envelops. The symbolic sense of the elements dissociates from their "proper" thematization in terms of the self-world structure; this dissociation is critical to allowing the tension of the polar quality of the elements to be overcome.[83]

Before delving into the implications of the unity of the ontological elements, we should pause and take stock of the movements in Tillich's theology thus far elaborated. For Tillich, God's living is akin to our living in that both reference the term life in its ontological sense as the actuality of being. This actualization is characterized in terms of the polar elements that indicate fundamental qualities of being in Tillich's ontology. The finitude of our living (that living being is always dying being) is contrasted to the eternity of the divine life. Our actualization of the polar elements, our living, always takes place within the tension-laden, "proper" sense dictated by the kinds of being that are self and world—our living is existential life; God's actualization of the polar elements, God's living, always takes place within the unified, "symbolic" sense dictated by being *beyond* the kinds of being that are self and world as the ground of being—God's living is essential life.

Now, Tillich calls the unity of the polar elements spirit. This spirit is contrasted with "Spirit," such that "Spirit is the symbolic application of spirit

---

82. Ibid., 1:244.

83. As an instance of this see the description Tillich offers of the doctrine of God as becoming. Ibid., 1:247.

to the divine life."[84] Life as spirit embraces a unity of the polar elements where neither is absorbed by its correlate; this spirit is the *telos* or fulfillment towards which life is driven. To say then that "God is Spirit means that life as spirit is the inclusive symbol for the divine life."[85]

To assert that the life of God is life as spirit means that the living God is always a unity of the power and meaning, divine depth and *logos*, that are related elements of the human intuition of the divine. Power and meaning as the actuality of God deepen the sensibility already expressed by "ultimacy" and "concern" in the phenomenological account of God. Power points to the ultimate basis of God as God—the intensity of the ground of being that without structure and meaning is an overwhelming chaos, even demonic; meaning points to the possibility of God being our concern—the concrete symbolization that makes access to God tenable. The Spirit is the actualization of these two principles. This should come as no surprise since life in the spirit involves overcoming the polar tension between the ontological elements through their mutual instantiation; divine life in the Spirit involves an analogous actualization of power and meaning—two terms that seem to stand as ultimate expressions of the polar elements.

God as living expresses the perfection of the qualities of our own living being. Instead of the polar elements of this quality being in tension, they are realized in dynamic fulfillment of one another. In order that this Living God is not a living being among other living beings, however, God is conceived as the ground of life. Not subject to the distinctions in kinds of being (self and world) governing the proper sense of the ontological elements, the symbolic sense of these elements finds their expression in an essentialized form beyond creaturely vicissitudes.

To conclude I will recap what we have found throughout this chapter before focusing on the potential importance of Tillich's contribution. With Barth and Moltmann, I found life cannot be sufficiently understood if it is circumscribed by an ontology of death. Theologically speaking, the problem with such circumscribing is that it limits the life-creating power of God and inadvertently makes the living God subject to the ultimate power of death. Moltmann's work in particular makes very clear that a theological vision that takes seriously resurrection hope has a vested interest in a natural scientific approach that can articulate principles of life that do not rely on an

---

84. Ibid., 1:249.

85. Ibid., 1:250. It is in terms of the ontological unity indicated by "spirit" and "life" as applied to God via the symbolic sense of the elements that Tillich posits a preparation for his own understanding of the doctrine of the Trinity. The Christian doctrine of the Trinity must proceed from Christological dogma; however, the Trinitarian principles can be addressed as "moments within the process of the divine life" (ibid.).

understanding of life as only resistance to death. A theology filled with resurrection hope needs a conception of life that can be articulated positively: an account where "life is," instead of an account of life as "not death."

For Zizioulas we asserted there was a connection between how he develops a unique sense of self and the radical interdependency of self and world at work in my account of life. For both God and life generally understood there is an interdependency of self and other. The uniqueness of the person of the Father relies on the loss of radical autonomy that comes with begetting Christ and bringing forth the Spirit; the continuing uniqueness of living things is able to persist through forming relationships of inextricable dependency that, though counterintuitive, preserve uniqueness through reciprocity and dependence.

In McFague as well we found a connection between her model of the world as God's body, human ecological responsibility, and the radical dependency of life that is a part of the increasing complexity of dynamical boundedness. McFague's approach implicates an understanding of God as living that is dynamically bound to the well-being of creation. The world as God's body—wherein the body serves as a marker of life and vitality—makes God's living interdependent with created life. Both McFague and Zizioulas provide models of understanding God's living that correlate to the affirmation that life is radically dependent, but the object of relationship or dependency is quite different: for Zizioulas it is the dynamics of the immanent Trinity and for McFague it is between the divine and creation.

Finally, Tillich's work can be made akin to the conclusion that life is dynamic flesh. His characterization of God's living as being-itself (forming the ground of life and actualizing being) is quite similar to the phenomenological account of life and its ontological meaning that I have developed previously: living being is phenomenologically understood as moving being and ontologically understood as desire (or flesh) that actualizes the senses of self and world fundamental to our experience of living. Symbolically, to understand God as living in Tillich's terms is quite similar to affirming that God is the ontological meaning we have been calling desire or flesh.

There are two aspects of this correlation that are important to emphasize and press Tillich's thought in constructive directions. First, to call God the ground of life is to treat God as the expansive horizon of living things that is enriched by the diversity of life and its actualization. God is a ground whose ultimacy and power is revealed by and explored through the variety of ways that life, as dynamic flesh, explores the contours of its world widening the possible meaning and concrete conceptualizations of concern. God as living, as the ground of life, grows in conjunction with the living movement of creation.

Second, Tillich is explicit about the important correlation between living and being. To understand God as living is to understand God as the ground of being; to understand God as living is *not* to understand God as *a* being or *a* living being. Instead, to call God living is to refer to God as the ground from which *a* being can arise. This emphasis that God's living is *beyond* being or is being-itself and not just *a* being is immensely important to keep in mind in theologically explicating the religious symbol God is living. While Tillich may or may not have understood his own work this way, I think his affirmation of God as living opens the door to understanding God as beyond being—as the primordial flesh from which kinds of being arise.

Finally, it is important to note that none of the thinkers addressed have connected themes of *hiddenness* or *absence* to the affirmation that God is living. Yet, it was the fourth conclusion in chapter 4 (life is abstential desire) that I claimed could encapsulate all of the rest. In all of the cases considered here, to affirm God is living is to make an affirmation about the presence of God's being: God's living is understood in each case to be some-thing. I would suggest that perhaps a part of the reason for this is the persistent tendency to circumscribe life to an ontology of death: to understand life as not dying or resistance to non-being. Even when theologians acknowledge that we are not bound to this approach, it casts a long shadow: death as an ultimate nothingness stands in contrast to life and makes us think life must be some-thing. If we are to continue to employ the religious affirmation that God is living, I believe we must begin to rethink this symbol in terms of the critical themes that emergence theory and phenomenology provide: absence and desire. If we can envision God's living in terms of absence and desire, then perhaps God's living is also like our own: a no-thing rather than a some-thing.

6

Where is This Living God?

Two themes that appeared in the philosophical and scientific analysis of life remained unaddressed by the treatment of theological themes traditionally related to the symbol of the living God in the previous chapter: absence and desire. First, I will address desire. Perhaps one of the most challenging aspects of treating desire is to overcome its traditional location in theological discourse as a uniquely human feature. Desire, especially as *eros*, is correlated to the theological analysis of love as it relates to human beings or the divine. However, I have been treating desire in a primordial form as a feature of life and living things: not just as in the human being or even in conscious animals—a feature in all life. So there is a challenge to be overcome in theologically thinking about desire as I am suggesting: desire, theologically speaking, traditionally relates to the religious affirmation "God is love" not the "living God."

Second, I will address absence. In all of the theological accounts above, life and living being remained, at least implicitly, conceived in opposition to death and nonbeing. The positive, constitutive place of absence as a critical facet of life was not developed. Certainly resources exist to deal with absence in the Christian tradition. There is a strong line of mystical and apophatic theology that takes the absence of God very seriously. In deconstructionist philosophy as well, there has been a renewed interest in understanding the absence of God. However, the theme of absence has not found much cross over with the theme of life in the theological imagination.

Both desire and absence are themes with a rich theological tradition, but a tradition not often paired with theological discourse about life. It is weaving these two themes together, as sieved through their critical place in living things, which is the task at hand. While the insights of many different theological and philosophical thinkers could be used to undertake this constructive project, I will make the most direct use of Jan-Olav Henriksen on desire and Simone Weil on absence.

Henriksen provides an understanding of desire that takes it far beyond its often stymied, sexualized interpretation. There are many recent writings in systematic theology that have also deftly avoided this tendency,[1] but Henriksen provides us with critical insights through his engagement with themes from postmodern discourse on desire. While Henriksen writes about desire from its particularly human facets, especially as related to Christology, his work provides critical theological insights about desire that can be of use to my constructive effort. Consider his basic account of desire: "[d]esire is what connects us to the world. Desire is shaping our orientations, giving us directions, suggesting aims to strive for. Our contemplation, consideration, and plans for action would mean nothing without desire."[2] His account, at least in its major themes, is akin to the account of desire that we have rehearsed in terms of life instead of human being. In both cases desire viscerally shapes the connection between self and world.

But why Weil? She is a nearly impossible thinker to engage in a strictly theological vein. Her writings span from political philosophy to mysticism, and they imbue such feverish intensity that they can be disorienting to read. Moreover, her theological tendencies often promote a brash heterodoxy. So why work closely with Weil when there are other more contemporary thinkers or less heterodox thinkers who could facilitate weaving together the themes of life, God as living, and absence?

As will become clear, Weil provides a particularly nuanced and multifaceted understanding of the absence of God. It touches on the ideas of God's relation to creation, our imitation of God's creative act, the role of absence in understanding the supernatural, and a distinctive means of giving an account of reality in terms of *metaxu*. These themes make Weil's work into an indispensable tool kit for constructive theological thinking about absence, especially as it regards life, in a post-metaphysical way.

Before delving into the content of this chapter, it behooves us to mention what I mean by post-metaphysical. I follow directly on Henriksen's clear description of the idea.

> The angle I am struggling to develop is thus post-metaphysical in the sense that it does not start with something before and beyond history. Rather, it starts with a history which, when we

---

1. For instance, see Farley, *The Wounding and Healing of Desire*; O'Murchu, *The Transformation of Desire*; and Brock, *Journeys by Heart*.

2. Henriksen, *Desire, Gift, and Recognition*, 28.

speak about it in certain ways, points to something beyond what happens, but still is present in what happens. This "something" is only accessible by a specific use of God-language, which both represents and opens up to a reality implied in what is given.³

The understandings of desire and absence that I am pursuing are post-metaphysical in this sense—they point beyond historical happenings but are still present in historical happenings.

With that in mind, I first want to consider Henriksen's account of desire and *eros*. While much of his work focuses on theological anthropology and Christology, he provides a mooring for understanding desire that places it within a Tillich-inspired approach to theological thinking.⁴ This will be followed by a brief recounting of critical themes to keep in mind when interpreting Weil's work with regard to Christianity, followed immediately by an analysis of her account of decreation. This concept is crucial to understanding the place Weil gives to absence in our lives as creatures, and I read it in relation to her account of the kenotic action of God in creation. Once these themes have been explicated, the place of absence or nothingness in them will be considered in terms of Weil's categories of the supernatural and *metaxu*. Developing the resources from these thinkers, I conclude that to affirm that God is living is to affirm an abstential correlation of God and life.

Henriksen and Desire

Henriksen's work is deeply concerned with engaging how phenomenological approaches to desire can contribute to emerging discourses about desire in theology. In this regard, his work weaving together Tillich's existential theology and Marion's phenomenological consideration of the erotic and desire is critical: it gives a frame of reference for theologically integrating the copious phenomenological literature directed to this topic.⁵ However, for my purposes it is important to highlight how anthropocentric such an approach is. Henriksen develops desire in terms of *eros* and its erotic features; however, these features are largely, if not entirely, construed in terms of human uniqueness and human culture.⁶ My goal has been to examine

3. Ibid., 25.
4. See especially Henriksen, "Eros And/as Desire," 220–42.
5. Ibid., 222.
6. Marion, one of Henriksen's primary philosophical dialogue partners, makes the case for love as a principle of human uniqueness quite explicitly: "Man [sic] loves—which is what distinguishes him from all other finite beings, if not the angels. Man is defined neither by the *logos,* nor by the being within him, but by this fact that he loves

where desire reaches into the very principles of life itself, not just human life. Noting that difference in what is to come, Henriksen's work remains an invaluable resource. For the time being, I will follow the anthropological character of his work and only begin culling out what features of it may be most useful for my purposes later.

Henriksen strongly emphasizes that desire does not result from *lack* or *need*. This makes his account amenable to what I have affirmed previously regarding desire through Barbaras. In Barbaras, need corresponds to the fulfillment of something lacking that provides direct and immediate satiation; however, desire is different from this relation of lack and need. The fulfillment of desire does not lead to satisfaction because the object of desire is only partially engaged; as a particular desire is fulfilled it is dispossessed from itself and inflamed to subsequent desire. Henriksen develops the distance between desire and need/lacking by linking the idea of desire to Marion's understanding of the erotic.

Marion introduces the idea of an "erotic reduction" as an alternative to the more typical epistemic reduction (i.e., a reduction to distinctive repeatable features) or ontological reduction (i.e., a reduction to that which has the status of being in order to work back to being itself). To be, on Marion's account, is not the vain being obtained through the ontological or epistemic reductions as they are performed in my own solitude; rather, *to be is to be loved*.[7] This shift from "to be" to "beloved" is indicative of a change in the way we ask a fundamental question about ourselves; instead of beginning with the question "Am I?" we now begin with "Does anybody love me?" But why make this shift? The question "Am I?" seems more fundamental than the question "Am I loved?" Marion argues that an assurance that I am loved provides something much more valuable than the pure certainty of an epistemic or ontological reduction. While certainty can be generated by me, as an *ego*,[8] the assurance of the erotic reduction is the assurance of the meaning of my being—an assurance of love, without which the question of my being, as it is baldly conceived, is mute.[9]

(or hates), whether he wants to or not" (*The Erotic Phenomenon*, 7).

7. Ibid., 24–25; See also Henriksen, "Eros And/as Desire," 223–24.

8. Imagine the Cartesian *ego cogito* here. While this phrase can perhaps produce some sense of the certainty of my being, it cannot help me answer "What is the use?" This is the question that most concerns Marion, because if the human being is unable to answer this question, a question that assures our being is not meaningless, then establishing the certainty of our being is inconsequential.

9. Marion calls pitting this question of "Am I?" against "Am I loved?" a sophism. The inclination to make the question "Am I loved?" subsidiary to the bald conception of being presupposes what it intends to conclude. To claim that my being loved is an addition to my more primordial ontological character is to assume from the outset

This assurance of love has to come from beyond me: it must come from a world or some "elsewhere."[10] Thus, to have my being reduced to being loved is to have my being given to me from beyond myself—to be always by a primordial relationality. By making this love primordial to my being, to make the assurance of my being loved more basic than the self-certainty of my being, Marion makes the openness to alterity of erotic desire a fundamental feature of our selfhood. In sum, I am as I am loved; thus, my being is dependent on more than myself insofar as my being loved must come from elsewhere.

But this question—does anybody love me?—is always at risk of being made merely reciprocal. It is constantly at risk of being reduced to an economy of love. In an economy of love, the love only serves to make a deal (it is bartered) in the assurance of my being (i.e., I love you so that I am loved and can thereby have control over my being). Recognizing the economy of love, we also recognize we are always at risk—at risk by rooting the very fundamental structure of our being in the question "Does anybody love me?"—of being subject to this economy and entering into love only partially. That is to say we are at risk of loving only in the face of fear; a fear stemming from the vanity of trying to establish or control the self-certainty of our being.[11]

To garner the full power of love's assurance, because the economy of love generates uncertainty regarding the motive of love, we must enter the question generated by the erotic reduction in a different way. Rather than beginning from "Does anybody love me?" we must instead ask "Can I love first?" If we begin from this later question we ameliorate the potential limitation of an economy of love without losing the alterity of the erotic reduction. Beginning from our being as a lover opens up the full depth of the erotic reduction and the assurance of love without making recourse to self-establishment through the self-certainty of being.[12]

We could blandly affirm that Marion is simply phenomenologically echoing a general religious sentiment that our being is not our own and all of creation is formed by the love of God. However, Henriksen helpfully links this account of love to Tillich's development of love as an ontological concept. This gives us a way to locate Marion's insights within a contemporary strand of theological thinking, and it allows us to see a potential value to

---

that my mode of being can simply be reduced to the same mode of being as objects in the world—it does not demonstrate this point but merely assumes it. See *The Erotic Phenomenon*, 21.

10. Ibid., 21–23.
11. Ibid., 68.
12. Ibid., 70–76.

his work that is more than a mere philosophical veneer to a religious claim. In part, Henriksen does this by analyzing a very important passage from Tillich's *Systematic Theology*.

> God is love. And, since God is being-itself, one must say that being-itself is love. This, however, is understandable only because the actuality of being is life. The process of the divine life has the character of love. According to the ontological polarity of individualization and participation, every life-process unites a trend toward separation with a trend toward reunion. The unbroken unity of these two trends is the ontological nature of love.[13]

There are three key features to this quote. First, Tillich affirms an equation between love and being-itself. His affirmation of God as being-itself is simultaneously a reference to God as the ground of being; a ground which can be interpreted, I would suggest, as that which is beyond being altogether and gives rise to it. This is what I emphasized in the conclusion of the previous chapter by analyzing Tillich's treatment of God as living. There I found that for Tillich, the quality of God's living is best described in terms of the symbolic sense of the polar elements that make up the second fold of his ontology. This symbolic sense of the polar elements as applied to God pointed to God's living as beyond subject to a distinction in kinds of being (i.e., between self and world). As such, to call God living was to make a statement about the ground of life or the ground of being. The ground of being or being-itself is not merely some facet of being that provides a firm foundation from which theology takes flight, but that which is entirely prior to the split between being and non-being that roots the question of "Am I?" It is what we might classically call *tremendum*—both creative and abysmal.[14] What Henriksen emphasizes is that as Tillich draws a firm connection between being-itself and love, his work implicitly formulates an ontology beyond ontology, if it is read with an eye towards a postmodern sensibility. What this means is that Tillich's affirmation of God as living or as being-itself represents a most fundamental reality of which the content is love: love is the *tremendum* from which being arises.[15]

---

13. Tillich, ST, 1:279; See also Tillich, *Love, Power, and Justice*, 24–34; Tillich, "That They May Have Life," 3–8; and Henriksen, "Eros And/as Desire," 224. Henriksen does not actually quote this passage, but is certainly dealing with it in some detail.

14. See Tillich, ST, 1:236–37.

15. It is somewhat ambiguous as to whether or not Tillich perceives himself as doing this. Repeatedly, we find Tillich refer to this line of argument that Henriksen is using as his way of stressing that love is a subsequent, not primordial, ontological concept. As a counter, Henriksen is suggesting that this deference to a classic ontologizing of love is a product of being a modern thinker that emphasizes the overarching role of love

This leads directly to the second feature: Tillich emphasizes that this quality of being-itself as love is intimately related to the actuality of life. I think we must assume that Tillich is referencing his earlier affirmation that life "is the process in which potential being becomes actual being."[16] Love is the "moving power" of life's procession: it drives the living thing beyond itself towards reunion with everything around it from which it has been separated.[17] This drive towards reunion is the actualization critical to life.

Tillich assures his readers that this conception of life can only symbolically be applied to God (as we have discussed with more detail above in chapter 5), because there is no separation of possibility and actuality in God. What is critical here is that this process of actualizing being, what Tillich calls life, manifests the character of love. Theologically speaking life and love are interrelated phenomena. More than that, they are interrelated in a very specific way: as Henriksen succinctly encapsulates it, "[l]ife is the manifestation of the possibility of love."[18]

But how is it that life manifests love? What kind of love does life manifest? What does Tillich mean that love drives the living thing outside itself towards reunion with features of its world? This leads to the third critical facet to be drawn out from our quote above. In its ontological understanding, Tillich affirms that love is characterized by the unbroken unity of separation and reunion.[19] This unbroken unity indicates that all forms of love are underscored by an element of *desire*: a desire that incessantly moves us towards reunion. It is this underpinning of desire in Tillich's account of love that makes life a manifestation of love. Life manifests love in the expression of desire.

To connect love and desire so robustly, it is critical to be aware of Tillich's sense of the meaning of love. An in depth analysis of Tillich's account of love would be beyond the scope of this work, but minimally we must understand that his account is primarily concerned to identify God with *agape*.[20] To explicate this identification, Tillich examines what is meant by each of the four kinds of love in Greek. In sum, he correlates *libido* with the fulfillment of a need, *philia* with union between equals, *eros* with the movement of something lower in power and meaning towards that which

---

as a drive toward unity. See ibid., 1:279; 2:71 and 176–7; 3:134–38; Tillich, *Love, Power, and Justice*, chap. 2; and Henriksen, "Eros And/as Desire," 225–26.

16. Tillich, *ST*, 1:242. Or, we could also think of his later statement that love is the "blood" of life. Tillich, *ST*, 3:134.

17. Tillich, *Love, Power, and Justice*, 25.

18. Henriksen, "Eros And/as Desire," 224.

19. Tillich, *ST*, 1:280.

20. See also Henriksen, "Eros And/as Desire," 225.

is higher, and *agape* with the fulfillment of longing in the beloved. These four forms of love are not unrelated; he finds that all of them express some sense of desire. What remains distinctive about the love of *agape* is that it affirms the other unconditionally.[21] So desire is the unifying principle of the different forms of love, and *agape* represents a perfection of love to which all the other forms can be sublated as their ultimate criterion. As the other forms of love are sublated they can also potentially express *agape* insofar as the desire that underpins each form is enacted with regard to this criterion.[22] It is this connection of desire to love and the sublation of desire to God's love as *agape* that underpins Tillich's affirmation of love as the moving power manifest in life. Desire is a principle present in all forms of love; this desire in love describes the drive towards reunion; this movement towards reunion is a critical facet of the actualization integral to life.

What I want to make clear is that Tillich's own writing makes desire a critical theological feature to our consideration of God as living. If (1) love is the moving power of life; (2) desire is the feature of all forms of love that describes the drive to reunion that is the critical facet of this moving power; and (3) God is living (even if this living is distinct from creaturely living in its symbolic instantiation of the polar elements instead of a proper instantiation); then (4) we can infer that desire is a crucial feature of God's living. As a result, we would expect a robust phenomenological account of desire with a subsequent consideration of its ontological implications (as most frequently happens in Tillich's consideration of other critical features in his systematic approach). Instead, Tillich offers a sparse account of desire that he frames in terms of the desire at work in created life but not considered in terms of God's living at all: "'desire' is the expression of unfulfillment."[23]

If desire is a core feature of love and life, then the banal presentation it receives in Tillich, as the unfulfilled, certainly needs to be enriched. *Henriksen uses Marion's work to enrich the phenomenological insight that roots Tillich's theological construction*; this creates new theological avenues to develop and allows this understanding of desire to deepen our theological articulation of Christian symbols in constructive ways.[24] In bringing Marion and Tillich together Henriksen offers a fairly radical reading of Tillich's work as presenting a God beyond God: a God as the love that is the

---

21. Tillich, *ST*, 1:280–81.
22. Henriksen, "Eros And/as Desire," 230.
23. Tillich, *ST*, 2:129; as cited in Henriksen, "Eros And/as Desire," 231.
24. Of course, Henriksen is very clear that the enrichment does not only stem from the deepened phenomenological insight of Marion to Tillich. Tillich provides a rich Christian theological framework for developing the ontological ramifications of Marion's work in constructive ways as well.

transcendent possibility of all being and the condition for the actualization of being. Merging their insights, Henriksen demonstrates that Tillich's God as being-itself is the *agape* love expressed in Marion's question that opens the full depth of the erotic reduction, "Can I love?" In bringing together these two thinkers Henriksen is providing a way of thinking about God as manifest in the love we enact—a love that makes our being possible.[25] Critical to this integration is to realize the place of desire in both accounts. For both Tillich and Marion, the distinction between various types of love (most notably as explored here between *eros* and *agape*) is not absolute. All forms of love manifest a rooting in desire; as such, desire is not at odds with our love or God's love.

While Marion, by Henriksen's account, provides this phenomenological enrichment, I will not follow him too far in this regard; instead, I will use the alternative account of desire developed from Barbaras that presents fewer anthropocentric biases. This is a necessary change to draw out the implications of desire for *life* as well as love.[26] Let us take a moment to remember what has already been claimed about desire via a phenomenology of life. Following Barbaras, the phenomenological meaning of life was characterized by movement, but to stop with that characterization would inadvertently ontologically inscribe life within death (i.e., movement as an act of self-preservation). Instead, the phenomenological meaning of life as movement had to give way to an ontological understanding of life as desire. Desire was understood not as the closed fulfillment of something lacking as with a need, but as a primordial incompleteness that is enflamed by the realization of needs. In short, the difference is that need is characterized by the lack of a specific incompleteness and desire is the presence of absence itself.

---

25. "The important outcome of this juxtaposition of Tillich and Marion is accordingly that God both transcends and conditions human love, and remains outside any determinable conditions for the lover's world. God is, exactly as love and as the possibility for my love, that which is not identifiable as being. Nor is God part of being, but must be seen as beyond being in order to manifest God as love and love's possibility in being" (Henriksen, "Eros And/as Desire," 229).

26. There is a critical caveat to this point, however. I am *not* suggesting that my work to connect desire to the understanding of God as living would contravene many of the implications of Henriksen's work, notably two. First, he finds that desire individualizes in establishing relationship to something other. Desire is always particular and specific: it is someone's or something's desire. To express a desire is to be a distinctive self as related to something other than one's self. Second, desire does not close itself off. The fulfillment of desire does not entail its ceasing but its intensification. The difference between Henriksen's work and my own is that I want to suggest there is a primordial instantiation of these same features of selfhood and desire's recursive intensification as a distinctive feature of living being itself and not of human being in particular. See Henriksen, *Desire, Gift, and Recognition*, 33 and 36–37.

This understanding of life as desire is a primordial expression of Merleau-Ponty's notion of the flesh. The flesh, or the flesh of the world, is the chiasmic concept that describes the mutual adventing of a self and a world. The mode of absence at work in desiring, which is characteristic of life, manifests a fundamentally alterior facet to the formation of the self. It is in this way that desire individualizes: desire individualizes insofar as it reaches out into its world towards a specific object that can never fully express desire. In the mode of absence characteristic of desire a sense of self and world advent together, which places something always alterior (always elsewhere) at the very center of the self.

I think the question that this line of thinking begs, with regard to understanding how God is living, is a profound one. I want to highlight four conclusions about how we understand the relationship between desire and God as living (two of these will be addressed again in the conclusion of the work as a whole). First, I think our analysis of Tillich's understanding of life and Henriksen's consideration of the place of desire in a Tillich inspired approach provides a robust home in the context of Christian theology for thinking about life and desire in constructive ways. To consider the theological significance of life and desire for God does not require us to strike out on our own and reject the tradition in its entirety; there is already a firm footing for engaging these topics theologically within the liberal theological tradition.

Second, Henriksen and Tillich affirm that desire is a fundamental feature of life. This desire is not antithetical to the movement of reunion that is a part of the fulfillment of God's *agape* love; rather, just the opposite was revealed: desire is a part of *agape* love. Desire is the unifying feature present across the different types of love and it is the feature of love that is manifested when Tillich affirms that "love is the moving power of life."[27] Insofar as desire plays a critical role in understanding what it means to live, *if God lives then God desires*.

Third, if God as living is also desiring, then there is a fundamental alterity in being-itself. I infer this as follows:

1. God as living is a religious symbol indicative of the actuality of God as being-itself.
2. The content of being-itself is love's moving power.
3. This indicates, as Tillich affirms, that God's living—God as being-itself—manifests the moving power of love.

---

27. Tillich, *Love, Power, and Justice*, 25.

4. The moving power of love is one which drives the living thing towards reunion with the world around it.

5. This feature of love is called desire and is a feature of all forms of love from *libido* to God's *agape* love.

6. God as *agape*, which is the content manifested by God's living, includes desire.

7. Desire, as a feature of love, implies an inherent sense of alterity (the need for a world to seek reunion with) and originary incompleteness (as desire was described in terms of the phenomenology of life).

8. Thus, insofar as the living God is being-itself and it is fundamental to living that life (both creaturely and divine life) as it is authentically understood manifests the desire of love, then the alterity and originary incompleteness that are a part of desire can be said to apply to being-itself.

However, this perhaps raises more questions than it answers. What is the living God's originary incompleteness? What is alterior to God's living desire? If we can identify something alterior to God, can we be more specific about the relationship of God to this alterity? These are legitimate questions. However, before endeavoring to deal with them, it is important to understand why I have not affirmed only desire but *abstential* desire (as with my fourth conclusion about life in chapter 4). Gaining a better sense of the potential meaning of absence for articulating what it means that God is living is a crucial next step.

Fourth, if we affirm with Tillich that to call God living is to mean that God is the ground of life, then there is theological significance to juxtaposing this with the affirmation from chapter 4 that life is dynamic flesh. There I suggested (following Barbaras and Merleau-Ponty) that life is a primordial instance of the flesh of the world, instantiating the chiasmic relation between self and world. *To call God the ground of life entails a connection to this idea of the flesh.* To call God the ground of dynamic flesh is to make those instances where we experience the flesh instances of God's presence. If this is the case, then there is a need to develop the idea of the transcendence of the divine within the fleshly action of the created order: a development of the divine within the flesh, or "a God beneath us rather than a God beyond us."[28] However, to develop this concept fully requires more than an analysis of desire alone; it requires a touch of Simone Weil's thinking, especially as it regards absence.

---

28. Kearney, *Anatheism*, 91.

Simone Weil's Crucial Themes

Three features of Weil's complex theological writing and spirituality are critical to understanding what she has to say about God and absence. First, Weil remains throughout her life in a liminal position as related to the church. Culturally Jewish, in her "Spiritual Autobiography" she writes of a mystical experience with Christ, but she herself is never baptized. Instead she considers herself a member of the church "by right but not by fact."[29] She remains beyond the bounds of confessional orthodoxy, but attuned to the goodness of God revealed in Christianity—stringently criticizing its unchecked dogmatic positions.

Second, Weil displays a dogged commitment to contradiction as a method for investigation. As she tersely puts it: "Method of investigation: as soon as we have thought something, try to see in what way the contrary is true."[30] The idea, methodologically, is that truth or goodness is really best understood by the union of opposites. However, the opposing positions to claims of dogmatic theology have been under-investigated because they are considered untenable or unorthodox. This circumscription of orthodoxy provides no boundary for Weil. As a result, her commitment to contradiction is intensely applied to the classic notion of God's aseity. If God is traditionally conceived in terms of absolute being or a supreme reality, Weil is interested in investigating the truth of its contrary claim, God is nothingness or absence, with the hope of discovering truth through the mediation of these contradictory principles.

Third, it is clear that Weil is committed in her Christian intimations to a form of materialism. As the work of Robert Chenavier and Inese Radzins[31] indicates, the challenge of this assertion is to appreciate the comprehensive scope of this materialism. It is a materialism that is not in the vein of some form of atomism or physical reductionism. Moreover, it is a materialism that does not take *being* in some pure sense as its fundamental unit. Weil's materialism is a vision rooted in labor and production. The concern in Weil's materialism is not for a bare sense of being, but the productivity of labor that marks the meaning of our engagement with the world: in the

---

29. Weil, *Waiting for God*, 32. By her reasoning, the church ought to be catholic (universal) and include all those things that God loves (everything in existence); however, many things remain outside of the Church or heretical to it. Insofar as the church can be catholic by right but not in fact, she feels it is legitimate and dutiful to be a member of the Church by right but not in fact until she feels so moved by God to change this status.

30. Weil, *Gravity and Grace*, 102.

31. Chenavier, "Simone Weil," 61–76; and Radzins, "Truly Incarnated," 221–39.

secondary literature this is presented as a radicalized Marxist materialism.[32] While her account of labor is certainly not a standard feature for literature correlating theology and natural science, a Weilian materialism is akin to other, more typical ontological positions found in this corpus, such as emergent monism or non-reductive physicalism.

Liminality in relation to the church, contradiction as a methodological principle, and a thorough-going materiality rooted in an account of labor are cornerstones of Weil's approach to Christianity. These form the axiomatic features for my account of Weil's potential use in constructive Christian theology. It is with these three concepts in mind that I offer an explication of the themes related to the absence of God in Weil's work.

Decreation and Kenosis

To examine the absence of God, one must consider its correlate in Weil's thinking: her notion of decreation. For this, it is most prudent to begin by examining how Weil invokes two themes: necessity and mechanism. These concepts have a very specific meaning within the context of Weil's thinking. I will focus on necessity.

There are two senses regarding necessity that need to be understood: exercising and enduring.[33] In terms of exercising, necessity points to the laws and order of the created universe. Weil's perception of the universe is one that is radically mechanistic, and as mechanistic it is both beautiful and filled with suffering. The radical independence of its operation is astounding, but this also promulgates suffering across all living things as a blind mechanism. We might say Weil echoes the Gospel of Matthew: the sun and rain fall on the good and the wicked alike; but she emphasizes it is practically miraculous that the sun shines and the rain falls in the first place.

In this act of creating a lawful universe that works through necessity, there is a correlate renunciation on the part of God in Weil's thinking. For God to create a universe that operates by its own necessity and mechanism entails that God no longer be the only reality and power in existence. Where

---

32. Radzins, "Truly Incarnated," 223–24. In giving an account of the relationship between Weil's materialism and Marx's materialism, Radzins astutely emphasizes that the materialism at play here is distinctively human (i.e., a feature of human uniqueness as compared to other creatures). My own reading of Weil will be constructive and I intentionally deemphasize these anthropocentric features of the work. This does not detract significantly from her account, because the important feature of labor and production is the radical singularity of its production. This radical singularity of work can be maintained without coordinating labor to human distinctiveness.

33. Weil, *Gravity and Grace*, 43.

there is the radical risk entailed by the non-specific suffering in the blind mechanism of the universe's necessity, there is also an independence that comes from God's self-removal.[34] By Weil's account, God's creation of the universe is like the notion of *tsimtsum* in the Kabalistic tradition.[35] Creation happens by the action of God's self-contracting; it involves forming a space for a power of existence and reality that is other than God. Creation appears in the absenting action of God.

In terms of enduring the blind necessity of the universe, Weil asserts that we have only one authentic choice: to realize our own nothingness and empty ourselves before God. In enduring the necessity of the universe our response is to be one of renunciation that imitates God's self-renunciation in the act of creation (bringing exercising and enduring necessity into parallel).[36] Our enduring necessity is an imitation of God's self-contraction that is constitutive of exercising necessity. Why does Weil believe this has to be the case?

To understand this, one must have a sense of the role that love plays in relation to this absence of God from creation. Beginning with the affirmation that God is love, Weil finds two indissoluble forms of this love: meeting and separation. The love of God seeks simultaneously (1) an infinite nearness approaching identity and (2) robustness such that there is no diminishment to love no matter how far apart a lover and the beloved might be. For Weil, these two forms of love are descriptive of God. God loves God's own self in infinite nearness and across an infinite distance. The infinite distance across which God loves is all of creation, which stands between Christ and God.[37] We, as created beings, stand in this infinite chasm across which God loves God's self.

It is critical to realize that in Weil's understanding God's self and power are completely hidden; the creation must be a true chasm across which love's separation does not break. If the chasm creation provides were insufficient, only a straw man chasm, then the two forms of love (in nearness and across infinite distance) would collapse into the unity sought in love's nearness.[38]

---

34. Ibid., 38; and Allen, *Three Outsiders*, 101.

35. See also Vetö, *The Religious Metaphysics of Simone Weil*, chap. 1; Dupré, "Simone Weil and Platonism," 15; Gabellieri, "Reconstructing Platonism," 146–48; and Radzins, "Truly Incarnated," 232.

36. Weil, *Gravity and Grace*, 33.

37. Weil, *Waiting for God*, 74.

38. If the love manifest across infinite distance does not vitally participate in the infinite distance, it becomes a foil for the love found in nearness; it would only be a kind of test case for the extremity to which the love of nearness could be stretched without breaking.

For the divine love to reach across an infinite distance, the chasm creation provides must truly cause a wrenching apart in the midst of God's own self. Without God being absent from the creation the required infinite distance could not be established.

Just as the absence of God from creation provides the infinite distance required to manifest the breadth of God's love for God's self, our being in the midst of this absence provides an opportunity for us to experience this love of God across an infinite distance as well. God's absence from creation provides the conditions that allow us to love God freely. Thus, creation has a double function: it is a chasm for (1) the love of God to God's self and (2) the love between God and created things. What is critical for Weil is that without this separation from God our love of God could be compulsory: we would love God for receiving rewards or fearing punishment. However, in a universe governed by the necessity of blind mechanism this compulsion to love is no longer a possibility.[39]

It is in the wake of these ideas (the utter absence of God in God's power within the creation and the creation's interposition between God and Christ across which separating love prevails) that our response to the exercising necessity in the blind mechanism of creation is the enduring necessity that is a renunciation of ourselves. By renouncing ourselves we provide an obedient space within creation. This obedient space represents a rejection of our reliance on the limited power constituting us[40] and allows us to be a channel for God's grace throughout creation. One of Weil's themes is particularly well-suited for developing the implications of this renunciation: decreation.

Decreation is what Weil calls our imitation of God's renunciation that occurs in the initial creation itself. In decreation we pass not into pure nothingness or non-being, but into the uncreated.[41] We give up the positive power of our being and existence in order to become a void; as this void, we become co-creators with God as participants in the creative power of God's love. By giving up ourselves, we refuse to exist outside of God and thereby most perfectly adore God and God's love.[42]

This is a particularly difficult concept to understand within Weil's work. It is easy to slip into a more classic conception of Christian theological anthropology when dealing with this issue. For instance, classically we might claim that we empty ourselves so that God might fill us with grace to

39. Weil, *Gravity and Grace*, 104–6.

40. Our power must be limited since it only arises in the space created by the self-removal of God's infinite power.

41. Weil, *Gravity and Grace*, 32.

42. Ibid., 36–37 and 40.

do God's work. *This is not what Weil means.* Decreation is a loss of the ego or the self to God. There is an emptying of the self not to be filled up again, but to be taken into God. If decreation is close to any classic Christian doctrine, it is perhaps most similar to a basic sense of *theosis*.[43]

It is important to pause at this point and note that while my description of decreation could sound voluntaristic, that is certainly not the intent. Here the work of Rebecca Rozelle-Stone can be helpful. She prevents us from interpreting decreation as a kind of willful act. Rozelle-Stone describes decreation in terms of the structure of a happening or an event. It is a first movement of grace that transfigures our way of being.[44] In short, decreation is a willing renunciation on our part to a new way of being, but it is revealed to us as a transcendent event and is not a process that we initiate. The curious part of decreation, which Weil keenly emphasizes, is that in relating this renunciation to a transcendent event we become the image of God. In our self-renunciation, or our decreation, we imitate the kenotic *tsimtsum* of God's creating.[45]

While this idea of decreation can seem counter-intuitive, it does emphasize a paradoxical tradition already within Christian theology. A good example of this tradition is the inverse dialectic of Christian existence that Kierkegaard develops through his later pseudonymous writings (especially as in Johannes Anti-Climacus). An example of his work with an inverse dialectic might help clarify what is at stake in Weil's notion of decreation.

This inverse dialectic occurs in a number of different places, but it is particularly clear in the remembering and forgetting that are a part of Kierkegaard's notion of forgiveness. On the one hand, he emphasizes the need for Christ as a prototype. Forgiveness relies upon remembering the love of

---

43. One of Weil's examples has helped me to try and conceptualize this point. "A woman looking at herself in a mirror and adorning herself does not feel the shame of reducing the self, that infinite being which surveys all things, to a small space. In the same way every time that we raise the *ego* (the social *ego*, the psychological *ego* etc.) as high as we raise it, we degrade ourselves to an infinite degree by confining ourselves to being no more than that. When the *ego* is abased (unless energy tends to raise it by desire), we know that we are not that" (ibid., 33).

44. In Weil's notes compiled as *Gravity and Grace*, she indicates there are two movements to grace: first an ascending and then a descending. Rozelle-Stone interprets these two movements in terms of decreation and subjectivation. The first movement of grace is a transfiguration in light of the graceful, decreative event. The second movement of grace treats the authentic subjectivating power that comes in the wake of this event. In the subjectivating power of the second, or descending, movement of grace we are transfigured to encounter the world in a revelatory way. See Rozelle-Stone, "The Event of Grace"; and Weil, *Gravity and Grace*, 4.

45. Weil, *Waiting for God*, 115.

Where is This Living God? 179

Christ that through an act of substitution brings the relief of forgiveness.[46] On the other hand, forgiveness requires that we forget the very consciousness of sin that brings us to realizing our need for forgiveness. This is because forgetting our sin is necessary if we are to fully accept the forgiveness offered to us by Christ. So while we constantly remember this forgiveness offered to us, the full acceptance of that forgiveness entails a forgetting or letting go of the sin that brought us to need that forgiveness.[47]

Here is an inverse dialectic in the remembering and forgetting of forgiveness.[48] We forget the ruling of sin over our past in remembering the love of Christ that is our forgiveness; in remembering this forgiveness the consciousness of sin that informs our past is erased and we are freed to emulate the love and forgiveness of Christ given to us. Yet, emulating this love entails a renewed confession and consciousness of our sin that deepens our awareness of our dependence on Christ's love and forgiveness. There is a perpetual deepening of our consciousness of sin (even in forgetting) that inversely brings us ever nearer to the love of Christ and an ability to practice that love in our lives. We forget sin to fully accept forgiveness; we accept forgiveness and thereby remember the depth of our sin.

There are three points I would emphasize in conceiving decreation in Weil as akin to the inverse dialectic in Kierkegaard: two points of similarity and one of distinction. First, decreation in Weil evidences the same paradoxical movement of inversing we find in Kierkegaard. Whereas in Kierkegaard we come closer to the love of Christ through a deepened consciousness of our sin, for Weil we come closer to imaging God as we renounce our ability to assert our personhood or our distinctive place in existence. We come closer to that which is most real as we give up our ability to assert our own reality.

Second, just as for Kierkegaard there is no synthetic moment to this inverse dialectic (i.e., there is no over-turning moving us past this tension of coming closer to God through a deepened consciousness of sin), for Weil there is no moment when we get beyond the ideal of obedience. The inverse dialectic is a continuous process that must be constantly re-engaged over and over. We never get past the dialectic; our best hope is to learn to live within it.[49] This is important in the context of Weil's work because it points

---

46. Kierkegaard, *Practice in Christianity*, 152–53.
47. Kierkegaard, *Upbuilding Discourses in Various Spirits*, 246–47.
48. See Walsh, *Living Christianly*.
49. This is consistent with Weil's rejection of the Marxist reliance on process in history. See Chenavier, "Simone Weil," 67–70; and Radzins, "Truly Incarnated," 228.

to creation and decreation being perpetual acts. Neither of these works are "one and done" events.

Finally, while for Kierkegaard the inverse dialectic establishes a point of dissimilarity between God and creation, for Weil there is a parallel in this inversion. In Kierkegaard I established the inverse dialectic in terms of the remembering and forgetting at work in the consciousness of sin as related to forgiveness; this consciousness of sin is a peculiarity of the creature though: it cannot find a direct parallel in the creator. The inverse dialectic establishes distinction and difference between creature and creator—direct acts of the creator (i.e., forgiveness) are only indirectly available to the creature (i.e., through the consciousness of sin). Instead, Weil establishes a parallel between God and creatures in terms of the inversion. The inverse structure of the self-effacing power at work in decreation parallels the inverse structure of the kenotic power at work in creation.

Death and the Supernatural

To stop our reading of Weil at this point would leave significant ambiguity about the meaning of *God's* absence or nothingness. Weil makes clear that the nothingness of *decreation* is total. The self-effacement of decreation is a complete annihilation of the self that makes our being into a total absence. We become a void or a space in the midst of creation for God's love; we freely give up our assertion of being, not as a strict negation to non-being, but to become a nothingness, a void, an absence, or a space. If there is a parallel in the inverse dialectic at work in both the kenotic act of God's self-emptying in creation and our creaturely decreation, *how complete is this parallel?* Is God's *tsimtsum* as radical an instance of self-effacement as our decreation? How do we understand God's kenosis in the continuous action of creation? These are important questions with notable consequences for the interpretation and constructive use of Weil's work. Let us take a moment to outline possible responses.

On the one hand, let us assume that the parallel between God's *tsimtsum* and our decreation is *not* complete. While decreation entails our total renunciation of selfhood and distinctive being in order to provide a space for God's love in the world, for whatever reason God's kenotic act in creation involves a renunciation of self but not at the expense of God's own being.[50] On this approach the kenotic renunciation would be partial; the creation would be like a hole in the otherwise ubiquitous presence of God.

---

50. We might resist such a negation of God's own being to avoid logical contradiction. For instance, in such a negation of God's own being the divine love formative of

For the kenotic act of creation to present renunciation this way leaves open the possibility of God's essential presence existing elsewhere outside creation. The implication is that Weil is pressing up against an *epistemological* boundary: her writing on God's nothingness would fit neatly into a classic understanding of God's being through apophatic theology because its true referent is not God in God's self but our human understanding of God. God's absence from creation is not a statement about God, but a statement about our limited understanding of God from within creation. Lurking behind the curtain of our experience of God's absence could be the omnipotent, ontotheological God—imperceptibly present all along.

Two consequences arise from this trajectory of argument worth highlighting. First, such an interpretation assumes a priority for love of nearness above the love over infinite distance in Weil's thinking. The love offered over an infinite distance would only be a kind of test case for the boundlessness of the fusing love of nearness. If this is the case, the implication seems to be that Weil falls prey to the critique of autarkic love that Julia Kristeva launches at ontotheological accounts of God and God's love: that the ontotheological God makes the ideal of love narcissistic. In short, she asserts there is a narcissistic quality to the God we understand as self-loving-love, in that the value of the other is lost. In such a model the power of the alterity of the other person being loved is lost. Alterity is lost as God's self-loving-love becomes exclusionary through an all-encompassing fusion; love fuses God to God's self without (an)other of any kind. Love becomes idealized as a fusion of two common elements. As Kristeva points out, even if our stake (as part of creation) in this model of God as self-loving-love is a denial of ourselves (i.e., even if there is a realization that such narcissistic love would be sinful for a creature), the ideal of love represented by God remains narcissistic.[51]

Weil's argument could be interpreted to fit within the structure of Kristeva's critique. For Weil, our ideal is to freely model the necessity of the created order. We are to deny our selfhood in order to become a space by which God's love might work through us in the midst of creation. By this self-annulment we are best able to participate in love's overcoming the separation between God and Christ, which is the chasm that is all of creation itself. In the self-loving union of God and Christ that overcomes the separating chasm of creation there is restored unity that removes alterity. The assumption then is that love overcomes the breach of infinite distance

---

creation, which we seek to inculcate through becoming a void, would be destroyed. How could God's love occur in the creation if the act of creation entails its destruction?

51. Kristeva, *Tales of Love*, chap. 3.

to restored unity instead of emphasizing that a critical part of love is how it manifests itself through or in the midst of the breach of infinite distance.

Second, to assume there remains an essential part of God not annulled in the kenotic act of creation tinges Weil's work with some kind of otherworldly supernaturalism. That remainder which was untouched by the kenotic act of creation would need some kind of existence beyond the created realm. I am not convinced either of these consequences are what Weil intends.

On the other hand, let us assume that the parallel between God's *tsimtsum* and our decreation *is* complete. Just as decreation entails our total renunciation of selfhood and distinctive being in order that we provide a space for God's love in the world, so also God's kenotic act in creation involves a total renunciation of God's own being. If the partial renunciation was like making a hole in the ubiquitous space that is otherwise God, this would be a total removal of God's self. *With this complete parallel, the implication would be that God's presence in the world could only be as a mode of absence.* The absence or nothingness of God would then represent the good, wherein nothingness' absence exceeds any conception of a binary between being's presence and non-being's lack of presence.

This point is immensely important for incorporating Weil's work within the larger aim of this project. To interpret Weil this way (i.e., with a complete parallel between decreation and God's absenting action in creation) makes her account of the nothingness or absence of God very similar to the characterization of God as being-itself in my interpretation of Tillich. In both cases, God stands for a reality that is beyond the distinction between being and non-being; God would have to be understood not just as a being but beyond being. This is important because it helps root Weil's work on this point into a particular style of theological thinking.

Given Weil's idea of the nothingness or absence of God as a conception of God beyond being who creates by an act of kenotic withdraw from the creation, the challenge for theological thinking is twofold. First, we must better understand what the constitutive place of this absence of God in our material/physical world means. Second, we must reconceive the supernatural in such a way that God is more than but not outside of material reality. In various ways, Weil takes on both of these challenges in articulating a vision of Christianity steeped in materialism. Given this proclivity in her own work and its overlap with the theological tradition I have been pursuing it is this second way of interpreting decreation that I intend to follow: that there is a complete parallel between the self-effacement of the creature in decreation and the self-effacement of God in the kenotic act of creation.

How then do we understand Weil's development of a Christian materialism? For Weil, as already noted, work is the central activity of human life. The production of this labor is "a broad category that defines our fundamental humanity."[52] All our actions can be a form of labor insofar as they shape our engagement with the world. Labor constitutes all the productive practices of living. These practices are never solitary though, and the social forces that shape our labor are a vital part of Weil's conception of materialism. These social forces constrain our labor and production. For Weil, this is not necessarily a bad thing. We need to live in communities; communities provide us with what she would call "roots." However, this rooting, even in its best formulations, constrains us, and at best we hope to live under social forces that promote liberty through these constraints.[53]

It is important to keep in mind that Weil rejects any revolutionary overturning from within the sphere of social forces (i.e., she rejects any Hegelian synthesis or Marxist hope in the progress of history).[54] There is no hope for overcoming the oppressive power of social forces in a materialist vein. The social forces are a robust part of her materialism, and no amount of time will yield such progress that we completely eliminate the oppressive potency of these forces. Instead, the only counter to the natural and material social force, for Weil, is a *super*natural force. The content of this supernatural force is, in typical Christian terms, grace; grace as conceptualized in terms of themes already outlined above (necessity, obedience, and decreation). *This supernaturalism is not of a different order from Weil's materialism.* The super- of supernatural force points to something beyond social force that brings us towards the idealization of our materiality; but, it is not an other-worldly supernaturalism.[55]

Conceptualizing this vision of supernaturalism is difficult. It certainly does not fit into a classically understood neo-Platonic framework or some species of Kantianism as is sometimes applied to Weil's work in secondary literature.[56] Instead, I think that this is a place where the existing literature in the dialogue between theology and natural science can be immensely helpful. I suggest Weil's materialist supernaturalism is akin to arguments

---

52. Radzins, "Truly Incarnated," 224.

53. See Weil, *Oppression and Liberty*, 53–54; *The Need for Roots*, 12–13; and Radzins, "Truly Incarnated," 227–28.

54. Weil, *Oppression and Liberty*, 52.

55. Radzins, "Truly Incarnated," 229.

56. For instance, see Vetö, *The Religious Metaphysics of Simone Weil*; and Springsted, *Simone Weil and the Suffering of Love*. My reading of the importance of the supernatural may be pressing beyond the bounds of historically interpreting Weil's work, advancing a Weil inspired concept of which her extant work only provides hints and traces.

for the various monistic approaches used in dialogue between theology and natural science (such as nonreductive physicalism, emergent monism, or ontological emergence). In short, these positions entail that while the world is composed of strictly physical matter, there is genuine ontological distinctiveness to complex phenomena that are irreducible to a description purely in terms of their basic matter. The connection I am drawing here is not thorough-going. I bring up these positions only to highlight that to advocate materialism does not necessarily imply one is advocating *reductive* materialism. If our reading of Weil's work is one where the *kenosis* of God in creating is a complete renunciation, a total absenting of God from the creation and not just an otherworldly withdraw, but we also affirm the reality of God's grace as a supernatural power that is not otherworldly and leads towards the idealization of our created order, we must generate more than an epistemic sense of God's absence. This absence must find its place within the account of materialism as a part of the supernaturalism that is beyond social force but not otherworldly.

The implications of God's absence appear as a fragment in Weil's notebooks. She connects God to the good and proffers a striking reading of Plato's affirmation (in book VI of the *Republic*) that the good is beyond being. Classically, Plato's affirmation is interpreted as meaning that God or the good is beyond comprehension. Weil, however, radicalizes this point and asserts that God as beyond being is nothing.[57]

> The good represents for us a nothingness, since no one thing is in itself good. But this nothingness is not a non-being, not something unreal. Everything which exists is unreal compared to it. This nothingness is at least as real as we are ourselves. For our very being itself is nothing else than this need for the good.[58]

She asserts that the good or God is a nothingness which animates our material reality as that towards which we strive. Still, where do we locate, for lack of a better term, God in Weil's account? This is a tricky question. It cannot be that God is found from within social force, within Weil's materialism, because the grace and love of God is a supernatural power. It also cannot be found outside her materialism as indicated by the strong parallel between decreation and the kenotic features of God's creation. If God is neither within nor outside materialism what can this mean? What does it mean to be an absence or nothingness within materiality? Weil's strong rejection

---

57. For two contrasting approaches to the significance of this piece of Weil's thinking, see Dupré, "Simone Weil and Platonism," 14–15; and Vetö, *The Religious Metaphysics of Simone Weil*, 52.

58. Weil, *The Notebooks of Simone Weil*, 491.

of resurrection and her view of death may help us articulate this paradoxical location for God.

Weil's writing about death's positive function, appealing specifically against Christian accounts of the power of resurrection, is one site where her aversion to an other-worldly conception of supernaturalism is made particularly clear. She vigorously resists the Christian appeal to the power of resurrection insofar as resurrection strips death of its meaning by imaginatively prolonging life.[59] Resurrection provides a pseudo-immortality, thereby displacing the suffering and affliction that is a part of the social forces that make up our material reality. By her estimation, hope in resurrection can and always will be an other-worldly escapism. Facilitating this other-worldly hope, Christendom's triumphalist Christology offers a variation on the theme of historical progress that she rejects: resurrection for Weil stands as an empty hope for an impending future better than the present.

By contrast, Weil finds a positive role for death. Put tersely she writes, "Death. An instantaneous state, without past or future. Indispensable for entering eternity."[60] Here death is an idealized point of utter detachment. At the moment of death we can truly become the void we emulate in decreation, because in death we experience something that is an end in itself. The challenge to decreation is our constant tendency to try and fill the void with our imagination and assert ourselves. In asserting ourselves we are unable to renounce ourselves and become a space for God's love in the midst of creation. However, at the moment of death we have an utter renunciation of the self and no need for pursuit of various means to prop up our assertion to be. In death there is only the present moment which is an expression of utter detachment and decreation. In that moment we no longer have the past and the future to fill the void we decreatively become.[61]

On this view, death becomes a moment of transition. It is a transition that in this life we are most keenly aware of in our suffering over the death of a loved one. Weil argues we suffer because in death the dead person's presence becomes imaginary. She is no longer able to be with us in existence; and, just as in death we are deprived of a potential future, so also in our

---

59. Though I have not discussed imagination in much detail, it bears noting that imagination is not often a positive faculty for Weil. Usually, she opposes imagination to the waiting and void-making that is the process of decreation; imagination fills up what could otherwise be a fruitful void for God's love. Theologically, Weil's conception of resurrection is quite impoverished and could easily be rehabilitated—it is a straw man understanding of resurrection she kicks over that does not treat theologically nuanced versions of this doctrine.

60. Weil, *Gravity and Grace*, 37; see also *Intimations of Christianity Among the Ancient Greek*, 82–83.

61. Weil, *Gravity and Grace*, 11–12 and 19.

suffering over the loss of a loved one we suffer because of the loss of a future in which the dead one is directly present. We can imagine a future with this dead loved one, but we realize that this is only imaginary and can never be real. Instead, the dead person can only appear to us as an absence, and our love of the dead one has to be love for this absence. That is to say that in our chaste love for the dead (i.e., where we love the dead without the prolongation of life that is resurrection) we are provided a glimpse into the possible meaning of the presence of absence: being without a future.[62]

In the passages where Weil discusses loving the dead, there is a constructive avenue for a wider argument about the supernatural. The dead, the good, God, and any number of things that are part of the supernatural are quite paradoxically *not outside the realm of the material, but beyond being.* They are beyond being in that they cannot appear as directly present to us. They are present as an absence; their mode of appearing is truly distinct from the presence of being. What the analysis of the dead and loving the dead indicates is that the difference between being as it appears directly present and that which appears as an absence has to do with its temporal dimensions. Something that occurs to us directly, with the force of being or presence, situates itself within a temporal context. It appears to us with a past and a future, especially with a future so that its existence is always conditioned as the means to an end. Those things that appear to us in absence *appear without a future*. To occur in the midst of materiality without a future is to inculcate the supernatural.

In sum, I suggest Weil is hinting at a three-tiered approach to reality. We might have being, non-being, and absence as three distinctive structures of reality. Those features of reality that inculcate the supernatural for Weil (such as the good, God, beauty, grace, decreation, affliction, etc.) appear as an absence or nothingness. This standing as absence or nothingness is neither being nor non-being; yet, it is a nothingness that is nonetheless that which is most real and efficacious. This is because it is without a future—this nothingness does not occur on the order of things as a means to some good end. As a nothingness, without a future, it is an end in itself.

Metaxu

Finally, there is one more critical theme in Weil's work to be discussed: *metaxu*. They form a critical category in Weil's work pointing to the principle of harmony or mediation. *Metaxu* are intermediaries between God and us. In principle, anything created can become an intermediary to God

---

62. Ibid., 18–23 and 65–66.

Where is This Living God? 187

so long as it is encountered in the spirit of decreation.⁶³ Thus, the *metaxu* characterize those interstitial points that manifest the supernatural in our material reality. They are the ecstatic places where the supernatural ruptures our reality: exemplars of a materiality beyond being. For my purpose, this is immensely important because it can provide a category through which we can think of the relation of life to its parts and the divine to the world.

What must be emphasized is that the mediation of a *metaxu* is not necessarily personal. Even though Christ is a critical example of mediation for Weil (a *metaxu par excellence*),⁶⁴ she also describes mediation in non-personal terms, such as in her other often used example: the Pythagorean notion of harmony as a geometric mean.⁶⁵ The geometric mean is particularly important for the concept of *metaxu* more generally; in various places in Weil's writing the formula for the geometric mean gets used as an ideal of mediating, harmonizing, or bridging that *metaxu* effect between God and the world.

Since the idea of the geometric mean holds this place of prominence in relation to mediation, it deserves to be described in some detail. The unique facet of the geometric mean (as opposed to the arithmetic or harmonic mean) is that it represents the relation between two ratios with a common term. The geometric means is the solution to the formula $a/b=b/c$. In Pythagoras's work, the special place of the geometric mean (as it is used in constructing scalar harmonies) is that it is the unifying relational principle around which all of the "absolute consonances" (root, fourth, fifth, and octave) are characterized. It mediates a relationship between the arithmetic and harmonic means; it mediates mediating relations.⁶⁶

---

63. Ibid., 145–46. I used the phrase the "spirit of decreation" as the proper way for encountering created things as intermediaries. Following Weil's language more strictly, we would say that it is through encountering created things in attention that such an intermediary experience is possible. The concept of "attention" is a well-treated topic in Weilian secondary sources and only occasionally related to my primary aim, so I have not treated it in detail. For helpful accounts of Weil's attention, see Aregay, "La Gratuidad," 567–93; and Von der Ruhr, "Simone Weil: An Apprenticeship in Attention," 374–9.

64. Weil, *Intimations of Christianity*, 169 and 176.

65. Weil's notion of Pythagorean mediation and harmony draws on the three part notion of mediation and harmony found in *Epinomis* 986b–992e, not the four part notion (introducing cause as separate from the unlimited, limited, and harmonious found in each *individual* thing) as found in *Philebus* 16c–30e, with one exception: Weil, *Intimations of Christianity*, 168–69.

66. A simple set of arbitrary frequencies assigned to tones can demonstrate this claim. First we must realize that the Pythagorean method for constructing the western twelve tone scale (the twelve keys between C and C' on a keyboard—where C' is the same tone as C but one octave higher) relies upon a variety of principles. The first

For my purposes, the critical factor is that the geometric mean mediates because the proportions of its formula rely on the *presence of a common term* that fit together the otherwise disparate elements. *Metaxu* serve as this common term. Weil provides an explicit example of this with regard to Christ as the *metaxu* between God and humankind; Christ is the common term in the mediating proportion between God and human beings: human being/Christ=Christ/God.[67]

---

important feature is that the harmonies are built off the "epimoric ratios." This is a ratio that is characterized as (N+1):N. The simplest epimoric ratio is 2:1 which establishes a simple octave. Let us assume a string being plucked has a vibrational frequency of 6 and let us call the tone it produces C. If I bridge the string directly in half (at the inverse of the epimoric ratio) I will double the vibrational frequency to 12 and produce the tone C.' This is because a shorter string gives less time for the vibrational wave to move up and down it, thus creating higher frequency; we can calculate the new frequency by multiplying the original frequency of the length of the unbridged string by the epimoric ratio: 6 x 2=12.

The next simplest epimoric ratio would be 3:2. Using the rule for calculating a frequency given above, we know that 6 x 3/2 =9. The vibrational frequency of 9 is the perfect fifth, which in our hypothetical case would be G. 9 is also the arithmetic mean between 6 and 12 (the arithmetic mean is the simple average). The arithmetic mean of frequencies of an octave will always yield a perfect fifth. The next simplest epimoric ratio is 4:3, which in our schema will yield a frequency of 8 (6 x 4/3 = 8) and is the perfect fourth, which for our case is F. 8 is also the harmonic mean between 6 and 12 (the harmonic mean is the reciprocal of the arithmetic mean of the reciprocals for a set). The harmonic mean of the frequencies of an octave will always yield a perfect fourth. Thus, the three simplest epimoric ratios, when applied to the vibrational frequency of any tone, will give the four cardinal tones of the Pythagorean scale (C, F, G, and C' in the example); they are called the absolute consonances. Moreover, the perfect fourth and the perfect fifth of these absolute consonances (F and G in our example) can also be calculated as the harmonic and arithmetic means of the frequencies of the octave.

There is one final form of mean critical to the Pythagorean approach (the one I am most concerned with here): the geometric mean. Unlike the arithmetic or harmonic means, the geometric mean does not produce a discernible tone when applied to our basic frequencies of 6 and 12, nor is it calculable by the next epimoric ratio. Instead the geometric mean is an irrational number in our example ($\sqrt{72}$—where the geometric mean is the nth root of the product of the numbers in the set). Curiously, the geometric mean of the frequencies of the octave (C and C'—6 and 12) is the same as the geometric mean that exists between the fourth and the fifth (F and G—8 and 9). The "absolute consonances" of the Pythagorean scale are symmetrically arranged around the geometric mean. *The whole tone between the fourth and the fifth in the scale is a proportional relation characterized by the geometric mean of its absolute consonances.* See Maziarz and Greenwood, *Greek Mathematical Philosophy*, 30–32; and Morgan, *Weaving the World*, 74–80.

67. "'Friendship is an equality made of harmony.' If one takes harmony in the sense of geometric mean, if one conceives that the only mediation between God and man is a being at once God and man, one passes directly from this Pythagorean equation to the marvelous precepts of the Gospel of St. John. By assimilation with the Christ, who is one with God, the human being, lying in the depths of his misery attains a sort of

This mediating image of Christ produces theologically surprising elements: primacy given to the cross instead of resurrection, a model of inert matter's obedience, and a Christological model wherein the mediator becomes the *logos alogos*—something different than the purely divine or the purely human.[68] These ideas are well addressed by other thinkers in other essays. What I want to draw attention to is the repeated way in which Weil uses this appeal to Pythagorean harmony and mediation. Is the analogy of Christ to the Pythagorean harmony simply a helpful heuristic tool, or does the Pythagorean harmony point towards a significant and necessary aspect of what it means more generally for Weil to mediate the relation of the good or God to creation?

I believe it is much more than a heuristic tool. The harmony of the geometric mean provides a critical insight into the vision of reality that Weil develops. Notably, I agree with Emmanuel Gabellieri who suggests that with regard to the very structure of reality Weil does not so much have a classic metaphysics, but a *metaxology*. How would a metaphysical approach be different from a metaxological approach?

It is helpful to remember that *meta-* can be understood in more than one way. Gabellieri sees Weil picking up on the ambiguity of this Greek prefix in her interpretation of classical sources. The prefix can denote both the traditional meaning "beyond" (i.e., metaphysics is beyond-physics) and the more forgotten meaning "between" as with the term *metaxu*.[69] Weil is emphasizing this idea of "between" as fundamental to a robust conception of reality. She is not after an idea, essence, or substance as the fundamental feature of reality; instead, the critical concepts are those that stand between or harmonize. But what do these *metaxu* stand between if Weil is a non-reductive materialist? These *metaxu* or bridges stand between the natural and the supernatural: *metaxu* offer the point at which the connection of materiality to the supernatural manifests.

The importance of these "bridges" is that they invoke the distinctive category by which Weil locates the supernatural within the material. *Metaxu* do not bridge the gap between the material and an otherworldly supernaturalism; rather, they characterize a particular way of relating material things such that they invoke the supernatural. They manifest the power of the supernatural in the midst of our materiality. This itself is not revolutionary, but the peculiar aspect is the "power" of the supernatural being

---

equality with God, an equality which is love" (Weil, *Intimations of Christianity*, 170).

68. Ibid., 162, 171–72, and 195; Weil, *Waiting for God*, 76–77; and Willox, "The Cross, the Flesh, and the Absent God," 62–67.

69. Gabellieri, "Reconstructing Platonism," 145 and 151.

manifested: the power of an absence or being without a future; the *metaxu* manifest absence.

Before tying together the diverse insights about absence, life, desire, and God, it behooves us to review the wide swatch of Weil's work on absence that I have treated here. I began by examining the potential connection between decreation and the kenotic action of God in creation as major concepts in which Weil develops the theme of absence. The focus was on explicating the parallel between these two concepts in order to ascertain how complete the absenting action of God would be in creation: does God's self-contraction from creation model the same radical degree of self-effacement involved in our decreation? It does; consequently, I suggested that Weil develops a view of God and creation that inculcates God's total self-removal. The only exceptions to this self-removal were in events that she would call supernatural. These supernatural events, or events of grace, entailed an in-breaking of God into the otherwise mechanical action of creation. Given Weil's views on the supernatural and her emphasis on a broadly conceived materiality, these supernatural phenomena were not an other-worldly in-breaking. The supernatural is material, but does not appear in the same way as being, baldly conceived. Instead of appearing as the presence of being, the supernatural appears as an absence in the midst of creation. Weil opens a space for us to consider the supernatural as beyond being but wholly material. To better understand what she could mean that something is beyond being but not other-worldly, I looked to her consideration of the dead and loving the dead. There she outlines a conception of absence or nothingness pertaining to those phenomena that appear to us without a future: they are phenomena that must be treated as ends in themselves. Finally, I proposed that her treatment of the dead is an instance within the more general framework of her *metaxology*. The *metaxu*, which are so critical to Weil's work, are instances that manifest the supernatural to us—they imbue the natural world with this supernatural hue.

Living God ~ Desiring God ~ Absent God

To examine God's living in terms of abstential desire, it is important to keep in mind a critical point only mentioned occasionally until now. *We should expect that the abstential desire of God's living will not manifest in God as it does in creaturely living, because God as living is not a being but being-itself: the ground of being and the ground of life.* While there is similarity in God's living and creaturely living in terms of the presence of desire, so long as we maintain that God is being-itself and not a being we must also affirm some form of fundamental difference between divine and creaturely living. To understand what it might mean to think of God's living as abstential desire, these similarities and differences must be made clear. How does God's living overlap with creaturely living? How does it go beyond our greatest expectations for life? With that in mind, I have created table 7 below; it posits a key similarity and a key difference to be explicated through the rest of this chapter regarding absence and desire in both divine and creaturely life.

Table 7: Similarity and Difference between Divine and Creaturely Living

	Desire	Absence
Similar	The inculcation of alterity	Whole-part relationship
Different	Love through infinite separation	Being without a future

The best place to begin explicating the religious concept that God is living, is to begin with Tillich's insight that God is the ground of life, especially as this insight can be understood in terms of Henriksen's encapsulation of Tillich: life is a manifestation of love's potential. In such an interpretation, God as living—like all living things—manifests the moving power at work in all forms of love: desire. Put concisely, desire drives life in the process of reunion that is life's actualization. If God's living manifests desire's power to move towards reunion, with what is God being reunited?

This is precisely the problem Tillich wants to avoid. To avoid it, he affirms there is a fundamental difference between divine and creaturely living through the application of the first-fold of his ontology: the distinction between self and world. He asserts that this fundamental difference in kinds of being could not even be symbolically applied to God as living, though it is the most fundamental feature of creaturely living. The implication within this restriction (i.e., the restriction of applying kinds of being, self and world, to God's living) is that *the alterity of self and world is not expressed in the fundamental unity comprising Tillich's vision of being-itself;* desire indicates an "unfulfilled" quality not applicable to being-itself and risks making God into *a* being that can only be understood in its dependency on a world.

I would follow Tillich in his claim that to call God living is to mean that God is the ground of life; further, I would affirm that he is right to note there is a fundamental difference that must be maintained between creaturely living as a being and divine living as being-itself. It is the way he conceives of this fundamental difference that is problematic. The problem is that Tillich's notion of desire is much too simplistic.

Henriksen's post-metaphysical interpretation of Tillich recognizes this problem, and with an enriched understanding of desire allows me to develop a very different understanding of God as living using Tillich's own categories. Henriksen emphasizes that to call God being-itself indicates God is beyond being. Not only is God beyond being, but God is beyond being in a very particular way: as love. Since God as being-itself is the ground of life and life is the manifestation of love's potential, being-itself is a manifestation of love's potential. Love is the most primordial structure or ground from which being arises. As Tillich himself notes, the critical feature driving the potential within love is desire; this same desire has been identified as the moving power of life. *If being-itself is concomitant to the desire that grounds the various forms of love (desire as a more basic principle than being), then the separation and reunion that are critical to understanding desire in living are a fundamental part of both creaturely living and God's living. This places alterity or otherness at the heart of God's living.* By Henriksen's account this is not problematic as long as desire means more than "unfulfillment."

What Tillich does not have at his disposal, which I have been developing in this work in terms of a phenomenology of life, is a distinction between desire and need. Tillich's understanding of desire as simple unfulfillment is much closer to the concept of need and lack as I have defined these terms: something we are without that is satiated by being made present. Now if we read Tillich's "desire as unfulfillment" in terms of the sense of need we have previously developed, I think it is clear why Tillich worries about applying the self-world fold of his ontology to God. To apply this facet of his ontology to God is to make God's self in need of the world, such that the world provides God some positive presence that God otherwise lacks. This presents a severe challenge to preserving any real sense of the classic meaning of aseity and seems to violate the abyss or *tremendum* that is a crucial part of the untamed sense of power comprising God as being-itself for Tillich.

The question is could this tension be avoided with a more robust understanding of desire? I think it can: a sense of God as being-itself, and not just a being, can be preserved while also allowing the alterity of the self-world structure to be symbolically applied to God as living. The crucial shift is to understand that the separation and reunion at work in the desire characteristic of God's living is not a need or lacking. The desire has to be construed in terms of the primordial incompleteness developed in the phenomenology of life. In this way the ontological meaning of life as desire, as described by Barbaras, is also manifest in God's living as the ground of life—there can be a complete parallel between creaturely living and divine living on this point. Thus, while in Tillich's original understanding it was improper to use the kinds of being (self and world) from his ontology to explicate the symbol "God is living" because it risks positing God as a being instead of being-itself, if desire is fundamental to being-itself, then the alterity it implies makes the kinds of being, self and world, important features for interpreting how God is living. Whether creaturely or divine, life's driving desire indicates alterity.

Interpreted this way, what difference is there between divine and creaturely living as related to desire? With Tillich the fundamental difference related to the self-world distinction, but taking that distinction as an indication of alterity takes away this option. How then do we characterize the difference?

Weil's two indissoluble forms of love—meeting and separation—are helpful at this point. The love of meeting characterizes love drawing the lovers together in nearness approaching identity, while the love of separation characterizes love's robustness across any distance. This is quite similar to separation and reunion as found in Tillich. However, it is crucial for Weil that the love of separation is not just a testing ground for the love of nearness; or to borrow language from Tillich, we do not affirm that love is reunion where the separation has the role of testing the indissolubility of love's bond. To address love this way risks making it autarkic.

Assuming with Tillich that (1) the moving power manifest in life is the desire underpinning the various forms of love and with Weil that (2) love has the characteristics of meeting and separation such that separation is not just a quality the nearness of meeting must overcome, we might affirm that (3) desire as the underpinning of the forms of love also has this character of meeting and separation. Further, insofar as desire is the underpinning of love manifest in life, we might assume that (4) the fullest expression of life would demonstrate both meeting and separation in desire. Put more succinctly, (5) *God as living indicates that being-itself manifests desire that seeks a union of infinite nearness without diminishment across infinite distance.*

However, this is *not* what we find in creaturely living. In creaturely living, the desire of living being appears to be distinctly autarkic. Think of the reciprocity of the dynamics in Deacon's model of emergence theory. Imagine his teleogens; we could say the shift from orthograde to contragrade in the dynamics that form the teleogen represents desire in its nearness. That is to say that the desire coextensive to the emergence of such a hypothetical living thing brings two otherwise independent processes into a unity by making their normally orthograde tendencies contragrade through constraining reciprocity; this forms a newly emergent identity, thereby realizing the ideal of the nearness of desire. The realization of the ideal of nearness in desire does not stop there. The teleogen that enters into some form of modular synergistic reciprocity demonstrates this nearness of desire again (forming increased complexity through incorporation). Even the evolution of the formed teleogen adapting to its environment illustrates the nearness of desire (i.e., incorporating features of the environment that the desiring teleogen explores).

In all of these cases there is a strong tendency towards localization. The desire the teleogen expresses and is formed into is one of incorporation and nearness. The alterity of its desire is one that works by overcoming separation to create identity in higher level complexity. This is precisely what we have affirmed our theological reflection intends to resist: the desiring of God's living does not only overcome separation but is manifested in and through separation itself. In sum while the alterity of desire in divine living and creaturely living is akin, the desire of creaturely living only exemplifies the ideal of nearness while the desire of God's living exemplifies the ideals of both nearness and separation.

Just as there is similarity and difference between creaturely and divine living as characterized in terms of desire, there is also similarity and difference in terms of the absence that characterizes life. There is a substantial similarity between life as abstential desire and a Weilian concept of God's nothingness. Weil's category of the supernatural provides crucial insight for making this connection.

God's nothingness in Weil's account parallels the relation of life to its constitutive parts in abstential desire. For Weil, God's nothingness is not an expression of non-being, but a total absence. No matter how we might imagine God, that imagining will always be restricted to the realm of being. However, God as nothingness or absence stands beyond the realm of being altogether, while nonetheless representing the "really real"—a most authentic reality. Just as God as nothingness represents a complete absence from the realm of being, life is completely absent from the parts of which it is constituted. Nonetheless, life is an authentic reality—an absent whole without which we cannot understand the parts of a living thing because being in the context of a living thing changes the parts in themselves (i.e., they shift from orthograde to contragrade tendencies in mutually constraining reciprocity). I illustrated this previously as the melody comprised of a series of notes: the melody is nothing other than the notes but is not reducible to the notes themselves. This is because we cannot consider the note in its point-like instantiation for the melody, but have to consider it as it bleeds over into the tones and rhythms comprised with the notes around it.

Just as life as the absent whole effects a change in its parts, we could say something similar about God as nothingness. The fundamental absence that God as nothingness represents has an effect on the realm of being which such a God stands beyond. Just as the living whole has the effect of reversing the natural tendencies of its constitutive parts, God's absenting action has the effect of reversing the natural tendency of human beings to assert their autonomy. In order to appreciate and experience God as nothingness we must engage in the attentive waiting of decreation: becoming a void that channels God's grace—manifesting God's absence that is beyond being. In sum, *the way life as an absent whole affects a change in its constitutive parts is analogous to the way an absent God affects materiality.* To affirm God is living is to affirm an analogy between the relationship of wholes to parts in living things and the relationship of God to all of creation.

This analogy between the relational structures of life to its material parts and God to all materiality fits neatly into the wider Weilian category of the supernatural. Weil's supernaturalism is not otherworldly; rather, it is an idealization of reality beyond the crushing power of social force. The supernatural manifests as an alternative force within materiality; it provides an alternative to the oppression of social force. For Weil, there is no way around the oppression of social being: to be in a community is to have the total freedom of one's actions constricted to some extent. However, if our materiality is informed by a supernatural force, instead of the oppressive, social force, then its communal structure will promote the liberty of its members. I suggest that elements deemed supernatural in a Weilian interpretation are those that promote or affect liberty among their constitutive parts. Both God and life as absent wholes affect their constitutive parts in such a way; they are supernatural.

How does life promote liberty amidst the constraining change it affects in its material parts? Think back to the claims made regarding life's radical dependency. The dependency of teleodynamics was modular: the possibilities of a component dynamic were constrained in its modular participation in a more complex dynamic, but only partially constrained. Constraint occurred to the specific extent that it aided the more complex dynamic; the participation in the more complex dynamic created a more stable environment for the component dynamic. I earlier called this part of the radical dependency of life; teleogens rely on the formation of radical dependency between their constitutive parts in order to generate more complex stability. Yet, as with modular synergistic reciprocity, the dependency is very specific and otherwise a wide degree of freedom is maintained for the parts of the teleogen. We might think of this dependency, in a basic sense, as a liberating dependency. Weil's value of liberty—a set of rules that restricts possibilities only to such an extent that they can promote the otherwise free action of the societal member—taken in a non-conscious way can be a means to thinking about the specific and reciprocal constraint of component dynamics in a teleogen.

This similarity regarding absence exemplifies a *metaxological* connection in a Weilian sense. This unique characterization of reality in terms of a *metaxology* is a key reason for using her approach. Remember *metaxu* are bridges or harmonies between the natural and the supernatural. On her approach, anything can be a *metaxu*; even a conception of the supernatural in one arena can operate as a *metaxu* for the realization of the supernatural in another arena. I suggest life could be a *metaxu* for God's relation to the world; vice versa, God's relation to the world could be a *metaxu* for the relation of life to its constitutive parts. Weil's metaxology provides a helpful framework for thinking through the connection between life and God, because it allows me to identify three distinct ways of relating God and life that could serve to interpret the religious affirmation "God is living": (1) God and life are both supernatural; (2) life is a *metaxu* for God; and (3) God is a *metaxu* for life.[70]

This metaxological approach inculcates a sense of the relation that Mayra Rivera has recently developed in terms of the touch of transcendence. She develops a model of God's transcendence that arises from within creation. For her, transcendence refers to the transformative creativity of creation that fosters itself in our midst. *It is transcendence coming from within the immanence of creaturely relations.*[71] The transcendent God for Rivera is not an otherworldly reality; it is akin to the immanence we see developed in Weil's supernaturalism, where *metaxu* foster a harmonious relationality that realizes the transcendent force of the supernatural as the *presence of an absence* in our materiality.

The difficulty of this approach is that it does not fit well with the classic models of God we tend to rely on in our theological thinking. Just try characterizing this conception of God via metaxology in terms of classic models of God. Certainly it is not a form of deism or classic theism insofar as there is a denial of otherworldliness in this conception of the supernatural. Weil assures us this is not pantheism either.[72] The world in its mechanism and necessity is bereft of God (even if the divine is manifest through these same features when approached with appropriate attention). The conception of God in process theology seems quite similar in many respects to this metaxological vision of God, but the metaxology is notably monist and not dipolar.

Perhaps the most relevant, often used, model of God correlate to this metaxological approach would be a form of panentheism. Here we might

---

70. Remember *metaxu* are not the same as metaphor. While a metaphor implies an epistemological confusion (i.e., holding two disparate concepts in the mind simultaneously), a *metaxu* implies an ontological confusion—harmonizing the natural with supernatural forces.

71. Rivera, *The Touch of Transcendence*, 131.

72. Weil, *Intimations of Christianity*, 103.

read with Philip Clayton, who is astutely aware that the "en" of panentheism is highly metaphorical. It indicates the irreducibly relational character constituting an intimacy between God and creation: God is in the world and the world is in God. The intent of this term is certainly not to be spatially locative;[73] the kenotic action of God in creation that would inspire a Weilian panentheism is more concerned with *how God is in the world*. To emphasize the side of panentheism where the world is in God almost inevitably makes recourse to a kind of standardized interpretation of panentheism where we claim "the world is in God but God is always more than the world." The image this produces is something like a bull's-eye: God as a surrounding that envelops creation. Instead, I think to call Weil a panentheist is to do so in a very particular way such that there is no remainder. It is not a panentheism where God is encompassing the universe. Instead, it emphasizes the reciprocity of relationship that panentheism indicates: God is in the world and the world is in God, but God is also not more than the world nor is the world more than God. There is not a remainder to God outside the world.

How do we identify the distinctiveness of God in this panentheism without remainder, such that it is not straightforward pantheism? Emphasizing that life is a *metaxu* to the divine helps answer this question. One of the four statements I used to describe life was "life is dynamic flesh." Flesh indicated the flesh of the world described by Merleau-Ponty: the chiasmic simultaneity of sensing and being-sensed that gives rise to a distinction between self and world. Instances where the divine is revealed within the context of the world could be moments where the authenticity of the flesh—as the elemental structure of reality—is realized across the separation of self and world. Instances of life coming to be, encounters of the flesh of the world, are inculcations of the divine as both are expressions of the supernatural.

What is interesting about this is such a panentheism results in inculcations of the divine that are both relatively rare and nearly ubiquitous. In terms of the rarity, it is with emergent transitions that the ontological confusion of metaxically connected phenomena occurs. Where new absenting dynamics creatively emerge in our world the expanse of God's living is increased. In terms of the ubiquity, to take a key example like life, living things cover the face of our world in our everyday experience; if encountered authentically, all of these living things bring the divine into our midst. It is not just their participation in the divine, but when encountered rightly life and the plethora of living things are ontologically confused with the divine.

---

73. Clayton, *Adventures in the Spirit*, 127–32.

This ontological confusion relies on "encountering authentically," which is important to keep in mind as we think about how divine living and creaturely living are different regarding absence. Previously I asserted that for Weil, to appear as an absence is to be without a future. However, in our day to day encounter with living things, they appear in the context of their future. It is only when living being is properly construed, understood as being without a future that its metaxological connection to divine living is manifest. So when properly construed, created living being and divine living being-itself are similar in that both are without a future, but the everyday experience of creaturely living being stands in contrast to divine living being-itself.

To conclude, let me offer four statements about what it means that God is living that parallel the four statements I offered in chapter 4 (life is dynamic flesh; life is radically dependent; life is always manifesting; life is abstential desire).

Life is dynamic flesh; the God who lives is the ground of dynamic flesh

Life is dynamic through and through. It is an expression of movement where the living being is incessantly pressing into the horizon of its world. This generates a chiasmic encounter where the living thing is both sensing and being sensed. In this way it is a primordial instance of this process of interaction between a self and a world that is descriptive of the flesh as a third kind of being, adventing an ontological sensibility. As this flesh of the world, the primordial chiasmic encounter of the living thing gives rise to the more traditional ways we conceive of life in terms of the functioning of a living thing and its lived-experience—the intransitive and transitive senses of living.

The God who lives is the ground of this dynamic flesh. This is a claim similar to Tillich's that God is the ground of life: God is the power out of which the meaning of living being takes shape. My shift in language implies two things. First, it indicates that God is an inchoate sense of desire that thereby manifests a primordial sense of alterity at the heart of being. Living being reflects the desiring structure of God as being-itself. At root, to affirm God is living is to associate God with the notion of the flesh from which the intransitive and transitive senses of living being emerge.

Second, God is incarnate in those moments where the elemental sense of flesh, expressed in the advent of life itself, is realized. The chiasmic encounter of the flesh is not only something deep within the history of living being; we can encounter it in our everyday existence—even in our most mundane moments. For human beings, the realization of these moments takes a great act of attention whereby there is a sense of reunion that overcomes the subject-object divide so typical of our natural attitude. Moments that manifest the flesh are in-breakings of God; or, we might say that God *happens* in these chiasmic encounters of the flesh.

Life is radically dependent; the God who lives makes alterity axiomatic

The radical dependency of life is evident in the indissoluble correlation of the intransitive and transitive senses of living being. These senses are totally interdependent. This correlation of the functioning of the living thing and the lived-experience of being reflects the interdependency of the adventing of a sense of self and a sense of world. Dynamically speaking, this pointed to the very specific reciprocity of component processes that yielded stable higher-order dynamics. Here, teleodynamics featured heavily in my claim. Teleodynamic emergence relies on the synergistic reciprocity of component morphodynamics; the orthograde tendencies of these morphodynamics are made contragrade in their relation to one another generating a stable sense of higher-level identity—a memory to a reference state that can be reformed.

The living God constitutes radical dependency. By correlating God as the ground of life and being-itself with desire as the feature present across all forms of love, alterity is made a fundamental feature of God as being-itself. Desire, and the necessary otherness of that which is desired, is a structure more basic than being as it is baldly conceived. A living God is a desiring God.

For Christian theology, this is particularly interesting because of its implications. What is so alterior to God that we can claim it stands as that which God desires? I consider the creation as that which is alterior to the God who lives. To make such a claim has a certain heterodox implication: if desire, and its implied alterity, is characteristic of God as living, and the creation is that which stands as alterior to God, then so far as God lives the creation stands as the other of God in a dynamically bound unity. God and creation would be as a pair of eternal lovers—the reciprocal objects of each other's desire; concomitantly, one could not be without the other.

When I claim that one could not be without the other, the idea of modular synergistic reciprocity (a key feature of my characterization of life as radically dependent) can be helpful to conceptualize this point. In modular synergistic reciprocity, two teleogens each partially degrade some specific feature of their orthograde independence to become contragrade to one another allowing for the formation of a more complex dynamically bounded structure. Perhaps we can make an analogous claim about God and creation: that each gives up some degree of independence so as to be dynamically bounded to each other. Weil's kenotic conception of God's act of creation and our decreation could exemplify this well. God withdraws in order to make room for creation and we make ourselves into a void so as to channel God's grace. In both cases, the degradation of radical independence implied by kenotic creation and decreation allows for the best realization of desire, as that which grounds being, through participation in this dynamical boundedness.

Life is always manifesting; God lives as possibility

Life is constantly in the process of manifestation. Manifestation is concomitant to the dispossession and dependency of desire in living being. The object of desire for living being is only partially engaged and so the presence of the supposedly desired object cannot satiate the desire, it only enflames desire, dispossessing it towards a different object. This dispossession is always directed towards the world of the living being, which emerges in dependent relation to the sense of self in a living being. The result is that living being undergoing desire's dispossession is constantly exploring or unfolding its world. Not only does living being perpetually widen the horizon of its world after its formation, its inception reflects the conditioning environment out of which it arises and is itself an initial instance of manifestation.

To adapt this aspect of life to God's living, in light of what has been proposed above, the manifestation at work in divine living would be directed toward creation. In trying to express the dynamical boundedness of God and creation, I suggested that the creation could be the desired object of God's living. If this is the case, then in the context of the divine life the creation is continually dispossessed as that which God's living desires. In the dispossession, the living God continually manifests new facets of the creation as an ever-expanding horizon probed by God's living as desire.

What would this mean that God manifests new facets of the creation? To answer this it is important to remember a key feature of Tillich's phenomenological account of life: living is a process of actualization. For Tillich this is only metaphorical as applied to God's living, because God as being-itself is total actuality: there is no unfulfilled possibility in being-itself. However, if desire and its alterity, as I have suggested, is a critical part of God's living as being-itself, possibility can have a part to play in God's living. On this point, reading with Richard Kearney is helpful, because he suggests that we must get beyond the binary opposition of potency and actuality to understand that in God "possibilizing is actualizing and actualizing is possibilizing."[74]

Following this line of thought, the claims that life is always manifesting and that God lives as possibility describe the dynamical boundedness that exists between God and living being. Living being co-accomplishes creation as the actualizing other to the free play of divine possibility. Living being constantly recreates the world for God who manifests a perpetually shifting realm of possibilities in response to the living being's actualizations. Put a bit more poetically, the living world is the manifesting horizon God's possibility explores, and God's utter possibility is the free space into which the living world manifests the future of its actualizations: God is the space of possibility living being explores, and living being is the actuality that expands the horizons of God's possibility.

Life is abstential desire; the God who lives is absent and without a future

To claim that life is abstential desire is to emphasize life's fundamental dispossession from itself; the mode of life's being is an effective absence that calls for a reconceptualization of the relation between the parts of a thing and the aspect of its "living" as a whole. Notably, life as an effective absence causes a change in its component parts such that they are not the same as they were before entering into the dependent relations of the organismic whole (they shift from an orthograde orientation to a contragrade orientation). The implicit assumption in such a change is that the parts cannot be understood as point-like and individual, but must always be considered within the context of their relations that form their radical dependency to other parts, including a consideration of the transversal communication with their past and future states.

Weil's claim that supernatural things (which would include God and life) are without a future seems particularly important to understanding the relation of God as living to abstential desire. As noted above, she focuses on breaking over-determination by causal efficacy. To be without a future is to be radically free on her account; it is to be opened to impossible possibilities that defy the expectations that an archonic causal history would generate.

In some sense the model of the autogen demonstrates this quality of being without a future, though we do not necessarily see this quality in our

74. Kearney, *The God Who May Be*, 102.

everyday encounter with living things. The autogen, as a living thing, breaks open the archonic causal history of its underlying morphodynamic processes (represented as their orthograde tendencies). A more Weil-inspired, poetic way of putting it would be that life is a supernatural force that liberates its morphodynamic processes from the limitations that arise as they assert their independence apart from being in the living thing.

In a similar way we could say the God who lives is absent and without a future. Like life in our creaturely sense, this God is nothing more than but irreducible to the parts of the world; a present absence that happens in those interactions that manifest the flesh of the world—that highlight the elemental connection we share with that which is Other. Just as life breaks open the archonic causal history of its underlying dynamics, God frees living being to realize otherwise improbable possibilities. To use Weil's term, God's present as absent quality is a supernatural force dynamically bound to living being—delimiting living being or imbuing it with grace.

However, this never occurs as something *present*—something substantially additional. Life does not add something to its dynamic components: it is a constitutive absence, an organizing supernatural force that makes something seemingly impossible possible (or more properly it makes probable an otherwise improbable possibility) through radical dependency. In this sense life happens without a future. For God to be without a future is to live into the risk and uncertainty of the Other as totally alterior to the self. It is to live with the uncertainty of God as a supernatural force of radically creative possibility that can only form itself from the entangling of a dynamical boundedness with creation. This is to affirm what I have already asserted, that God's axiomatic alterity and utter possibility found an Other in the world.

The God who lives is without a future in that there is a constant repose with the world. This kenotic vision of God, a God emptied before the vicissitudes of the world, puts herself at the constant risk of a rupture between God's own living self and the world towards which she is opening. The God who lives does not have the safety valve of a radical eschatology; there is no end that will certainly come that mitigates the risk of alterior dependence. Instead, the God who lives is radically and ultimately with us, related to us, emptied of a future in the risky possibility of opening herself to being in relation with the created order.

Bibliography

Ackrill, John L. "Aristotle's Definition of *Psuchē*." In *Articles on Aristotle*, ed. Jonathan Barnes, Malcolm Schofield, and Richard Sorabji, 4:65–75. London: Duckworth, 1979.
Alexander, Samuel. *Space, Time, and Deity*. 2 vols. Gifford Lectures 1916–1918. London: Macmillan, 1920.
Allen, Diogenes. *Three Outsiders: Pascal, Kierkegaard, Simone Weil*. Eugene, OR: Wipf & Stock, 1983.
Allison, Henry. "Kant's Antinomy of Teleological Judgment." *The Southern Journal of Philosophy* 30 (1991) 25–42.
Aquinas, Thomas. *Summa Theologiae*. Trans. Fathers of the English Dominican Province. London: Burns, Oates & Washbourne, 1914–1920.
Aristotle. *The Complete Works of Aristotle*. Ed. Jonathan Barnes. 2 vols. Princeton: Princeton University Press, 1971–1984.
Barbaras, Renaud. *The Being of the Phenomenon: Merleau-Ponty's Ontology*. Trans. Ted Toadvine and Leonard Lawlor. Bloomington: Indiana University Press, 2004.
———. *Desire and Distance: Introduction to a Phenomenology of Perception*. Trans. Paul Milan. Stanford: Stanford University Press, 2005.
———. "Life and Perceptual Intentionality." *Research in Phenomenology* 33, no. 1 (2003) 157–66.
———. "Life, Movement, and Desire." *Research in Phenomenology* 38, no. 1 (2008) 3–17.
———. "A Phenomenology of Life." In *The Cambridge Companion to Merleau-Ponty*, ed. Taylor Carman and Mark B. N. Hansen, 206–30. New York: Cambridge University Press, 2005.
Barbour, Ian. *Myths, Models and Paradigms: A Comparative Study in Science and Religion*. New York: Harper & Row, 1974.
———. *Religion and Science: Historical and Contemporary Issues*. Gifford Lectures 1989–1991. San Francisco: HarperOne, 1997.
Barth, Karl. *Church Dogmatics*. 2/1, *The Doctrine of God*. Ed. G. W. Bromiley and T. F. Torrance. Trans. T. H. L. Parker et al. Edinburgh: T. & T. Clark, 1957.
Beckermann, Ansgar. "Supervenience, Emergence, and Reduction." In *Emergence or Reduction? Essays on the Prospects of Nonreductive Physicalism*, ed. Ansgar Beckermann, Hans Flohr, and Jaegwon Kim, 94–118. Berlin: de Gruyter, 1992.
Bernal, J. D. "Discussion." In *The Origin of Prebiological Systems and of Their Molecular Matrices*, ed. S. W. Fox, 65–88. New York: Academic, 1965.

Bitbol-Hespériès, Annie. "Le Principe De Vie Dans Les 'Passions De L'âme.'" *Revue Philosophique* 178 (1988) 415–31.

———. *Les Principe De Vie Chez Descartes*. Paris: Vrin, 1990.

Blumenbach, Johann Friedrich. *Handbuch Der Naturgeschichte*. 10th ed. Göttingen: Dietrich, 1821.

———. *Über Den Bildungstrieb*. Göttingen: Dietrich, 1789.

Broad, C. D. *The Mind and Its Place in Nature*. International Library of Psychology, Philosophy, and Scientific Method 1923. New York: Harcourt, Brace, 1925.

Brock, Rita Nakashima. *Journeys by Heart: A Christology of Erotic Power*. Eugene, OR: Wipf & Stock Publishers, 2008.

Burnyeat, M. F. "Is an Aristotelian Philosophy of Mind Still Credible? A Draft." In *Essays on Aristotle's De Anima*, ed. Martha C. Nussbaum and Amélie Oskenberg Rorty, 57–73. Oxford: Oxford University Press, 1992.

Cairns-Smith, A. G. *Seven Clues to the Origin of Life: A Scientific Detective Story*. Cambridge: Cambridge University Press, 1990.

Caum Aregay, Nuria. "La Gratuidad, Paso Por La Contradicción, Como Acceso a Dios: En Torno a Las Formas Del Amor Implícito a Dios De Simone Weil." *Estudios Eclesiásticos* 81, no. 3 (2006) 567–93.

Charlton, Willie. "Aristotle's Definition of Soul." *Phronesis* 25 (1980) 170–86.

Chenavier, Robert. "Simone Weil: Completing Platonism Through a Consistent Materialism." In *The Christian Platonism of Simone Weil*, ed. E. Jane Doering and Eric O. Springsted, trans. Aedín Ní Loingsigh, 61–76. Notre Dame: University of Notre Dame Press, 2004.

Clayton, Philip. *Adventures in the Spirit: God, World, Divine Action*. Minneapolis: Fortress, 2008.

———. "Conceptual Foundations of Emergence Theory." In *The Re-Emergence of Emergence: The Emergentist Hypothesis from Science to Religion*, ed. Philip Clayton and Paul Davies, 1–31. London; New York: Oxford University Press, 2008.

———. "Emergence from Quantum Physics to Religion: A Critical Appraisal." In *The Re-Emergence of Emergence: The Emergentist Hypothesis from Science to Religion*, ed. Philip Clayton and Paul Davies, 303–22. London: Oxford University Press, 2008.

———. *Mind & Emergence: From Quantum to Consciousness*. Oxford: Oxford University Press, 2004.

Code, A. "The Persistence of Aristotelian Matter." *Philosophical Studies* 29 (1976) 356–67.

Code, A., and J. Moravcsik. "Explaining Various Forms of Living." In *Essays on Aristotle's De Anima*, ed. Martha C. Nussbaum and Amélie Oskenberg Rorty, 129–45. Oxford: Oxford University Press, 1992.

Cogan, John. "The Phenomenological Reduction." *The Internet Encyclopedia of Philosophy*, 2006. http://www.iep.utm.edu/phen-red/#H5.

Cohen, S. Marc. "Aristotle's Doctrine of the Material Substrate." *Philosophical Review* 93 (1984) 171–94.

———. "Hylomorphism and Functionalism." In *Essays on Aristotle's De Anima*, ed. Martha C. Nussbaum and Amélie Oskenberg Rorty, 57–73. Oxford: Oxford University Press, 1992.

Corrigan, Kevin. "Love of God, Love of Self, and Love of Neighbor: Augustine's Critical Dialogue with Platonism." *Augustinian Studies* 34, no. 1 (2003) 97–106.

Dasgupta, Sudhir Ranjan. *A Study of Alexander's Space, Time and Deity*. 1st ed. Serampore: Sahityasree, 1965.

Deacon, Terrence. "Emergence: The Hole at the Wheel's Hub." In *The Re-Emergence of Emergence: The Emergentist Hypothesis from Science to Religion*, ed. Philip Clayton and Paul Davies, 111–50. New York; Oxford: Oxford University Press, 2006.

———. "The Hierarchic Logic of Emergence: Untangling the Interdependence of Evolution and Self-Organization." In *Evolution and Learning: The Baldwin Effect Reconsidered*, ed. Bruce H Weber and David J Depew, 273–308. Cambridge, MA: MIT Press, 2003.

———. *Incomplete Nature: How Mind Emerged from Matter*. New York: Norton, 2011.

———. "Reciprocal Linkage Between Self-organizing Processes Is Sufficient for Self-reproduction and Evolvability." *Biological Theory* 1, no. 2 (2006) 136–49.

Deacon, Terrence, and Jeremy Sherman. "The Pattern Which Connects Pleroma to Creatura: The Autocell Bridge from Physics to Life." In *A Legacy for Living Systems: Gregory Bateson as Precursor to Biosemiotics*, ed. Jesper Hoffmeyer, 59–76. 1st ed. Biosemiotics 2. Dordrecht, Netherlands: Springer, 2008.

Derrida, Jacques. *Le Toucher—Jean-Luc Nancy*. Paris: Galilée, 1998.

Descartes, René. "La Description Du Corps Humain." In *Oeuvres De Descartes*, ed. Charles Ernest Adam and Paul Tannery, 11:223–86. New ed. Paris: Vrin, 1964.

———. *The Philosophical Writings of Descartes*. Trans. John Cottingham et al. 3 vols. Cambridge: Cambridge University Press, 1985–1991.

———. *Principles of Philosophy*. Trans. R. P. Miller and V. R. Miller. Dordrecht, Netherlands: Kluwer Academic, 1984.

———. *Treatise of Man*. Trans. Thomas Steele Hall. Harvard Monographs in the History of Science. Cambridge: Harvard University Press, 1972.

———. "Treatise on Light." In *Descartes: The World and Other Writings*, ed. Stephen Gaukroger, 3–75. Cambridge: Cambridge University Press, 1998.

Des Chene, Dennis. *Spirits and Clocks: Machine and Organism in Descartes*. Ithaca: Cornell University Press, 2001.

Dupré, Louis. "Simone Weil and Platonism." In *The Christian Platonism of Simone Weil*, ed. E. Jane Doering and Eric O. Springsted, 9–22. Notre Dame: University of Notre Dame Press, 2004.

Dyson, Freeman. *Origins of Life*. 2nd ed. Cambridge: Cambridge University Press, 1999.

Eigen, Manfred. "Self-Organization of Matter and the Evolution of Biological Macromolecules." *Naturwissenschaften* 58 (1971) 465–523.

———. *Steps Towards Life*. Oxford: Oxford University Press, 1992.

Falcon, Andrea. "Aristotle on Causality." *Stanford Encyclopedia of Philosophy*, January 25, 2011. http://plato.stanford.edu/entries/aristotle-causality/.

Farley, Wendy. *The Wounding and Healing of Desire: Weaving Heaven and Earth*. Louisville: Westminster John Knox, 2005.

Fink, Eugen. "The Phenomenological Philosophy of Edmund Husserl and Contemporary Criticism." In *The Phenomenology of Husserl*, ed. R. O Elveton, 73–147. Chicago: Quadrangle, 1970.

Fox, S. W. "Protenoid Experiments and Evolutionary Theory." In *Beyond Neo-Darwinism*, ed. M. W. Ho and P. T. Saunders, 15–60. London: Academic, 1984.

Franks, Christopher A. "The Simplicity of the Living God: Aquinas, Barth, and Some Philosophers." *Modern Theology* 21, no. 2 (2005) 275–300.

Friedman, Michael. "Regulative and Constitutive." *The Southern Journal of Philosophy* 30 (1991) 73–102.

Fry, Iris. "Are the Different Hypotheses on the Emergence of Life as Different as They Seem?" *Biology and Philosophy* 10 (1995) 389–417.

Gabellieri, Emmanuel. "Reconstructing Platonism: The Trinitarian Metaxology of Simone Weil." In *The Christian Platonism of Simone Weil*, ed. E. Jane Doering and Eric O. Springsted, trans. Céline Bally and Chris Callahan, 133–58. Notre Dame: University of Notre Dame Press, 2004.

Gadamer, Hans-Georg. *Truth And Method*. Trans. Joel Weinsheimer and Donald G. Marshall. 2nd rev. ed. London; New York: Continuum, 2005.

Garber, Daniel. *Descartes' Metaphysical Physics*. Chicago: University Of Chicago Press, 1992.

———. "Descartes' Physics." In *The Cambridge Companion to Descartes*, ed. John Cottingham, 286–334. Cambridge: Cambridge University Press, 1992.

Gaukroger, Stephen. *Descartes' System of Natural Philosophy*. London: Routledge, 2000.

Ginsborg, Hannah. "Kant on Understanding Organisms as Natural Purposes." In *Kant and the Sciences*, ed. Eric Watkins, 231–58. Oxford: Oxford University Press, 2001.

———. "Kant's Aesthetics and Teleology." *Stanford Encyclopedia of Philosophy*, July 2, 2005. http://plato.stanford.edu/entries/kant-aesthetics.

Gregersen, Niels Henrik. "Emergence: What Is at Stake for Religious Reflection?" In *The Re-Emergence of Emergence: The Emergentist Hypothesis from Science to Religion*, ed. Philip Clayton and Paul Davies, 279–302. New York; Oxford: Oxford University Press, 2006.

Haag, James W., Terrence Deacon, and Jay Ogilvy. "The Emergence of Self." In *In Search of Self: Interdisciplinary Perspectives on Personhood*, ed. J. Wentzel Van Huyssteen and Erik P. Wiebe. Grand Rapids: Eerdmans, 2011.

Hartman, Edwin. *Substance, Body, and Soul: Aristotelian Investigations*. Princeton: Princeton University Press, 1977.

Heidegger, Martin. *Sein Und Zeit*. Frankfurt: Klostermann, 1977.

Henriksen, Jan-Olav. *Desire, Gift, and Recognition: Christology and Postmodern Philosophy*. Grand Rapids: Eerdmans, 2009.

———. "Eros And/as Desire—A Theological Affirmation: Paul Tillich Read in the Light of Jean-Luc Marion's The Erotic Phenomenon." *Modern Theology* 26, no. 2 (2010) 220–42.

Husserl, Edmund. *Husserliana*. Ed. W. Biemel. 41 vols. The Hague: Martinus Nijhoff, 1950–2012.

Irwin, T. H. "Homonymy in Aristotle." *Review of Metaphysics* 34 (1981) 523–44.

Johnson, Elizabeth A. *Quest for the Living God: Mapping Frontiers in the Theology of God*. New York: Continuum, 2008.

Jonas, Hans. *The Phenomenon of Life: Toward a Philosophical Biology*. Trans. Eleonore Jonas. Evanston, IL: Northwestern University Press, 2001.

Jones, B. "Aristotle's Introduction of Matter." *Philosophical Review* 83 (1974) 474–500.

Kant, Immanuel. *Critique of Pure Reason*. Ed. Paul Guyer and Allen W. Wood. Cambridge: Cambridge University Press, 1999.

———. *Critique of the Power of Judgment*. Ed. Paul Guyer. Trans. Paul Guyer and Eric Matthews. Cambridge: Cambridge University Press, 2000.

———. *Kants Gesammelte Schriften*. 23 vols. Berlin: Reimer, 1902.

Kauffman, Stuart A. *Investigations*. London: Oxford University Press, 2002.

———. *The Origins of Order: Self-Organization and Selection In Evolution*. New York: Oxford University Press, 1993.
Kauffman, Stuart, and Philip Clayton. "On Emergence, Agency, and Organization." *Biology and Philosophy* 21, no. 4 (2006) 501–21.
Kearney, Richard. *Anatheism {Returning to God After God}*. New York: Columbia University Press, 2010.
———. *The God Who May Be*. Bloomington: Indiana University Press, 2001.
Kenney, John Peter. "Augustine's Inner Self." *Augustinian Studies* 33, no. 1 (2002) 79–90.
Kierkegaard, Søren. *Practice in Christianity*. Trans. Howard Hong and Edna Hong. Kierkegaard's Writings 20. Princeton: Princeton University Press, 1991.
———. *Upbuilding Discourses in Various Spirits*. Trans. Howard Hong and Edna Hong. Kierkegaard's Writings 15. Princeton: Princeton University Press, 2005.
Kim, Jaegwon. "Being Realistic About Emergence." In *The Re-Emergence of Emergence: The Emergentist Hypothesis from Science to Religion*, ed. Philip Clayton and Paul Davies, 189–202. London: Oxford University Press, 2008.
———. "'Downward Causation' and Emergence." In *Emergence or Reduction? Essays on the Prospects of Nonreductive Physicalism*, ed. Ansgar Beckermann, Hans Flohr, and Jaegwon Kim, 119–38. Berlin: de Gruyter, 1992.
———. "Making Sense of Emergence." *Philosophical Studies* 95, nos. 1–2 (1999) 3–36.
Kreeft, Peter. "Aquinas and the Angels." Lecture, Christi Fidelis, April 1999. http://www.peterkreeft.com/audio/10_aquinas-angels.htm.
Kristeva, Julia. *Tales of Love*. Trans. Leon S. Roudiez. New York: Columbia University Press, 1987.
Lawlor, Leonard. *The Implications of Immanence: Toward a New Concept of Life*. 3rd ed. Fordham University Press, 2006.
Levinas, Emmanuel. *Totality and Infinity*. Trans. Alphonso Lingis. Pittsburg: Duquesne University Press, 2007.
Lewes, G. H. *Problems of Life and Mind*. Vol. 2. Series 1: The Foundations of a Creed. London: Trubner, 1875.
Malysz, Piotr J. "From Divine Sovereignty to Divine Conversation: Karl Barth and Robert Jenson on God's Being and Analogy." *Concordia Theological Quarterly* 71, no. 1 (2007) 29–55.
Margulis, Lynn, and Dorion Sagan. *What Is Life?* Berkeley: University of California Press, 2000.
Marion, Jean-Luc. *The Erotic Phenomenon*. Trans. Stephen E. Lewis. Chicago: University of Chicago Press, 2007.
Matthews, Gareth B. "Anselm, Augustine, and Platonism." In *The Cambridge Companion to Anselm*, ed. Brian Davies and Brian Leftow, 61–83. Cambridge: Cambridge University Press, 2005.
———. "De Anima 2. 2–4 and the Meaning of Life." In *Essays on Aristotle's De Anima*, ed. Martha C. Nussbaum and Amélie Oskenberg Rorty, 185–93. Oxford: Oxford University Press, 1992.
Maziarz, Edward A, and Thomas Greenwood. *Greek Mathematical Philosophy*. New York: Ungar, 1968.
McFague, Sallie. *The Body of God: An Ecological Theology*. Minneapolis: Fortress, 1993.
———. *Metaphorical Theology: Models of God in Religious Language*. Philadelphia: Fortress, 1982.

———. *Models of God: Theology for an Ecological, Nuclear Age*. Philadelphia: Fortress, 1987.
McLaughlin, Brian P. "The Rise and Fall of British Emergentism." In *Emergence or Reduction? Essays on the Prospects of Nonreductive Physicalism*, ed. Ansgar Beckermann, Hans Flohr, and Jaegwon Kim, 49–93. Berlin: de Gruyter, 1992.
McLaughlin, Peter. *Kant's Critique of Teleology in Biological Explanation*. Lewiston, NY: Mellen, 1990.
Merleau-Ponty, Maurice. *Phenomenology of Perception*. Trans. Colin Smith. New York: Routledge & Kegan Paul, 1962.
———. *The Structure of Behavior*. Trans. Alden L. Fisher. Pittsburg: Duquesne University Press, 1983.
———. *The Visible and the Invisible*. Trans. Alphonso Lingis. Chicago: Northwestern University Press, 1968.
Mill, John Stuart. *A System of Logic, Ratiocinative and Inductive*. 8th ed. New York and London: Longmans, 1965.
Modrak, D. "An Aristotelian Theory of Consciousness?" *Ancient Philosophy* 1 (1981) 160–70.
Moltmann, Jürgen. *The Crucified God: The Cross of Christ as the Foundation and Criticism of Christian Theology*. Trans. Margaret Kohl. Minneapolis: Fortress, 1993.
———. *God in Creation*. Trans. Margaret Kohl. Minneapolis: Fortress, 1993.
———. *The Source of Life*. Trans. Margaret Kohl. Minneapolis: Fortress, 1997.
———. *Theology of Hope*. Trans. James Leitch. Minneapolis: Fortress, 1993.
———. *The Trinity and the Kingdom*. Trans. Margaret Kohl. Minneapolis: Fortress, 1993.
Monod, Jacques. *Chance and Necessity: An Essay on the Natural Philosophy of Modern Biology*. New York: Vintage, 1972.
Morgan, C. Lloyd. *Emergent Evolution*. Gifford Lectures 1922. New York: Holt, 1931.
Morgan, Vance G. *Weaving the World: Simone Weil on Science, Mathematics, And Love*. Notre Dame: University of Notre Dame Press, 2005.
Morowitz, Harold J. *Beginnings of Cellular Life: Metabolism Recapitulates Biogenesis*. 1st ed. New Haven: Yale University Press, 2004.
Morrison, Ronald P. "Kant, Husserl, and Heidegger on Time and the Unity of 'Consciousness.'" *Philosophy and Phenomenological Research* 39, no. 2 (1978) 182–98.
Müller-Fahrenholz, Geiko. *The Kingdom and the Power: The Theology of Jürgen Moltmann*. Minneapolis: Fortress, 2001.
Murphy, Nancey. "Emergence and Mental Causation." In *The Re-Emergence of Emergence: The Emergentist Hypothesis from Science to Religion*, ed. Philip Clayton and Paul Davies, 227–43. London: Oxford University Press, 2008.
O'Connor, Timothy, and Hong Yu Wong. "Emergent Properties." *Stanford Encyclopedia of Philosophy*, August 24, 2010. http://plato.stanford.edu/entries/properties-emergent/#SumBriEme.
Oden, Thomas C. *The Living God*. 1st ed. San Francisco: Harper & Row, 1987.
O'Murchu, Diarmuid. *The Transformation of Desire: How Desire Became Corrupted—And How We Can Reclaim It*. Maryknoll, NY: Orbis, 2007.
Pannenberg, Wolfhart. *Systematic Theology*. Trans. Geoffrey W. Bromiley. Vol. 1. Grand Rapids: Eerdmans, 1991.

Pichot, André. *Historie De La Notion De Vie*. Paris: Gallimard, 1993.
Pryor, Adam. "God as Still Living: An Analysis of Paul Tillich's Concept of the Divine Life in Light of Mark Taylor's Infinitization of the Finite." *Bulletin of the North American Paul Tillich Society* 38, no. 4 (2012) 14–20.
———. "Tillichian Teleodynamics: An Examination of the Multidimensional Unity of Emergent Life." *Zygon: Journal of Religion & Science* 46, no. 4 (2011) 835–56.
Putnam, Hilary. *Representation and Reality*. Cambridge, MA: MIT Press, 1988.
Radzins, Inese. "Truly Incarnated: Simone Weil's Revised Christianity." In *The Relevance of the Radical: Simone Weil 100 Years Later*, ed. A. Rebecca Rozelle-Stone and Lucian Stone, 221–39. New York: Continuum, 2010.
Richards, Robert John. "Kant and Blumenbach on Bildungstrieb." *Studies in History and Philosophy of Biological and Biomedical Sciences* 31 (2000) 11–32.
Ricoeur, Paul. *Husserl: An Analysis of His Phenomenology*. Trans. Edward G. Ballard and Lester E. Embree. Evanston, IL: Northwestern University Press, 1967.
Rivera, Mayra. *The Touch of Transcendence: A Postcolonial Theology of God*. Louisville: Westminster John Knox, 2007.
Roesler, Tabea. "Reconstructing Paul Tillich's Anthropology: Multidimensional Life in Dialogue with Feminist Process Theology." *Dialog: A Journal of Theology* 45, no. 1 (2006) 63–73.
Rozelle-Stone, Rebecca. "The Event of Grace." Paper presented at the conference "Simone Weil: The Drama of Grace in the Gravity of Contemporary Society," University of Notre Dame, March 22–25, 2012.
Russell, Matheson. *Husserl: A Guide for the Perplexed*. London: Continuum, 2006.
Russell, Robert J. *Cosmology—from Alpha to Omega: The Creative Mutual Interaction of Theology and Science*. Theology and the Sciences. Minneapolis: Fortress, 2008.
Sartre, Jean-Paul. *La Transcendance De L'Ego: Esquisse D'une Description Phénoménologique*. Paris: Vrin, 1965.
———. *L'Être Et Le Néant: Essai d'Ontologie Phénoménologique*. Paris: Gallimard, 1976.
Schrag, Calvin O. *The Resources of Rationality: A Response to the Postmodern Challenge*. Bloomington: Indiana University Press, 1992.
———. "Transversal Rationality." In *The Question of Hermeneutics: Essays in Honor of Joseph J. Kockelmans*, ed. Timothy J Stapleton. Dordrecht, Netherlands: Kluwer Academic, 1994.
Shea, William R. *The Magic of Numbers and Motion: The Scientific Career of René Descartes*. Sagamore Beach, MA: Science History, 1991.
Shields, Christopher. "Aristotle's Psychology." *Stanford Encyclopedia of Philosophy*, August 23, 2010. http://plato.stanford.edu/entries/aristotle-psychology/.
Silberstein, Michael. "In Defence of Ontological Emergence and Mental Causation." In *The Re-Emergence of Emergence: The Emergentist Hypothesis from Science to Religion*, ed. Philip Clayton and Paul Davies, 203–26. London: Oxford University Press, 2008.
Silberstein, Michael, and John McGeever. "The Search for Ontological Emergence." *Philosophical Quarterly* 49, no. 195 (1999) 182–200.
Slowik, Edward. "Descartes' Physics." *Stanford Encyclopedia of Philosophy*, June 27, 2009. http://plato.stanford.edu/entries/descartes-physics/.
Smith, David Woodruff. "Phenomenology." *Stanford Encyclopedia of Philosophy*, July 28, 2008. http://plato.stanford.edu/entries/phenomenology/#4.
Sorabji, Richard. "Body and Soul in Aristotle." *Philosophy* 49 (1974) 63–89.

Springsted, Eric O. *Simone Weil & the Suffering of Love*. Eugene, OR: Wipf & Stock, 2010.

Steinbock, Anthony J. *Home and Beyond: Generative Phenomenology After Husserl*. 1st ed. Northwestern University Press, 1995.

Stratis, Justin. "Speculating About Divinity? God's Immanent Life and Actualistic Ontology." *International Journal of Systematic Theology* 12, no. 1 (2010) 20–32.

Taylor, Mark C. "End the University as We Know It." *The New York Times*, April 27, 2009, sec. Opinion. http://www.nytimes.com/2009/04/27/opinion/27taylor.html.

Taylor, Mark C., and Carl A. Raschke. "About *About Religion*: A Conversation with Mark C. Taylor." *Journal for Cultural and Religious Theory* 2, no. 2 (2001). http://www.jcrt.org/archives/02.2/taylor_raschke.shtml.

Tillich, Paul. *Love, Power, and Justice*. Oxford; New York: Oxford University Press, 1954.

———. "Rejoinder." *Journal of Religion* 46, no. 1 (1966) 184–96.

———. *Religiöse Verwirklichung*. Berlin: Furche, 1930.

———. *Systematic Theology*. 3 vols. Chicago: University of Chicago Press, 1951–1963.

———. "That They May Have Life." *Union Seminary Quarterly Review* 20, no. 1 (1964) 3–8.

Tracy, David. *The Analogical Imagination*. New York: Crossroad, 1981.

van Huyssteen, Wentzel. *The Shaping of Rationality: Toward Interdisciplinarity in Theology and Science*. Grand Rapids: Eerdmans, 1999.

Vetö, Miklos. *The Religious Metaphysics of Simone Weil*. Trans. Joan Dargan. Albany: SUNY Press, 1994.

Von der Ruhr, Mario. "Simone Weil: An Apprenticeship in Attention." *Philosophical Investigations* 31, no. 4 (2008) 374–79.

Walsh, Sylvia. *Living Christianly: Kierkegaard's Dialectic of Christian Existence*. University Park: Pennsylvania State University Press, 2005.

Weber, Bruce. "On the Emergence of Living Systems." *Biosemiotics* 2, no. 3 (2009) 343–59.

Weil, Simone. *Gravity and Grace*. Trans. Emma Crawford and Mario Von der Ruhr. New York: Routledge, 2002.

———. *Intimations of Christianity Among the Ancient Greeks*. Trans. Elisabeth Geissbuhler. New York: Routledge, 1998.

———. *The Need for Roots; Prelude to a Declaration of Duties Toward Mankind*. Trans. Arthur Willis. New York: Routledge, 1952.

———. *The Notebooks of Simone Weil*. Trans. Arthur Wills. 2 vols. London: Routledge, 1956.

———. *Oppression and Liberty*. Trans. Arthur Wills and John Petrie. London: Routledge, 2001.

———. *Waiting for God*. Trans. Emma Craufurd. Harper Perennial Modern Classics. New York: HarperCollins, 2009.

White, David E. "Phenomenology." *The Internet Encyclopedia of Philosophy*, 2009. http://www.iep.utm.edu/phenom/#H2.

Whiting, Jennifer. "Living Bodies." In *Essays on Aristotle's De Anima*, ed. Martha C. Nussbaum and Amélie Oskenberg Rorty, 75–91. Oxford: Oxford University Press, 1992.

Wickens, J. *Evolution, Thermodynamics and Information*. New York: Stanford University Press, 1987.

Willox, Ashlee Cunsolo. "The Cross, the Flesh, and the Absent God: Finding Justice Through Love and Affliction in Simone Weil's Writings." *Journal of Religion* 88, no. 1 (2008) 53–74.

Zahavi, Dan. "Internalism, Externalism, and Transcendental Idealism." *Synthese: An International Journal for Epistemology, Methodology and Philosophy of Science* 160, no. 3 (2008) 355–74.

Zizioulas, John D. *Being as Communion: Studies in Personhood and the Church.* Contemporary Greek Theologians 4. Crestwood, NY: St. Vladimir's Seminary Press, 1985.